Trail Riding Arizona

Help Us Keep This Guide Up to Date

Every effort has been made by the author and editors to make this guide as accurate and useful as possible. However, many things can change after a guide is published—trails are rerouted, regulations change, techniques evolve, facilities come under new management, etc.

We would love to hear from you concerning your experiences with this guide and how you feel it could be improved and kept up to date. Although we may not be able to respond to all comments and suggestions, we'll take them to heart, and we'll also make certain to share them with the author. Please send your comments and suggestions to the following address:

> The Globe Pequot Press
> Reader Response/Editorial Department
> P.O. Box 480
> Guilford, CT 06437

Or you may e-mail us at:

> editorial@GlobePequot.com

Thanks for your input, and happy trails!

A FALCON GUIDE ®

Trail Riding
Arizona

Wynne Brown

FALCON GUIDE ®

GUILFORD, CONNECTICUT
HELENA, MONTANA
AN IMPRINT OF THE GLOBE PEQUOT PRESS

Photos by Wynne Brown except as noted
Maps by Bruce Grubbs © Morris Book Publishing, LLC

Library of Congress Cataloging-in-Publication Data
Brown, Wynne L.
  Trail riding Arizona / Wynne Brown.– 1st ed.
      p. cm.
  ISBN-13: 978-0-7627-3073-5
  ISBN-10: 0-7627-3073-0
  1. Trail riding–Arizona–Guidebooks. 2. Trails–
Arizona–Guidebooks. 3. Arizona–Guidebooks. I. Title.
  SF309.256.A6B76 2006
  798.2'309791–dc22
                                                    2006004818

Manufactured in the United States of America
First Edition/First Printing

For Hedley—

it would never have happened without you.

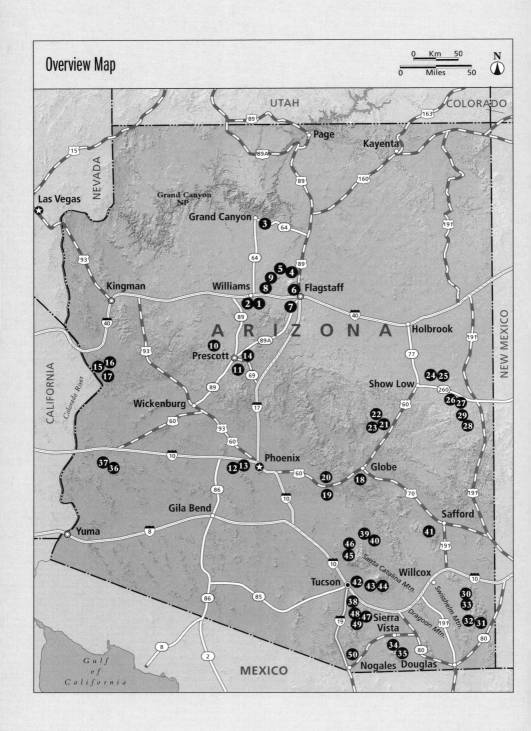

Contents

Preface

This is the book I wish I'd had when I moved back to Arizona.

Or so I used to think before recognizing how much I'd have missed: seeing Lake Havasu's hills ablaze with brittlebush, Douglas Spring draped in fog, and the late-afternoon light slanting through the Los Burros aspens onto a perfect iris; scampering across Pole Knoll's summit to dodge the lightning; being turned back by snow on Mount Wrightson; admiring the Gila monster in Alamo Canyon; riding across the rugged spine of the Chiricahuas . . . and relishing the company of all the truly fine people and horses who've shared the journey with me.

I've learned that writers of trail guides have a fine line to walk—or ride—in sharing the splendor of this state, yet not spoiling the special places by revealing them. Many, many trail-riding gems still lie out there, awaiting discovery by you and your equine companion.

After thousands of miles on the road, hundreds of hours on the trails, and more gallons of diesel than I care to count, this book is by no means a full listing of Arizona's trails; nor does it even come close. I think of it more as a menu of appetizers, a sampler platter of trails sprinkled around the state.

May you savor them as much as I did.

Acknowledgments

For sharing the load ("Sure, I'll do the maps—how much work can that be?") and for running/measuring/describing 300-plus miles of trail: Hedley Bond.

For carrying me hundreds of miles for this book: Kheegan. This project took us from wary strangers to a comfortable, trusting team.

For carrying me thousands of miles for the past twenty-two years and for willingly carrying others to help out with this book: Salazar.

For putting in ground-truthing trail time, either on foot or by hoof, for what sometimes turned out to be many more hours than expected: Susan Anderson (Salazar); Beth Brinkley (Jubilee); Anne Britt (Kip); Patty Danley (Rushcreek Dee); Stefanie Daratony (Cowboy); Sheryl Geis (Scorpion); Jan Gingold (Salazar and Harmony); Kathy Kelly (Gabriel); Ginger Kleespie (Buddy); Marilyn McCoy (Kid); Susan Cummins Miller; Maryna Ozuna (Raffik); Terry Parker (Dillon); Marge Pracht-Gehrmann (Salazar); Carol Simon; Mike Van Buskirk; Heidi Vanderbilt (with Ben, Cyrus, Delyte, Desi, and Levi); Karen and Paul Vanderjagt (Nugget and Redfern); Adele Youmans (Dreamweaver).

For providing a serene, solicitous, and comfortable home for Kheegan and Salazar with three meals a day: Jean Bagley and Aristeros Cardenas ("Tio") of Gentleman's Acres, Tucson.

For geological fact-checking, reading (and re-reading), and reassurances that the book *would* be finished one day: Susan Cummins Miller.

For general trail recommendations, guidance, background, and/or advice: Patricia Armstrong, Estrella Mountain Regional Park; Sherrie Barfield, Pima County Natural Resources Parks and Recreation; Paul Beakley; Cindy Barnes, BLM Field Office, Lake Havasu City; Ron Barrett; Beth Brinkley; Sinclair ("Zeke") Browning; Rita Cantu; Jan Cleere; Stefanie Daratony; Sheryl Geis; Bill Gillespie, USDA Forest Service; Jan Hancock; Valarie Hannemann; Kathy Kelly; Marilyn McCoy; R. W. Morrow; Patty Rickard, DVM; Bev Showalter; Kelly Tighe; Heidi Vanderbilt; Vicki Warner; Loren Weaver, DVM; Bea Wilts; Adele Youmans.

For keeping Kheegan shod for these many miles of trails, and for providing a working mantra for the book: John Russell, Sonoita.

For keeping both Salazar and Kheegan healthy: Darryl Dunn, DVM, Tucson.

For keeping the trailer in one piece (in spite of the roads I insist on traveling) and for advice about tires, tools, and trailer maintenance: Rick Prefling of Cholla Metal Craft, Tucson.

For their hospitality (and the occasional much-needed shower): Rita Cantu; Patty Danley; Kathy Kelly; Anne Harrington of Little Thumb Butte B&B, Paulden; and Astrid Sheil.

For their generosity in sharing family information on John, Frank, and Alfred Hands: Glenn Whitehead and Ruth Reed Whitehead.

For providing multiple horse-, cat-, dog-, garden-, and house-sittings during our frequent trail-research trips: Frances and Peter Grill.

For their infinite patience, flexibility, and willingness to put up with an employee who'd rather be riding on weekdays: Steven Moore and Kris Rees of the Center for Image Processing in Education (CIPE), Tucson.

For her careful and eagle-eyed copyediting, Laura Jorstad.

For her enthusiasm and editorial support at the beginning, middle, and end of the project, Erin Turner; and for their graceful and tactful guidance, Scott Adams and Jan Cronan.

Introduction

Consider this book a launching pad for more exploration.

Arizona's equestrians have 5,000 miles of trails to choose from—and the ones listed here are only a fraction. The criteria to include them were as follows:

- The trails are on state or federal land so they should remain open to the public for years to come, keeping the book relevant.

- Most of the trails are not listed in Jan Hancock's *Horse Trails in Arizona* (why walk in someone else's hoofprints?). To be a truly useful addition to a trail rider's library, I wanted this book to be a companion volume to Jan's, not a replacement.

- The trailheads are accessible for large gooseneck multihorse rigs and provide sufficient space for at least three trailers.

- The trailheads have access to more than one route and, preferably, routes with varying skill requirements. Most locations I selected are ideal for group expeditions in which the rider–horse combinations differ in ability and/or fitness.

How to Use This Guide

This book is not a guide to horsepacking; instead, I've assumed you're just out for a day (if sometimes a *long* day!). The selected routes vary in length from 3 to 25 miles.

Just like people, every geographic location has a story to tell. A short narrative provides riders with some background of each area and its characters or culture.

Each trail, then, includes the following categories:

Ride summary: A brief, at-a-glance listing of the location, length, type, and highlights of the trail.

Start: Where the trailhead is in relation to a nearby town or other landmark, as well as the county it's found in.

Distance: The extent of the trail and if it's an out-and-back, one-way, lollipop, or loop route.

Approximate riding time: Don't be surprised if you get back to the trailhead before the listed time—I've assumed you're riding these trails at a leisurely, take-time-for-lunch pace.

Total ascent: Satellite reception can vary from day to day and between global positioning system (GPS) receivers, so sometimes this number is approximate. But it'll serve to let you know roughly what you and your horse are in for.

Difficulty: No one ever agrees on the degree of difficulty of any trail. But in this book "easy" indicates that the route is mostly flat with no unusual hazards; under normal circumstances it's suitable for riders or equines new to the trail experience.

"Moderate" trails are appropriate for horses and equestrians who are of average condition and experience.

"Difficult" trails should only be undertaken if both rider and equine are experienced and in good physical condition. Any extremely difficult sections are noted here. These locations are only for highly experienced and fit horse-and-human teams, and riders should be prepared to dismount and lead their mounts.

Each difficulty listing includes some elaboration. For instance, a particular trail might be "easy"—except for one challenging section.

Seasons: One of the many benefits of trail riding in Arizona is that we can ride somewhere in the state at any time of year. This section lets you know what time of year is best for each route.

Water availability: The availability of horse, dog, and people water at the trailhead and along the route.

Other trail users: This lets you know if you'll be encountering other people, such as hikers or ATVers.

Canine compatibility: If the route is suitable for dogs. The Bureau of Land Management and Prescott and Tonto National Forests permit off-leash dogs as long as they are "under control," but dogs must be contained or leashed in Coconino and Coronado National Forests, U.S. Fish and Wildlife Service wildlife refuges, and the Cayuse day-use area.

Fees and permits: Daily fee, if applicable. Arizona requires an annual recreation pass to access state land ($15 per individual, $20 per family), but the requirement is waived on certain routes. This section clarifies which permits, if any, are required for each route.

Facilities: The availability of corrals, picnic tables, portable toilets, barbecue pits, and so on.

USGS maps: Which maps apply to the trail. Additional trail maps are available at USDA Forest Service offices, National Forest ranger stations, Bureau of Land Management field offices, National Wildlife Refuge Web sites, park visitor centers, city recreation departments, trailhead campgrounds, and local outdoors retailers.

Contact: Which public lands office has jurisdiction, along with a phone number. Complete contact information, including Web sites, is available in Appendix B.

Reaching the trailhead: Specific travel directions to the trailhead, including any special hazards for horse trailers (narrow bridges, tight turns, and the like). The *DeLorme: Arizona Atlas and Gazetteer* is an invaluable resource for any outdoor enthusiast. Accordingly, the appropriate page and grid numbers are included for every trail.

Trailhead parking: The amount of parking space, whether it's appropriate for extra-long rigs, and whether it's pull-through parking or there's sufficient room to turn around.

The Ride: Many of these trails are so steeped in history, beauty, or fascinating ecology that each deserves its own book. This section is a grab bag of miscellaneous environmental, cultural, historical, or geological snippets about the area.

Kheegan and Salazar grab a mouthful of spring grass among the poppies at Catalina State Park. Pusch Ridge is in the background.

Miles and Directions: Unless indicated otherwise, my husband and I have ridden, hiked, run, driven, and/or biked every mile in this book at least once. (Thanks to the challenges of learning to use a GPS unit, we covered some three or four times.) Each trail is measured to 0.1 mile; however, your GPS receiver may not give the exact mileages as mine—and conditions may well have changed since I rode the trail.

Horses and humans alike have days when we set out believing we can take on the world, and then . . . something happens. The trail is more demanding than expected, the weather falls in a hole—or your horse does, and you have to lead him, hoofing it home on your own two feet. When possible, then, the trail descriptions include **Bail-outs,** letting you know the shortest way back to the trailhead.

Endurance riders, who ride 50 to 100 miles in one day in competition, often do one-day conditioning rides of 15 to 20 miles or more and will find many of the rides in this book too short. When available, connecting points for riders who want more than the basic mileage are listed under the heading **Options.**

How to Use the Maps

All maps are to scale and based on GPS tracks superimposed on USGS topo maps.

Techie details: With a digital camera, GPS unit, and equine heart monitor, I found myself becoming quite the Equi-Geek while researching this book. For those who care about the electronic nuts and bolts, I used two Garmin GPS eTrex units to capture my waypoints and track logs, then used MapTech on a Dell laptop to create the draft base maps. (As a fiercely loyal Mac user, I was saddened to have to resort to the dark side, but MapTech was the best choice at the time.) I took notes the low-tech way with pencil and paper since tape recorders tend to rebel in bouncy or rain-drenched conditions. All photos were taken with a Canon PowerShot S50.

The maps in this book that depict a detailed close-up of an area use elevation tints, called hypsometry, to portray relief. Each gray tone represents a range of equal elevation, as shown in the scale key with the map. These maps will give you a good idea of elevation gain and loss. The darker tones are lower elevations, and the lighter grays are higher elevations. The lighter the tone, the higher the elevation. Narrow bands of different gray tones spaced closely together indicate steep terrain, whereas wider bands indicate areas of more gradual slope.

Maps that show larger geographic areas use shaded, or shadow, relief. Shadow relief does not represent elevation; it demonstrates slope or relative steepness. This gives an almost 3-D perspective of the physiography of a region and will help you see where ranges and valleys are.

Selecting Your Equine Trail Companion

Companion is the operative word here, and it should be linked to another word: *safe*.

The best breed, gender, size, and temperament of trail horse is the one that's the best fit for your particular skill level and personality. Do keep an open mind and remember that a less experienced rider needs a more experienced horse. Start gradually on your career together: Begin with leisurely, short expeditions until you're both fit enough to venture out faster and farther.

Trail Clothes That Work—For Both of You

Be sure that your equine companion is "dressed" comfortably with:

- Appropriate braking power for your level of skill with your particular horse—under stressful circumstances. A well-fitted, correctly adjusted bit, vosal, or hackamore is best; riding in a halter is only a good idea if you *always* have perfect control over your horse. Runaway horses are as much of a danger to the surrounding trail users as they are to themselves and their own rider.
- A saddle (English, Western, or endurance) that fits you both and doesn't cause hot spots, hair loss, or eventual white patches.
- A girth that fits your horse and doesn't pinch or cause rubs.

- A pad that works well with the saddle and doesn't slip out from underneath.
- A properly fitted breast collar. Not only is it useful for attaching a sponge you can use to cool your horse, but it's also vital for keeping the saddle on your horse's back instead of his belly, should the girth break or become loose.
- Tack that's clean and in good condition. Leather equipment may be the traditional route, but dunking your bridle and breast collar in a bucket of soapy water sure is easier maintenance than going the saddle-soap-and-LeatherNew route. Your choice.
- Hoofwear that's trail ready for the terrain you'll be riding. Carrying the correct size Easyboot and a tool to apply it may save you some walking miles.

As for the human half of the closet, the key word is, again, *safety*—and that includes a helmet. Study after study has shown that the major cause of death and severe injury among equestrians is head trauma resulting from a fall from the horse. Here are a few facts courtesy of the American Riding Instructors Association (www.riding-instructor.com):

- The most common reason among riders for admission to hospital and/or death is head injuries.
- A fall from 2 feet can cause permanent brain damage. A horse elevates a rider 8 feet, or more, above the ground.
- A human skull can be shattered by an impact of 4 to 6 miles per hour. Horses can gallop at 40 mph.
- A rider who has one head injury has a 40 percent chance of suffering a second one. Children, teens, and young adults are most vulnerable to sudden death from "second impact syndrome": severe brain swelling as a result of suffering a second head injury before recovery from the first.
- Death is not the only serious outcome of unprotected head injuries. Those who survive with brain injury may suffer epilepsy, intellectual and memory impairment, and personality changes.
- Hospital costs for an acute head injury can be in the range of $25,000 per day. Lifetime extended-care costs may easily exceed $3 million. Insurance doesn't cover the physical and emotional rehabilitation that occurs outside the medical setting.

Another layer of riding safely is to dress in, well, layers: Always, *always* bring one more layer than you think you'll need.

Padded tights are marvelously comfortable, even though they feel at first as if you're riding through the desert in nothing but a diaper. However, in a fight with mesquite and catclaw, tights lose every time—there's a reason jeans won the West. (Here's a wet-weather tip for riders of either gender: Planning a long ride in the rain? Don't be too proud to wear pantyhose under those jeans. You'll be spared some raw, painful rubs, and no one will ever know.)

Cowboy boots may fit the image you want, but make sure they fit your feet as well. Ideally, like the old song, your boots should "be made for walkin'."

Don't forget sun protection for your arms, hands, lips, and the part of your nose that sticks out beyond your helmet (the helmet that you'll, of course, be wearing).

And, ladies: Trotting doesn't have to be torture. Sport bras have (fortunately) come a long way from the uni-boob look and are available for every size, shape, and color/pattern preference.

Veterinary Care for Vehicles

One of the more disconcerting adventures in travel is to watch your own wheel roll past you doing 80 as you're driving down the interstate at 70.

Believe me—I know.

The lesson? *Check the lug nuts* after replacing a tire—even if it was a trusted spouse who changed it. (Yes, we're still married.)

Just as your horse should be well shod, so should your truck and trailer. One benefit of living in Arizona is the almost constant sunlight, but we pay for it in tires. Cracked tires are likely to blow out, sending bits of tread rocketing toward the open trailer window and your horse's face. Check both your truck and trailer often to be sure there's no cracking—and when you do replace them, make sure they all match, or you'll be right back at the tire store buying new ones.

Make sure both truck and trailer tires are inflated properly: Check your owner's manuals, look on the tire sidewalls for recommended and maximum inflation pressure, and ask your local trusted tire dealer.

If you do any traveling with your horse, you *will* have to change a tire. Get used to it. If you're lucky, you'll be on a quiet side road on a comfortably cool day with a competent friend, and the flat will be on the passenger's side. However, in Real Life, you'll be alone (except for the two horses, one dog, and three cats) on a narrow stretch of interstate between exits, in a cell phone dead hole, in rain or maybe a 109-degree afternoon, and the flat will be on the driver's side 3 feet from the passing eighteen-wheelers.

Your best bet is to train for this inevitable event by practicing tire changes on a pleasant mild day—serenely—in your own driveway.

Your tire-changing weaponry should include:

- A star wrench—one of those four-way lug wrenches that will fit the lugs on your spare, your truck, and your trailer.
- A good jack for the truck and the knowledge to use it.
- A Trailer-Aid for changing a trailer tire without a jack or the need to unload the horses.
- A flashlight.
- A few 2-by-6-inch cutoffs in case you need to raise or level the jack.
- A couple of substantial chocks.

- A can of Tire Seal for temporarily patching punctures won't go amiss, either.

Other useful tools that should live in your truck include:
- Screwdrivers—flat and Phillips.
- Pliers (needle-nose and multigrip).
- Vise grips.
- At least one crescent wrench. In time your wrench collection will grow—English or metric—according to which sizes you use most.
- WD-40 and a few old rags.
- A quart or two of extra engine oil.

If you're towing a horse trailer in Arizona, your vehicle should be serviced under a "severe duty" schedule, which simply means checking and changing the oil, oil filter, transmission fluid (for an automatic), and air filter more often.

Also, keep in mind that if you belong to AAA, you'll need RV+ coverage to have your truck and trailer towed. The extra coverage also provides more miles of towing.

Here are some useful checklists for truck/trailer maintenance:

Day Trips

1. Check tire pressure and look for any cracking on both the truck and trailer tires (including the spares).
2. Check for wasp nests in the upper inside corners of the trailer.
3. Check that the manger doesn't have old, muddy clumps of hay.
4. Check trailer connections (is the hitch locked down, and are the safety chains and breakaway cable attached?) and lights.
5. After the horse is loaded, make sure all the trailer doors and windows are secured and latched. (Did you *really* check all the trailer connections?)
6. After the trip, clean out the trailer thoroughly: Hose the floor and mats, making sure no water is trapped under a mat, allow everything to dry, and inspect the floor carefully. (In a perfect world, we'd all hose our trailers out after every day trip. Okay, so in Real Life, no one cleans out the trailer after every trip. It's still a good goal to aim for.)

Longer Trips

1. Items 1 through 5 on the Day Trip list.
2. Check fluids—coolant, windshield washer, brake, engine oil, transmission.
3. Make sure the trailer ball is well greased.
4. After the horse is loaded, check trailer connections and make sure all the trailer doors and windows are secured and latched. (Some things can't be said too often.)

5. After the trip, clean out the trailer thoroughly.

6. If it's a very long trip, check when your oil and oil filter were last changed—will they need to be changed before you get home?

Every Six Months

1. Check trailer connections, doors, and windows for loose screws, dried-out caulking, and so forth.

2. Get the truck lubed.

3. Rotate the tires (or every 6,000 to 8,000 miles—whichever comes first).

4. Check the air filter, particularly if you do a lot of driving on gravel roads.

5. Check the battery fluid level and that the battery terminals are clean (although most new batteries require little to no maintenance).

Every Year

1. Change the transmission fluid if appropriate (or every 20,000 to 25,000 miles).

2. Check the brakes.

3. Replace the windshield wipers. The Arizona sun is hard on wiper blades; plan to replace them just before the summer monsoons (*if* you can get a whole year out of them).

4. Pack the bearings on the trailer wheels.

Confirm Trail Status

For Arizonans, fire is a fact of life.

In 1990 the Dude Fire killed six firefighters and burned 24,000 acres near the edge of the Mogollon Rim.

In 1994, the Rattlesnake Fire ravaged 28,000 acres of the Chiricahuas.

In 2002 the combined Rodeo-Chediski Fire, the largest in Arizona history, took out 460,000 acres and 491 structures.

In 2003 Tucsonans watched from their living room windows in despair as flames swallowed 86,000 acres of the Santa Catalinas, along with the community of Summerhaven.

And in 2005 the Cave Creek Complex Fire burnt through Tonto National Forest north of Phoenix, and the Florida Fire charred 23,000 acres of the Santa Rita trails southeast of Tucson.

Less dramatic events, such as trail renovation or campground construction, can close a trail just as effectively. Unless you live near the area and know it well, it's worth the extra effort to call the ranger station or state park office—or check the Web site—to verify trail status. Sometimes trails are closed for surprising reasons: In early May 2005 the Forest Service closed every trail, every trailhead, and every road to every trailhead in the White Mountains because the copious (and very welcome) winter rains had generated copious (and less welcome) amounts of mud.

Also, on either printed maps or the Web, many trails look as if they're viable routes. They may not be. One call to the appropriate land manager can save you a trip to somewhere that's closed or impassable due to regeneration, lack of maintenance, or storm damage.

Got Permit?

Most of the trails in this book are on federal land managed by either the USDA Forest Service or the Bureau of Land Management. Those that are on state lands require a permit. Arizona requires an annual recreation pass to access state land ($15 for individuals, $20 for families); these are easily obtained by calling (602) 542–4174. An easy way to find out if the ride you're planning is on state land is to look at *DeLorme: Arizona Atlas and Gazetteer.*

Are You Packing? (A Gun, That Is)

Arizona gun laws are easy to memorize. Basically, there aren't any although gun buyers must undergo state and federal backgound checks, and minors are restricted from owning guns.

You do have to have a permit to carry a concealed weapon or to carry a handgun.

Sharing the Trail–Safely

Generally, the other trail users you're likely to encounter—hikers, mountain bikers, trail runners—are out there for the same reasons we all are: to enjoy the scenery, the quiet, the wildlife, and the required exertion to reach the destination. Technically horses—which have been defined as "1,000 pounds of flight response"—have right-of-way. But trail riding is also a public relations opportunity. Not everyone shares our obsession for large, impulsive, metal-footed manure droppers—so a cheerful "Good morning!" and pausing for a quick chat can go a long way toward averting a complaint about horses on the trail.

Often, hikers are not Horse People, and many are unaware that standing rock still in total silence, or waving hello with their walking stick, or lumbering toward you wearing a gargantuan backpack may send your horse into whirling hysteria. Asking a question that will elicit a conversation—"Hi there, and isn't it a perfect day to be out here?"—will help relax you, your horse, and the hiker. (Telling them to "Please speak so that my horse will know you're human" tends to throw people into a self-conscious, silent struggle to think of something to say.)

If you're on the Arizona Trail, you may well encounter through-hikers (those who are walking the entire 780-mile length). Some may have pack animals—usually llamas. Even the calmest trail horse may bolt when trotting around a corner to confront a 7-foot furball decked out in pots and pans.

On rare occasions you may find mountain bikers hurtling down the hill toward you, brakes shrieking, earphones flapping, and scaring the bejeepers out of your horse (and you). But for the most part, they're courteous, and as a group they build and maintain many trails. So be kind. Even though you have the right-of-way, when you see bikers struggling to pedal up a rocky hill, and if you can do so safely, move off the trail so that they won't lose momentum.

All-terrain vehicles (also known as OHVs, or off-highway vehicles) can be another monster in the eyes of your four-hoofed trail companion. Here's what the ATV Safety Institute recommends for their drivers:

> Be courteous to others you may meet on the trail. Always give right-of-way to hikers and horseback riders. Pull off the trail and stop your engine for horses. In most areas, horses are not permitted on trails unless they are accustomed to vehicles, but don't take a chance. The rider will likely talk soothingly to the horse. It doesn't hurt for you to do the same to assure the horse you are no threat. Horses respond very positively to a calm, human voice.

Cattle are frequent residents of the trails; generally they're not a problem once your horse is accustomed to them.

What if you run into someone who deliberately wants to hurt you or your horse? First of all, it's highly unlikely. Muggers have better luck in mall parking lots than 8 miles up a broiling, rocky trail. Chances are that drug smugglers, other criminals, or would-be immigrants would vastly prefer to hide from you than attack.

Nevertheless, here are some tips:

- Don't go without "filing a flight plan": Be sure that someone knows where you're planning to go and when you plan to be back.
- Don't ride alone.
- Don't count on your cell phone working.
- Don't gallop off at breakneck speed, unless the footing is good, and you and your horse are both used to speed.
- Don't get off your horse. Try to keep as much distance as possible between you and your would-be assailant.
- Don't kick at an assailant or try to hit him with your reins or crop. Once he grabs your leg or arm, he has the leverage to yank you off your horse.
- Don't count on your horse for help; after all, look at all the time you've spent training him to *not* bite or kick. You can, however, lie and say, "Don't come any closer—this horse hates people and will kick you!"

Life on the Wild Side

In thirty years of trail riding, I have never run into a human being who wished me harm. I have, however, been the victim of many a sociopathic plant.

Many southwestern plants have teeth. Jeans and long sleeves will protect you much of the time from mesquite and catclaw acacia, but you should also carry a readily accessible comb to flick off cholla sections that have attached themselves to you or your horse.

Poison ivy ("Leaves of three? Let it be!") isn't as much of a problem here in the Southwest as it is back east—but it is expanding in damp creekside habitats.

Arizona does have its share of poisonous animals, but in most cases trail riders have little to fear from them. As long as you aren't lifting up rocks and logs, you're unlikely to see scorpions. After the summer rains, you may well see male tarantulas trekking across the desert, but they have way more important things on their mind than you: They're in search of female tarantulas, who remain in their burrows most of their lives waiting for their annual suitors. (The males you see will die soon after mating, while the females often live to be twenty years old.)

You'll see many lizards, but Arizona's only poisonous one is the Gila monster, a sluggish, shy reptile. They have been protected since 1952, and severe penalties apply for any attempt to catch or harass them.

The reptiles you'll want to steer clear of are, of course, rattlesnakes. Arizona has eleven species, and for the most part they'd far rather get out of your way than in it. According to the Arizona Herpetological Association, the ones you're most likely to see are the western diamondback, western, Mojave, blacktail, and sidewinder.

If a rattler is in the trail—and if you see it in time—stop, and let it move on. If it's asleep, or too well fed to move, ride around it, leaving plenty of room. If there's no room to ride around it safely, dismount, keeping a safe distance. Toss a stone in its direction, while being prepared to get out of the way *fast* if it chooses to escape toward you. *Do not try to pick it up,* even with a stick: Some snakes can climb up a branch faster than you can drop it.

Most horses that have spent time in the desert tend to be snake savvy. However, if yours does get bitten, keep in mind that rattlesnake bites are rarely fatal for equines (or humans). Keep reminding yourself of this fact to stay calm as you proceed slowly back to the trailhead, and call for veterinary advice.

The same strategy applies if you or another rider is bitten:

- Do try to stay calm. Panicking only distributes the venom faster.
- Do remove any jewelry or other constricting items.
- Do immobilize the limb (if possible), keeping it below the heart.
- Do proceed slowly back to the trailhead.
- Do get medical help as efficiently as possible.
- Don't cut into the wound.
- Don't use a tourniquet or other form of constriction.
- Don't apply ice.
- Don't take alcohol or drugs.

Generally, you have more reason to fear bees than snakes. The venom of African-ized ("killer") bees is no more toxic than the European honeybee—the danger is the number of stings. Stay alert as you ride through thick brush: According to the National Park Service, most Arizona colonies are all or part Africanized bees. Park authorities recommend:

- Do get away as quickly as possible—perhaps as far as 0.5 mile. (This advice puts equestrians in a quandary: You want to get the heck out of there ASAP, but you don't want to put yourself in more danger by riding so fast you fall off or endanger your horse. This may be easier said than done, but do your best to find a happy medium.)
- Do cover your head, as the bees target moist areas such as eyes, nose, and mouth. (Again—galloping a panicked horse down a rocky trail with both hands over your face could be a Really Bad Idea. Use your judgment.)
- Don't kill any bees. Although your instinct may to be swat them, resist the urge. Dying bees release an alarm pheromone that attracts their friends and family members.

If you are stung, remove stingers by scraping them off with something resembling a credit card. Don't try to remove with fingernails or tweezers, since that will force more venom in.

Mountain lions made the news in southern Arizona when wildfires drove them down into populated areas. Most of the time, however, you're unlikely to see any.

You may encounter black bears and may be lucky enough to spot a youngster asleep in a tree. Keep on moving through efficiently, and be sure that you and your horse are not between a mother bear and her cub.

Weathering the Weather

Cold

All the trails in this book are either in the desert or in the mountains; both locales are notorious for sudden weather changes and abrupt drops in temperature. In one day's ride you could experience a range of fifty degrees! It's worth repeating: Always take one more layer than you think you'll need. A cheap poncho takes up almost no space on your saddle and should be a permanent fixture. At the very least, tucking a large garbage bag into your saddle bag can make the difference between unfashionable discomfort and fatal hypothermia. If you frequently do all-day rides in the mountains, consider keeping a space blanket in one of your bags as well.

Heat

It hardly seems necessary to mention that Arizona gets hot—and sometimes *really* hot. Plan your trips accordingly, in terms of both where you go and what time you ride.

Some things are worth getting up early for, and southern Arizona sunrises are

The southern section of the Pedersen Trail is beautiful in its desolation but can be brutally hot and exposed in summer.

among them. Dawn brings comfortable temperatures, cool ground underfoot, and, once the monsoons start, an improved chance of getting home before getting wet.

Besides, how better to start your day?

Here's a vital piece of cooling trail equipment that's cheap, takes up no room, and can even be personalized. Keep a bandanna tied to your saddle or tucked in your cantle bag. When temperatures rise, wrap it around your neck, pour a couple of tablespoons of water on it, and voilà! You're fifteen degrees cooler—well, for a few minutes anyway. You can also drape it under your chosen headgear to shield your neck and ears from the sun.

Another option is to ride late, starting at sundown. Yes, it *will* get dark, so pick a route that doesn't include ducking under mesquite branches. Wide-open washes and riverbeds are perfect for night riding as long as you're careful of abandoned shopping carts and other bits of assorted trash.

If you have to access the wash by road, make sure both you and your horse are visible. Mark your helmet permanently with reflective tape in case you're unexpectedly out after dark. Adding reflective tape to your horse's browband, breast collar, splint boots, and the back of the saddle isn't a bad idea, either.

Take a small flashlight, in case you need to adjust tack or read a sign. But for the most part, both you and your horse will see better if you let all four eyes adjust to the night light. It may be unnerving at first, but remember that your horse can see better than you can. Riding in the dark provides an interesting power shift—relax, and let him be the pilot (within reason).

That said, night riding is best done with a human companion . . . just in case.

Lightning

Starting in late June or July, the monsoons roll in with awe-inspiring thunderstorms and lightning displays. You really don't want to be on a ridge at these times—especially not on a creature in metal shoes.

Again, plan your rides accordingly. If you do get caught out, try to get off the exposed area to a lower elevation and avoid taking shelter under the tallest thing around.

Staying Hydrated

Newcomers to Arizona often think that because they're not sweating, they must not be thirsty. It's almost impossible to carry too much water when riding in summer. Here in the desert you *are* sweating; you're just not as aware of it, because the perspiration dries so fast. Active human beings can lose as much as two quarts, or four pounds, per hour. A 5 percent loss in body weight can result in heatstroke.

People Water

Always, always keep people water in your truck. Even stale, hot water will do the job if you return to the trailhead in a dehydrated state.

Fortunately for trail riders, the equestrian accessory companies have cooperated, making water-bottle bags that attach to the front, back, or sides of every kind of saddle.

But here's a thought. What happens if your normally trustworthy steed suddenly spooks, leaving you on the ground as he bolts for home? Consider investing in one of the shoulder- or hip-harness hydration systems. My CamelBak holds seventy ounces and features padded shoulder straps, a waist belt so it doesn't bounce around at the trot, straps for tying on an overshirt, a map/snack pocket, and a wide mouth for ice cubes and easy cleaning.

I don't leave home without it.

Horse Water

Many trails listed in this book have limited or no water on the trail, especially in late spring or summer. Get in the habit of keeping an empty bucket and a five-gallon plastic container of water in your trailer that you can offer your horse before and after hitting the trail.

Electrolytes, Human and Equine

Anytime Gatorade tastes ambrosial, I know I haven't consumed enough water or electrolytes. Keep a ziplock bag full of Gatorade powder in your trailer that you can add to your water bottle as needed.

You may think that equine electrolytes are only for equine athletes and that only endurance horses need them. On the contrary, look at the amount of crusty salt left on your horse from just standing and sweating in the corral when the temperature is over 100 degrees. If you ride more than a couple hours a day in the hot season, consider adding a tablespoon or two of powdered electrolytes to your horse's feed every day. Start gradually so you don't put him off his feed, or use a brand your horse finds palatable. (Mine enjoy AccuLytes.)

In hot weather and doing hard work, your horse also may need electrolytes on the trail. *However, be sure the horse has drunk recently before dosing.* Several veterinary supply companies make ready-to-use electrolyte paste, which is a convenient but expensive way to go. You can also easily carry electrolyte powder (a plastic Advil container works well) and a 60cc syringe in your saddlebag. When it comes time to electrolyte your horse, simply add two tablespoons of powder to the syringe, fill with water, shake—and squirt the contents into his mouth. (The squirt-in-his-mouth part tends to go better if you practice at home with something yummy like straight applesauce.)

When Things Go Wrong (And They Will)

Here are a few items no saddle should be without.

For Horse *and* Human

- At the very least, a knife sharp enough to cut a lead rope—fast.
- A multiuse tool, such as a Leatherman.
- Compression wraps, such as Vet Wrap.
- A comb to remove cactus.
- Electrolytes.
- Vaseline.
- A ziplock bag with a couple of large gauze pads, in case of cuts.
- Baling twine or rawhide, in case of tack repairs.
- A hoof pick.

Equine First Aid

- Triple-antibiotic eye ointment.
- Wound salve, such as Fura-Zone.

Rider First Aid

- Advil or some other NSAID (nonsteroidal anti-inflammatory drug).
- Benadryl for insect stings.

Treating the Land with Love

Open public land is the canvas on which our trails are sketched. No land, no trails. It's up to all of us to protect that canvas and keep it blemish-free.

Human Waste

When I tell non-horse-people that I often ride all day and into the night, one question is invariably: "Wow . . . umm, what happens if you have to go to the bathroom?"

It's not *if,* it's *when.*

The males of our species have an obvious advantage here, although many trail-riding women are happy to just dismount, squat, pee, "shake the dew off the lily" (as one Georgia friend of mine used to say), and hop back in the saddle.

But what about more lasting evidence? Both genders are well advised to carry toilet paper (you can get away with a maple leaf in other parts of the country, but desert plants tend toward tiny leaves with teeth). Carry a small plastic ziplock bag for used toilet paper and tampons. Digging a hole just doesn't work in most of Arizona's terrain. The only place that's easy to dig is a sandy wash, and any human waste should be at least 200 feet from a watercourse.

Equine Waste

The combination of Arizona's sun and wind decomposes manure fast, especially if it's scattered, but depending on the area, the seeds may be considered undesirable. When you camp, check ahead of time to see if the authorities want you to bring seed-free feed and to haul away your old hay and manure.

Campfires

Sitting around the fire after a long day of riding while watching the sparks blend with the nighttime sky is one of life's pure joys. However, some of Arizona's worst wildfires (Radio, Rodeo-Chediski, Aspen, and more) were caused by humans, and often an out-of-control campfire is the culprit. If you think there's *any* chance of causing a wildfire, leave your matches in your pocket.

Keeping Your Stock Contained

In earlier times when people camped with their equine family members, their only options were to set up a picket line, hobble the horses, or tie them to the trailer or a nearby tree. These days many people attach portable corral panels to their trailer and set up a roomy home-away-from-home for their stock. Other people use electric fencing—but remember that although it's lightweight and easy to set up, the prospect of a brief electric shock won't stop a panicked horse. Another option is a HiTie, or a homemade version of the same system, where the horse is attached to an arm that swings out from the trailer.

Do not tie your equines to trees. They're likely to chew or rub off the bark, which can kill the tree.

Riding on Indian Lands

Twenty-seven percent of Arizona is owned by Arizona's twenty-one Native American tribes. Non-tribal-members are allowed to ride on much of that land—but not without permission and/or a permit. Each tribe usually has a Web site where you can find out more.

Proactivism

If you've come this far in this book (thank you!), chances are good you enjoy trails in some way, either as a horseback rider, a bird-watcher or other naturalist, a trail runner, a mountain biker, or a hiker.

Here's a question. When was the last time you helped support your trails?

Recently? Good for you! Statistically—and sadly—that means you're probably not a horseback rider.

Nationwide, equestrians have a lousy reputation. We're notorious for not contributing money, time, or effort to sustain the trails we use. Most of us don't attend meetings. We don't go to trail work parties. We don't cough up money for new projects. We don't write letters. Federal and state agencies alike have said horse people can't be counted on—in one conversation a state land-use manager called equestrian volunteers "umm, fluid." (Translation? Unreliable.)

Our excuses are good ones: kids' schedules . . . a nights-and-weekends job . . . going back to school . . . starting a new business . . . writing a trail guide while working full-time . . .

Yet somehow we do still manage to find the time to ride.

On trails that someone else maintained.

So how come all those mountain bikers can be out there building trail alignments? How do those hikers find time to prune scrub and move rocks?

And what about that small number of truly dedicated and often unthanked horse people who are doing their share of the trail work—and ours?

Now that this book is (almost) done, I resolve to join them, even if it's only once a year.

See you out there!

Map Legend

Boundaries

————·———— International Border

————··———··· State Border

National/Wilderness Boundary

National Forest/Park Boundary

Transportation

══⟨40⟩══ Interstate

══⟨93⟩══ U.S. Highway

══⟨64⟩══ State Highway

————— Primary Roads

——⟨709⟩—— Other Roads

══⟨709⟩══ Unpaved Road

= = = = = Unimproved Road

▬▬▬▬▬ Featured Unimproved Trail

▬ ▬ ▬ ▬ Featured Trail

•••••••••• Optional Featured Trail

- - - - - - Other Trail

· · · · · · Cross Country Route

——┼——┼—— Tunnel

┼┼┼┼┼┼┼ Railroad

— — — — Ski Lift

Hydrology

River/Creek

Intermittent Stream

Spring

Falls

Lake

Physiography

× Spot Elevation

)(Pass

▲ Peak

Symbols

START Featured Trail Start

❷ Trail Locator

⤴ Turnaround

🅿 Parking

✈ Airport

≍ Bridge

🚌 Bus Stop

⚑ Cabin/Lodge

△ Campground

† Cemetery

•—• Gate

🯰 Lookout

⚒ Mine

🐾 Natural Preserve

🎪 Picnic Area

▪ Point of Interest

🛈 Ranger Station

🚻 Restroom/Toilet

⚲ Ski Area

○ Town

👁 Viewpoint

Northern Arizona
Bill Williams Mountain

S o who was Bill Williams?

Born William Sherley Williams on January 3, 1787, in Rutherford County, North Carolina, "Old Bill" was an itinerant preacher, trader, trapper, interpreter, and guide. When he was still a child, his family moved to Missouri, where he developed the woodland skills that he would rely on for the rest of his life. At sixteen he settled in with the Great Osage tribe, learning the language, marrying, and fathering two daughters.

When the snow melts and the mud dries, the gently graded cross-country ski trails near Parks are ideal for equestrians.

In 1824 he joined a government-sponsored survey of the Fort Osage–Santa Fe trade route. From then on, he made his living by trapping, and he established his home base in Taos, having moved in with a Mexican widow and her three children.

In 1848 Old Bill made the unfortunate decision to guide Capt. John C. Frémont's expedition across the Rockies in the quest for a railroad route to California. They started in November—late for a mountain crossing—and the expedition foundered, leaving ten men and 120 mules dead. Old Bill and three others made it back to Taos alive, amid accusations and speculations about whom to blame. In spring he and a few others returned to the area to try to salvage what they could, but were attacked and killed by a warring band of Ute Indians.

Another famous guide, Antoine Leroux, met Old Bill during what's thought to be his only trip to Arizona. On Leroux's recommendation, two years later a mountain and a river were named for Old Bill on the map made for the Sitgreaves survey by Richard H. Kern.

1 Benham/Bill Williams Mountain Trail

This out-and-back ride starts at the Benham Trailhead 4 miles south of Williams. From there, the Benham Trail ascends gradually before dead-ending at the Bill Williams Trail at the highest point of the ride. You'll then drop about 2,000 feet to the Bill Williams Ranger Station for a one-way total of 7.4 miles.

Start: 4 miles south of Williams; Coconino County.
Distance: 14.8 miles out and back.
Approximate riding time: 4 to 5 hours.
Total ascent: 3,700 feet.
Difficulty: Difficult. The footing is good for the most part, but most horses will find the climb challenging.
Seasons: Best in late spring and fall.
Water availability: None.

Other trail users: Hikers.
Canine compatibility: Best left at home.
Fees and permits: None.
Facilities: Two picnic tables, three pipe corrals (in excellent condition), vault toilet. Camping with your horse is permitted.
USGS maps: Williams South, McLellan Reservoir.
Contact: USDA Forest Service, Kaibab National Forest, Williams Ranger District, (928) 635-2633.

Reaching the trailhead: In downtown Williams, historic Route 66 parallels Interstate 40. From the intersection of Route 66 and South Fourth Street, follow the sign for SKI AREA, WHITEHORSE LAKE, and go south for 3.5 miles on South Fourth Street. This road is also known as County Road 73, Forest Road 173, and Perkinsville Road. At the sign on CR 73 for BENHAM TRAIL, go right onto Forest Road 140 to the Benham Trailhead, which will be on your right. *DeLorme: Arizona Atlas and Gazetteer:* Page 41 A5.

Trailhead parking: This trailhead features a roomy pull-through parking area with space for four to five trailers. Although space has been allocated for horse trailers at the Bill Williams Trailhead, there's barely enough room for one trailer to turn around.

The Ride

This is a beautiful and challenging ride that winds up, down, and more than halfway around Bill Williams Mountain. It features magnificent views of Sycamore Canyon and the Mingus and Woodchute Mountains to the south, the San Francisco Peaks to the east, and—on a clear day—the Grand Canyon to the north.

The Benham Trail originated as a 1920 toll road to the top of Bill Williams Mountain and was used by the Forest Service to maintain the lookout tower. It was abandoned in 1951 with completion of the new road, then reopened in 1976 as a recreation trail. It's named for H. L. Benham, who was the Williams forest ranger from 1920 to 1921.

The route starts due east of the mountain with a gradual climb through dry, open ponderosa pine forest with occasional thickets of Gambel oak. As you climb, you'll cross over to the west- and north-facing slopes, which are steeper and covered with

Riders of the Benham and Bill Williams Mountain Trails will spend most of their time in deeply shaded mixed-conifer forests and occasional patches of aspen.

dense mixed conifers, along with patches of aspens and the occasional thick carpet of ferns.

The trail is very popular with hikers, but most start at the Bill Williams Ranger Station at the bottom of the Bill Williams Trail. Even so, particularly on weekends, you may find yourself sharing the trail with groups of hikers, some of whom will have dogs (which are supposed to be on leashes).

If you plan to go in late spring or early summer, be sure to check with the ranger station to confirm that the area hasn't been closed due to the threat of forest fires. Also, use common sense during the summer rainy season to avoid exposed ridges during lightning storms.

Miles and Directions

0.0 The trail starts at a red gate behind the Benham Trail information kiosk and begins with a gradual climb through a dry pine and oak forest.

2.1 Cross a gravel road.

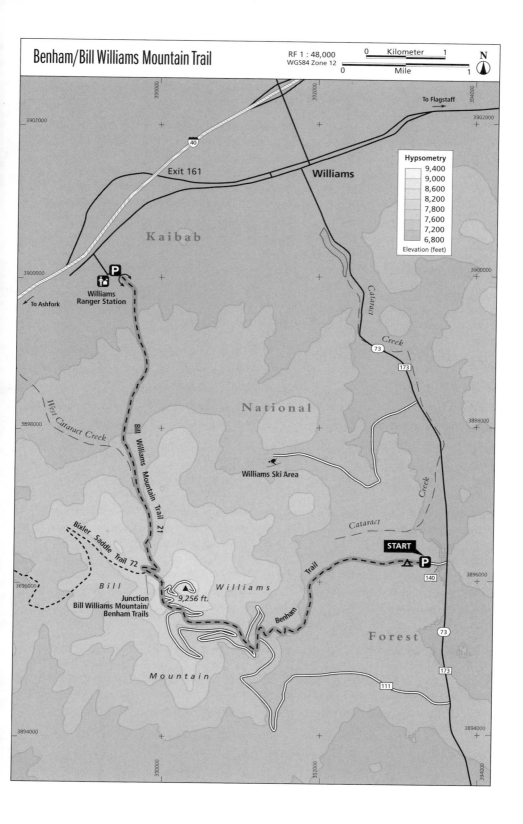

Benham/Bill Williams Mountain Trail

RF 1 : 48,000
WGS84 Zone 12

Kilometer
Mile

N

To Flagstaff

40

Exit 161

Williams

K a i b a b

Hypsometry

9,400
9,000
8,600
8,200
7,800
7,600
7,200
6,800
Elevation (feet)

3902000

3900000

3898000

3896000

3894000

Williams
Ranger Station

To Ashfork

West Cataract Creek

Bill Williams Mountain Trail 21

Bixler Saddle Trail 72

N a t i o n a l

Williams Ski Area

Cataract Creek

73

173

Cataract

Creek

START

P

140

73

173

111

B i l l   W i l l i a m s

9,256 ft.

Junction
Bill Williams Mountain/
Benham Trails

M o u n t a i n

Benham Trail

Benham

F o r e s t

2.5 Cross another gravel road; the trail picks up almost directly across the road. Be alert, as the trail can be easily missed here.

3.5 The trail crosses another gravel road.

4.1 The Benham Trail ends; at 8,860 feet, this is the highest point of your ride. Head up the road 100 yards to pick up the Bill Williams Mountain Trail on the left side of the road. **Bail-out:** Should you decide you and your horse have had enough, you can turn around at this point for a total ride of 8.2 miles, having climbed 1,600 feet.

4.4 The Bixler Saddle Trail comes in on your left. Go straight, remaining on the Bill Williams Mountain Trail. The trail is slow and narrow, but well graded through switchbacks and a dense forest of aspen, pine, and fir. This part of the trail is more challenging and will require more experience—particularly on weekends, when you are likely to encounter hikers.

7.4 The trail descends to the Bill Williams Trailhead, which is at 6,820 feet. Retrace your steps (a 2,000-foot climb) to the Benham Trailhead.

14.8 Arrive back at the trailhead.

Options: For more miles, you can also connect to the Bixler Saddle Trail.

2 Bixler Saddle Trail

This out-and-back route starts at the intersection of Bixler Saddle Road and Forest Road 45, which is 6 miles west of Williams. The first 3.4 miles are on a rarely used, gently ascending two-wheel-drive road; from the Bixler Saddle Trailhead, the trail climbs more steeply to the intersection of the Bill Williams Mountain Trail.

Start: 6 miles west of Williams; Coconino County.

Distance: 10.8 miles out and back.

Approximate riding time: 3 to 4 hours.

Total ascent: 2,000 feet.

Difficulty: Moderate. Most of the footing is good, but flatland horses will notice the climb.

Seasons: Best in late spring and fall.

Water availability: None.

Other trail users: Hikers and vehicles on Forest Road 45 on weekends.

Canine compatibility: Well-conditioned dogs will enjoy this trail. Bring water.

Fees and permits: None.

Facilities: None.

USGS maps: Williams South.

Contact: USDA Forest Service, Kaibab National Forest, Williams Ranger District, (928) 635-2633.

Reaching the trailhead: From Williams, travel west on Interstate 40 to Devil Dog Road (Exit 157). Go back under the highway, drive 0.5 mile, and turn left onto Forest Road 108. Go 2 miles, and FR 45 will take off to your left. Cross the creekbed to the parking area on your right. *DeLorme: Arizona Atlas and Gazetteer:* Page 41 A5.

Trailhead parking: There's a dirt pull-through campsite large enough for several trailers.

On the Bixler Saddle Trail, riders can enjoy seeing claret cup cacti and the view north over the Coconino Plateau toward the Grand Canyon.

The Ride

Although this trail may seem underwhelming at the beginning, the views at the top are well worth the less inspiring terrain at the bottom.

The route starts out as a rutted rocky doubletrack that's negotiable in a passenger car, assuming the vehicle has high clearance and an intrepid driver. *Do not* be tempted to drive your horse trailer up this road—turnaround space is limited.

The road ascends gently through thick stands of Gambel oak and increasing numbers of ponderosa pine, other conifers, and aspen. The footing becomes less rocky with quite a few trottable stretches as the road approaches the Bixler Saddle Trailhead. From then on, the trail is slow, narrow, and quite beautiful as it winds around the side of Bill Williams Mountain with outstanding views of the rock formations of Bixler Mountain itself and of the country to the west and south. Use common sense during the summer rainy season to avoid exposed ridges during lightning storms.

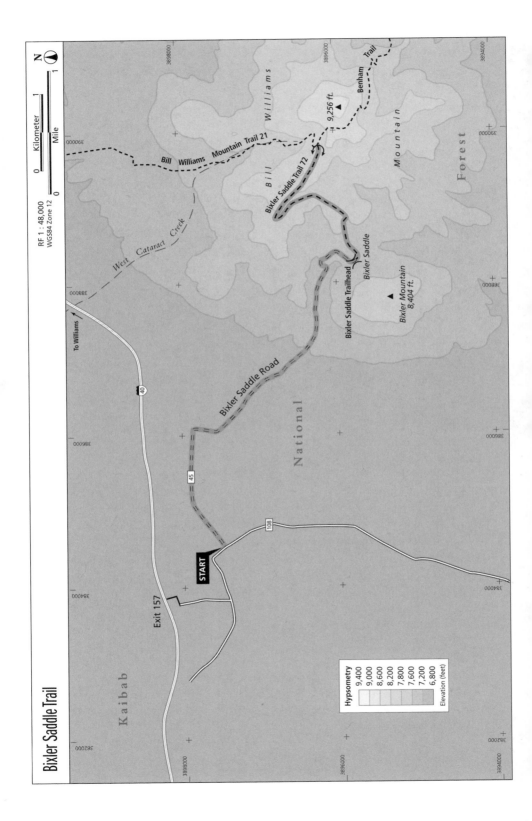

Bixler Saddle Trail

RF 1 : 48,000
WGS84 Zone 12

N

0   Kilometer   1

0   Mile   1

To Williams

40

45

Exit 157

START

108

Bixler Saddle Road

Bixler Saddle Trailhead

Bixler Saddle

Bixler Mountain
8,404 ft.

West Cataract Creek

Bill Williams Mountain Trail 21

Bill Williams

Bixler Saddle Trail 72

9,256 ft.

Benham Trail

Mountain

Kaibab

National

Forest

Hypsometry
9,400
9,000
8,600
8,200
7,800
7,600
7,200
6,800
Elevation (feet)

Because this trail is lightly used, your chances of seeing wildlife are excellent; one reward for walking along quietly was seeing both a tassel-eared squirrel and a mother Merriam's turkey with her babies. Smaller birds you might see include the noisy and nosy mountain chickadee, shiny black ravens, nuthatches, flickers, and the hairy woodpecker. The Bill Williams Mountain area is also some of the best bear habitat in northern Arizona, while javelina tend to be found in the lower elevations.

If you think you might extend your ride to all or part of the Bill Williams Mountain Trail, your canine companion should stay home. That particular trail is very heavily used by hikers, and all dogs should be leashed.

Miles and Directions

0.0 Continue on up FR 45 past the gate. You'll be following a two-wheel-drive road for the next 3.4 miles. Although some sections are rocky and rough, others are gently ascending with good footing.

3.4 Bixler Saddle Trailhead. **Bail-out:** Even if you decide you and your horse have had enough, this trailhead itself is a lovely destination with magnificent views of the rocky escarpment of Bill Williams Mountain. In June, however, it's worth going just a few hundred yards farther up the trail from this point to see if the claret cup cacti are flowering. If you do retrace your steps, you'll have done 6.8 miles with a 1,000-foot climb. To continue on, take Bixler Saddle Trail 72, directly behind the KAIBAB NATIONAL FOREST sign.

4.1 A wide saddle with scattered ponderosa pines, grass for the horses, and a great view of Bill Williams Mountain. If you're planning to picnic, this area is a much more inviting lunch stop than the intersection of the Bixler Saddle and Bill Williams Mountain Trails.

5.4 Intersection of Bixler Saddle Trail 72 and Bill Williams Mountain Trail 21. Retrace your steps to the trailhead. (To continue on, see Benham/Bill Williams Mountain Trail.)

10.8 Arrive back at the intersection of Bixler Saddle Road and FR 45.

Options: From the intersection of Bixler Saddle and Bill Williams Mountain Trails, you can choose to either go down to the Bill Williams Ranger Station and back (a 6-mile round trip, for a total ride of 17.8 miles) or continue on to the Benham Trailhead (an additional 8.8-mile round trip, for a total of 20.8 miles). For less distance, there are also several tempting and exploration-worthy four-wheel-drive double-tracks that take off from FR 45.

The Far North

O kay, so once you go north of Flagstaff maybe there aren't glaciers or moose or igloos. But the North Rim and the even more remote Arizona Strip—the piece of land that runs parallel to the equator just south of Utah—are still a *long* (and expensive) haul for most Grand Canyon State horse owners.

In fact, this piece of Arizona is so far from the "civilized" parts of the state that it almost became Utah instead. In 1866 the three-sided piece of land just northwest of the Grand Canyon had become a part of the new state of Nevada—an acquisition that annoyed many early Arizonans. By 1911 the Utah delegates were hungrily eyeing the Arizona Strip. Their argument was that residents of Fredonia would only have to travel 8 miles to reach Kanab, Utah, while it's a 300-mile round trip to the county seat in Flagstaff.

Nearly a century later, trail riders still have to go almost to Utah to get to the North Rim. Flagstaff residents can get there in five hours; Phoenicians in eight; and for Tucsonans, it's a two-day event just to reach the trailhead.

Detailed trail descriptions for this area will have to wait for some other book, but here are some suggestions for northern areas to investigate, along with one trail to get you started.

Monument Valley

Ironically, this redrock and sandstone landscape that defines Arizona for so many people belongs not to the United States, but to the Navajo Nation, which owns most of the northeast corner of the state. (Considering the rapid despoiling of America's unpopulated regions, perhaps more of our most precious landmarks should be given to tribal authorities for safekeeping.)

Fortunately, realizing the dream of riding your horse through the crimson towers of Monument Valley is still a possibility. Although you'll be required to ride with a guide, for a reasonable fee you are permitted to bring your own horses to this area.

For more information contact the Navajo Parks and Recreation Department, Window Rock Office, (928) 871–6647.

Buckskin Mountain Passage (Arizona Trail)

The Buckskin Mountain Passage is the 10-mile northernmost section of the Arizona Trail that descends the Kaibab Plateau to the Utah/Arizona state line in Coyote Valley.

Access to the state line trailhead is via U.S. Highway 89A between Marble Canyon and Jacob Lake, via Bureau of Land Management Road 1065.

For more information contact the Bureau of Land Management, Arizona Strip BLM District, (435) 688–3200.

Point Sublime

This overlook earns its name. It's a point of land that juts out into the Grand Canyon from which many a famous photograph has been shot. To get to the edge is a 17-mile trip each way over a rough, sometimes impassable, doubletrack better suited to hooves than wheels. Keep in mind that the North Rim within the park is only open mid-May through late October.

Access to the trailhead is from the Widfross Trail parking lot, 2.7 miles north of the Grand Canyon Lodge.

For more information the park has an informative Web site at www.nps .gov/grca/grandcanyon/index.htm.

In addition, the North Rim Backcountry Information Center is open mid-May to mid-October for walk-in visitors from 8:00 A.M. to noon and 1:00 to 5:00 P.M. Mountain Standard Time. Backcountry Information Center staff answer telephone inquiries at (928) 638–7875 between 1:00 and 5:00 P.M. Monday through Friday, except on federal holidays. This telephone number is for information only, not reservations.

3 Russell Tank/Grandview Lookout Passage

This scenic historic trail takes you to the southern edge of the Grand Canyon National Park past vistas where on clear days you can see all the way across the Coconino Plateau to the Painted Desert. You're also more than likely to see elk and deer.

Start: 15 miles southeast of Tusayan; Coconino County.
Distance: 22 miles out and back.
Approximate riding time: 4 to 5 hours.
Total ascent: 500 feet.
Difficulty: Easy, with one steep drainage.
Seasons: Best in late spring, summer, and fall.
Water availability: Stock tank at Russell.

Other trail users: Mountain bikers and hikers.
Canine compatibility: Best left at home.
Fees and permits: None.
Facilities: Vault toilet, stock tank.
USGS maps: Grandview Point.
Contact: USDA Forest Service, Tusayan Ranger District, (928) 638-2443; Arizona Trail Association, (602) 252-4794.

Reaching the trailhead: From Arizona Highway 64/180 (0.8 mile north of the Grand Canyon Airport and just south of Tusayan), go east on Forest Road 302. Take it about 10 miles to Forest Road 301A. Turn right, and go 3 miles to Forest Road 301. Turn right (south), and follow it 5 miles to the intersection of Forest Road 320 and FR 311. Turn left (north) onto FR 311, and travel 2.5 miles to the signed turnoff for Russell Tank. *DeLorme: Arizona Atlas and Gazetteer:* Page 32 B1.

    Trailhead parking: There's room for three or four trailers to pull through, with a little grass and shade.

The Ride

This historic trail follows much of the same route as the Flagstaff–Grand Canyon Stageline run in 1892. The coach ran three times a week, pulled by six horses and dragging a trailer behind. The $20 ride took twelve hours, and in 1897 members of the Coconino Cycling Club rode the same trail in their heavy, no-gear bicycles. How they must have hooted in delight when they beat the stage!

    The stagecoach was discontinued in 1901, when the Grand Canyon Railroad reached Williams.

    The ride begins at Russell Tank, a lovely camping spot nestled among ponderosa pines where elk have left tracks in every section of loose dirt. (Remember that by law, no camping is permitted within 0.25 mile of a stock tank, pond, or spring.)

    The trail is mostly singletrack as it twists, turns, dips, and rises toward the Grand Canyon. Be sure to allow time for Kodak moments to record stunning vistas of the distant canyon. The Painted Desert lurks in the distant haze, while Vishnu Temple points toward the sky.

    Your final destination is Grandview Lookout Tower, where you can celebrate by climbing the 105 steps to the top, near where the now gone Grandview Hotel

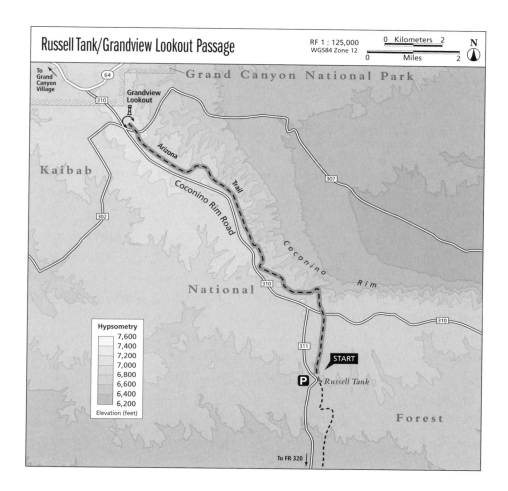

Russell Tank/Grandview Lookout Passage

RF 1 : 125,000
WGS84 Zone 12

0 Kilometers 2

0 Miles 2

N

perched near the South Rim. In the far distance is Humphreys Peak, still barely visible. There's no water at Grandview Tower, but you can take an extra 1.5-mile side trip to water your horse at Hunt Tank.

Miles and Directions

0.0   Head north along the singletrack trail next to Russell Tank, passing through a gate.

1.8   Cross straight over Forest Road 310 to pick up the trail on the other side. Continue heading north as you descend into a drainage and climb back out again.

2.3   A gap in the forest allows your first of a series of glimpses of the Grand Canyon.

3.0   A series of six or seven switchbacks takes you to the bottom of a deep drainage, then another brings you back up. **Bail-out:** You can return to Russell Tank by connecting to FR 310 here, then going south to FR 311.

5.8   After several gates, the trail continues to wander on a mostly level course through ponderosa pines and occasional oaks.

6.0 Along this section you'll be able to see the San Francisco Peaks to the southeast and more Grand Canyon vistas to the north. (Unfortunately, you'll also be able to hear the Grand Canyon planes doing sightseeing tours.)

9.0 "The Dying Forest" section has been clear-cut by the Forest Service to remove ponderosa pines affected by dwarf mistletoe. New trees have been planted, as the interpretive signs explain.

10.0 Intersection of the Arizona Trail with Forest Road 307. You may want to turn right (east) and go an extra 1.5 miles to water your horse at Hull Tank. (Hull Cabin, built in 1888, has been used by the Forest Service since 1907. It still houses seasonal crews who appreciate those who respect their privacy.) Otherwise, turn left and go through the gate next to the cattle guard to continue north.

10.5 The trail widens to a gravel path that intersects with the Vishnu Trail.

11.0 You've reached the Grandview Lookout. Celebrate by climbing the tower to see the San Franciscos, the Painted Desert, and the Grand Canyon. (The tower was built by the Civilian Conservation Corps in 1936.)

22.0 Arrive back at Russell Tank.

Options: If you follow the Arizona Trail 6.7 miles south from Russell Tank, you'll reach the old Moqui Stage Station where the Flagstaff–Grand Canyon stagecoach used to stop.

San Francisco Peaks

N o, the Golden Gate Bridge is nowhere nearby, and the name has nothing to do with the Bay Area.

Born of volcanoes six million years ago, these mountains are visible from more than 100 miles away. They bear one of Arizona's oldest names, having been christened in 1629 by the Franciscan order in Oraibe in honor of St. Francis of Assisi. It wasn't the first time mortals connected the peaks with the divine: Several Indian tribes consider the mountains holy. In 1887, in *Arizona as It Is: The Coming Country,* Hiram Hodge wrote that the Zunis considered San Francisco Peak to be one end of the earth. For the Hopi, *Nuvatukaovi,* "the place of snow on the very top," is winter home for the ancestral kachina spirits. The Navajo call these peaks *Doko'oo'sliid,* "Shining On Top," and see San Francisco Mountain as the western boundary of their lands, as well as a source for medicinal and ceremonial herbs.

The San Francisco Peaks consist of three mountains: Mount Fremont (11,940 feet), Mount Agassiz (12,340 feet), and Humphreys Peak, which at 12,633 feet is Arizona's highest mountain. The three peaks are what remain of what was originally one giant 16,000-foot volcano that erupted about 400,000 years ago.

In 1889 early ecologist C. Hart Merriam proposed that "life zones" change with elevation and latitude in a predictable pattern. He even managed to convince the U.S. Department of Agriculture to allow him to test his theory in the San Francisco Mountains. Today equestrians can duplicate his experience as they ascend through different biotic communities from piñon-juniper woodlands to ponderosa pine, mixed-conifer, aspen, and spruce-fir forests, and finally to alpine tundra atop the two highest peaks, Mounts Humphreys and Agassiz.

Not surprisingly, these mountains have been the site of land-use struggles starting back in the 1880s with logging and grazing, continuing into the 1930s with a ski lodge and access road, and into the '80s with the establishment of a now closed pumice mine. The pressure continues today as recreation, religious freedom, and greed all elbow one another for space on the aspen-and-ponderosa-clad mountainsides.

4 Little Elden/Little Bear Loop Trail

This beautiful and vista-rich 12.1-mile loop leaves from the Little Elden Springs Horse Camp. Much of it is wide and gently graded, but the Heart Trail includes a very steep ascent on a treacherously narrow and rocky trail and should not be attempted by novice horses or riders.

Start: 5 miles northeast of Flagstaff; Coconino County.
Distance: 12.1-mile loop.
Approximate riding time: 5 to 7 hours.
Total ascent: 2,100 feet.
Difficulty: Difficult. The Heart Trail is steep, narrow, and rocky.
Seasons: Best in late spring, summer, and fall.
Water availability: Limited supply at Little Elden Spring at 1.9 miles.
Other trail users: Hikers, trail runners, and mountain bikers.

Canine compatibility: Best left at home.
Fees and permits: $6.00 for day use, $15.00 per night.
Facilities: Restrooms (solar toilets), water faucets, trash dumpster, and 15 sites with picket line, picnic table, grill, and sturdy hitching rails.
USGS maps: Sunset Crater West.
Contact: USDA Forest Service, Coconino National Forest, Peaks District Ranger Station, (928) 526-0866.

Reaching the trailhead: From Flagstaff, travel east on Interstate 40 to Exit 201. Take U.S. Highway 89 north 4.5 miles and turn left (west) onto Elden Springs Road, which is also Forest Road 556. (The turnoff is 0.5 mile north of the traffic light at Silver Saddle Road. If you get to the landfill, you've gone too far.) Go 2 miles on FR 556 to the Little Elden Springs Horse Camp.

If you're parking for the day only, you can also drive up the road an additional 0.3 mile to the Little Elden Trailhead where there's limited pull-through parking for one or two trailers at no charge. *DeLorme: Arizona Atlas and Gazetteer:* Page 42 A2.

Trailhead parking: The Little Elden Springs Horse Camp, open May through mid-October, is one of the best horse camps in the state and highly recommended. Each site has ample room for large rigs to pull through as well as a picket line long enough for two horses. No permits are needed, but reservations are strongly recommended, especially for weekends; (877) 444-6777. Several campsites are also available on a first-come, first-served basis.

The Ride

This route includes the Heart Trail, which is officially not recommended for horses since it is steep, narrow, and rocky, and also includes the potential of meeting hikers and their (mostly) leashed dogs. Do not attempt this trail unless your equine companion is sensible, fit, and well shod, and do be prepared to dismount and lead your horse.

This trail is both lovely and dramatic in its variety and contrasts. It starts out in open ponderosa woodlands with scattered junipers and Gambel oaks, then ascends with nonstop vistas from the steep northern and eastern slopes of Mount Elden.

Given its narrow width and cardiac-stressing 1,450-foot climb in 2.4 miles, the appropriately named Heart Trail should only be attempted by sensible, well-conditioned horse-and-rider teams. However, the vista looking south over Flagstaff and beyond is worth the effort.

Until the top, riders have an unobstructed view thanks to the devastating human-caused 1977 Radio Fire, which burned 4,500 acres along the east slope of Mount Elden. Gambel oak is now returning to the area and lines the trail.

Once you've negotiated your way through the boulders just past the summit, the route meanders through lovely pine meadows with a wide choice of fallen logs to sit on while enjoying lunch. You'll then head downhill on the gently graded slope of the Little Bear Trail. This new, beautifully constructed trail—completed in 1998 by dedicated hikers, bikers, and equestrians—takes you down through the north-facing slopes densely forested with mixed conifers until you rejoin the Little Elden Trail.

All these trails are heavily used on weekends by hikers, trail runners, and mountain bikers, most of whom are extremely considerate of equestrians. However, although horses have right-of-way, be prepared to give up that right, particularly to novice mountain bikers with little control—or to those wearing headphones who may not be aware of your presence.

Little Elden/Little Bear Loop Trail

RF 1 : 62,500
WGS84 Zone 12

Use common sense during the summer rainy season to avoid exposed ridges during lightning storms.

Miles and Directions

0.0   The trail heads west through a gate near the campground entrance on the connector to the Little Elden Trail.

0.7   Little Elden Trailhead. The trail will soon cross over FR 556.

1.0   Intersection of the Little Elden Trailhead connector and the Little Elden Trail. Go left (southeast)—*do not* attempt this trail in the other direction. It's much safer to ride *up* the Heart Trail. The narrow width, rocky terrain, and steep slope of the switchbacks combine to make riding down this trail a definite Bad Idea.

1.9   Although Little Elden Spring does have water, it's not an ideal watering place for horses: The trough is a rusty half barrel with sharp edges and may or may not have sufficient water.

3.5 Intersection of the Little Elden and Heart Trails. The trail takes a hard right (north) turn then twists toward the west. You'll ride past the sign that reads NOT RECOMMENDED FOR HORSES. Again, be *sure* you and your horse are ready for the 1,450-foot climb. **Bail-out:** Should you decide that maybe you and/or your horse aren't quite ready for this challenge on top of the 700 feet you've already climbed, consider going left and heading toward the Sandy Seep, Christmas Tree, Fatman's Loop, or Elden Lookout Trails. You'll still have a lovely ride.

5.9 Intersection of the Heart and Sunset Trails. At 8,700 feet, this is the highest elevation of this ride, and you and your horse have climbed more than 2,000 feet. Go right (north) downhill on the Sunset Trail. The footing is somewhat tricky for the first 0.5 mile since the trail winds between, over, and around large round boulders.

6.8 Intersection of the Sunset and Little Bear Trails (both of which are popular with mountain bikers). Go right (north); you'll be heading downhill through a forested north-facing slope for the next 4 miles.

10.7 Intersection of the Little Bear and Little Elden Trails. Go right (east).

11.4 Turnoff to the Little Elden Trailhead and Little Elden Springs Horse Camp. Go left (north), following the sign that reads HORSE CAMP .7 MILES.

12.1 Arrive back at the horse camp.

Options: The Kachina Peaks Wilderness and Mount Elden/Dry Lake Hills area is arguably the state's finest trail riding. From the Little Elden Springs Horse Camp, you can connect to more than 200 miles of spectacular trails ranging from the very easy to the highly challenging.

5 Little Elden/Weatherford Trail

If you and your equine companion are up for a long and challenging day with stunning views of snow-covered peaks, this out-and-back trail from the Little Elden Springs Horse Camp to Fremont Saddle is it. At 21.4 miles with 4,000 feet of climbing, it's among the longest trails in this book.

Start: 5 miles northeast of Flagstaff; Coconino County.

Distance: 21.4 miles out and back.

Approximate riding time: All day.

Total ascent: 4,100 feet.

Difficulty: Difficult, due to the length, the challenging climb, and the possibility of snowdrifts much of the year.

Seasons: Best in fall to avoid mud, snow, and thunderstorms.

Water availability: Schultz Tank at 3.3 and 18.1 miles.

Other trail users: Hikers, mountain bikers, and trail runners.

Canine compatibility: Best left at home.

Fees and permits: $6.00 for day use, $15.00 per night.

Facilities: Restrooms (solar toilets), water faucets, trash dumpster, and 15 sites with picket line, picnic table, grill, and sturdy hitching rails.

USGS maps: Sunset Crater, West Humphreys Peak.

Contact: USDA Forest Service, Coconino National Forest, Peaks District Ranger Station, (928) 526-0866.

Reaching the trailhead: From Flagstaff, travel east on Interstate 40 to Exit 201. Take U.S. Highway 89 north 4.5 miles and turn left (west) onto Elden Springs Road, which is also Forest Road 556. (The turnoff is 0.5 mile north of the traffic light at Silver Saddle Road. If you get to the landfill, you've gone too far.) Go 2 miles on FR 556 to the Little Elden Springs Horse Camp.

If you're parking for the day only, you can also drive up the road an additional 0.3 mile to the Little Elden Trailhead where there's limited pull-through parking for one or two trailers at no charge. *DeLorme: Arizona Atlas and Gazetteer:* Page 42 A2.

Trailhead parking: The Little Elden Springs Horse Camp, open May through mid-October, is one of the best horse camps in the state and highly recommended. Each site has ample room for large rigs to pull through as well as a picket line long enough for two horses. No permits are needed, but reservations are strongly recommended, especially for weekends; (877) 444-6777. Several campsites are also available on a first-come, first-served basis.

The Ride

What with early and late snows, mud, forest closings due to fire danger, and thunderstorms, the window to ride this entire trail is narrow. (I was unable to reach Doyle Saddle in mid-June because of numerous snowdrifts across the trail, some as deep as 5 feet.) Even if you're forced to turn back at some point in the upper elevations of this trail, you still will have had a stunningly satisfying ride with superb views and magnificent scenery.

Mountain bikers, a common sight on the Little Elden and Schultz Tank Trails, take a break at Schultz Tank. Humphreys Peak, still with snow in mid-June, is in the background.

The first 3.5 miles—a gentle ascent with occasional short trotting stretches from the horse camp to Schultz Tank—is an ideal distance for warming up your horse before tackling the Weatherford Trail itself. From the low ponderosa pine and Gambel oak woodland, the trail moves into open meadows dotted with distinctive western white pines, then heads up into spruce forests. As it approaches the pass, it moves into a dense spruce forest. Then the trees gradually become less dense, revealing more of the incredible panoramas stretching 50 miles over to Flagstaff and beyond.

The Little Elden, Schultz Tank, and Weatherford Trails are all popular with hikers, mountain bikers, and trail runners, especially on weekends. Once you reach the Kachina Peaks Wilderness, however, mountain bikers are no longer permitted on the trail. Although the Weatherford Trail goes most of the way to Humphreys Peak, horses are not permitted beyond Doyle Saddle, approximately 4 miles below the peak.

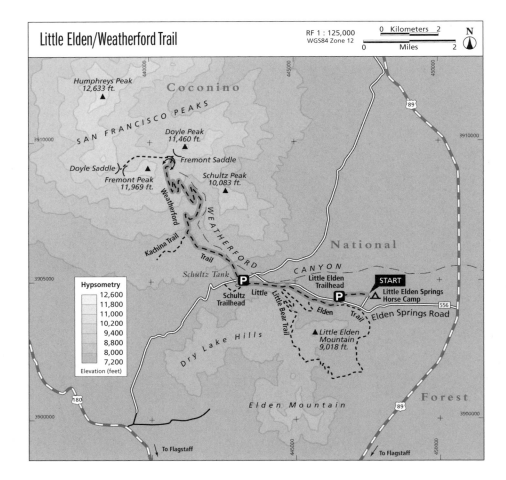

Little Elden/Weatherford Trail

RF 1 : 125,000
WGS84 Zone 12

0 Kilometers 2

0 Miles 2

N

Miles and Directions

0.0 The trail heads west through a gate near the campground entrance on the connector to the Little Elden Trail.

0.7 Little Elden Trailhead. The trail will soon cross over FR 556.

1.0 Intersection of the Little Elden Trailhead connector and the Little Elden Trail. Go right (west), following the sign to the Schultz Tank (the Heart Trail is to your left).

1.6 Intersection of Little Elden and Little Bear Trails. Continue to go straight (west).

3.0 Fence with a gate (always leave gates open or closed, as you found them).

3.3 Intersection of the Little Elden and Schultz Tank connector trails. Schultz Tank is to your right, with a sign. Turn right here, following the trail over a dam wall to the Schultz Trailhead. Continue on through the parking lot and across a gravel road to the start of the Weatherford Trail.

3.8 The Weatherford Trail, which is labeled with a sign, begins here and heads uphill toward Doyle Pass.

5.7 Intersection of the Weatherford and Kachina Trails. Continue on straight (north) on the Weatherford Trail. At this point you and your horse have climbed 1,700 feet.

5.8 Enter Kachina Peaks Wilderness (marked with a sign). The trail continues to climb, but soon after entering the wilderness, you'll start a series of wide, long switchbacks—what remains of an old road that was closed to traffic when this area was established as wilderness. Within the next 2 miles, you may encounter snow even as late as mid-June. Also, the trail may be blocked by the occasional tree fall.

10.7 Fremont Saddle and an elevation of 10,630 feet (a total climb of 3,500 feet), just below Doyle Pass. You can turn around here or proceed another 0.5 mile to Doyle Saddle, which is as far as horses are permitted to go. Retrace your steps to the trailhead.

15.7 Intersection with the Kachina Trail; bear left.

17.6 End of the Weatherford Trail. Cross the gravel road, pass through the Schultz Trailhead parking lot, and ride past Schultz Tank.

18.1 Rejoin the Little Elden Trail; turn left.

19.8 Intersection of the Little Elden and Little Bear Trails. Keep going straight.

20.5 Intersection of the Little Elden Trail and Little Elden Trailhead connector. Go left, following a sign that reads HORSE CAMP .7 MILES.

21.4 Arrive back at Little Elden Springs Horse Camp.

Options: After this ride it's unlikely you'll want more miles in the same day; however, from the Little Elden Springs Horse Camp, you can connect to more than 200 miles of spectacular trails ranging from the very easy to the highly challenging.

6 Flagstaff Urban Trail System (FUTS)

As someone whose favorite activity is futzing about in the woods, I have to ask: How can anyone not like a trail system called FUTS?

Even though I didn't test-ride any of the trails that make up the Flagstaff Urban Trail System, it's still well worth a mention—and even more worthy of emulation by many other American cities.

The city of Flagstaff should be commended for seeing trails not only as recreational assets, but also as transportation elements and as a way to assemble what will eventually be a 50-mile trail system connecting residential and commercial areas, cultural centers, schools (including Northern Arizona University), recreational areas, and public lands. FUTS also allows access to the Arizona Trail, to 200 miles within the Coconino National Forest, and the Flagstaff Bikeways Network. Since the 1980s, about 25 miles have been completed.

Even at the county level, trail awareness is high: The 2001 Coconino County Parks and Recreation Strategic Plan includes plans to "identify and develop feasible FUTS (Flagstaff Urban Trail System) trail extensions to communities outside the Flagstaff city limits as opportunities arise."

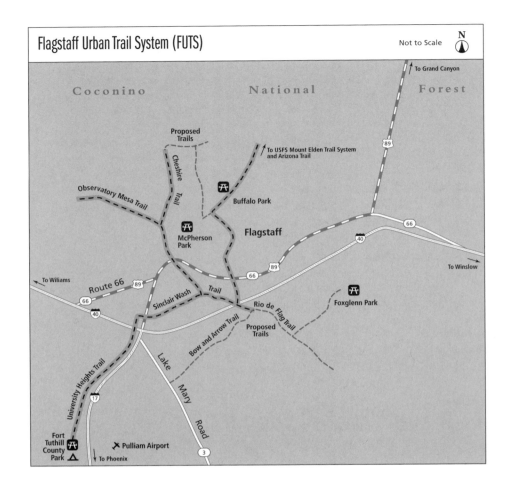

The trail is designed for walkers, pedestrian commuters, runners, bikers, and equestrians—who are asked to use the natural surfacing adjacent to the trails. With 108 inches of snow each winter in Flagstaff, the trail is also popular with cross-country skiers.

For more information or to pick up a FUTS map ($2.00), contact Flagstaff Parks and Recreation, (928) 779–7690, or check the Web at www.flagstaff.az.gov.

7 Soldiers Trail

This is a fun, easygoing 5-mile loop trail through the ponderosa pines right outside Flagstaff. Its mix of flat trottable stretches with a couple of challenging climbs is ideal for novice horses and riders.

Start: 3 miles south of Flagstaff; Coconino County.
Distance: 5-mile loop.
Approximate riding time: 1 to 2 hours.
Total ascent: Approximately 500 feet.
Difficulty: Easy with good footing.
Seasons: Best in summer and fall. Park authorities have asked that users avoid these trails during the snowmelt season.

Water availability: None.
Other trail users: Hikers and mountain bikers.
Canine compatibility: Best left at home; only leashed dogs are allowed in the park.
Fees and permits: None for day use.
Facilities: Two portable toilets.
USGS maps: Flagstaff West.
Contact: Flagstaff Parks and Recreation, (928) 774-2572.

Reaching the trailhead: From Flagstaff, travel south on Interstate 17 to Exit 337, labeled COCONINO COUNTY FAIRGROUNDS. Go right (east), and cross over U.S. Highway 89 to the county park. Follow signs to the trailhead. *DeLorme: Arizona Atlas and Gazetteer:* Page 42 A1.

Trailhead parking: Fort Tuthill County Park is home of the Coconino County Fair and Coconino County Horse Races, so there's room for hundreds of rigs.

The Ride

This pleasant, easy urban trail loops around the edge of the park named for the soldiers who were at Fort Tuthill when it was a National Guard facility before World War II. In addition to the main trail, riders have access to the cross-country course, which adds about 3 miles of wide, flat paths with excellent footing.

Camping with your horse is permitted at the stables from May through September. Fees run $11.00 per stall, $9.00 per campsite without utilities, $13.00 with utilities, $2.00 for a shower. Be sure to call first, as the facilities close for special events; (928) 774–5139.

The county park includes an amphitheater; fairgrounds (the Coconino County Fair takes place on Labor Day weekend); a 1,600-seat grandstand with 144 box seats; a ⅝-mile dirt racetrack (quarterhorse racing takes place on the July 4 weekend); a 309-by-157-foot rodeo arena; a 0.96-acre infield jumping arena; basketball, tennis, racquetball, and volleyball courts; and six picnic armadas, each of which has around ten picnic tables and a capacity of 350 people.

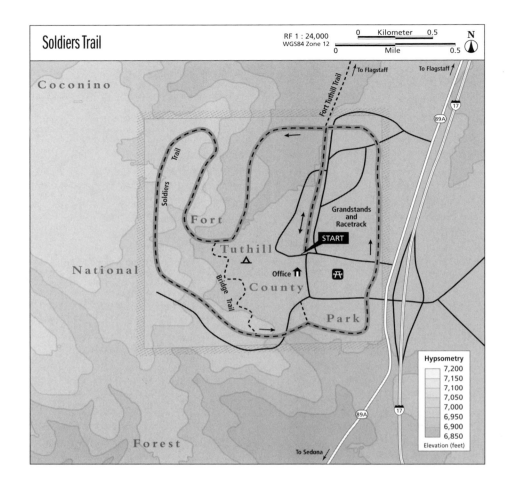

Miles and Directions

Because this trail is part of an urban trail system, it is signed and very obvious where to go. One point to watch out for: At approximately 2 miles out, you'll encounter the intersection of Soldiers and Bridge Trails. Be sure to remain on the Soldiers Trail. The Bridge Trail is a nature trail meant for hikers and not recommended for equestrians.

Options: Soldiers Trail connects to FUTS, the Flagstaff Urban Trail System via the Sinclair Wash Urban Trail. There are also occasional connections to various Forest Service roads.

Spring Valley
Cross-Country Ski Trails

T he next time you reach for your knife (you *do* carry one when you work around horses, don't you?), consider what the equivalent might have been 1,000 years ago. Chances are excellent the prehistoric Leatherman blade was made of obsidian—and in Arizona, chances are also good that it might have come from these very Spring Valley trails.

Obsidian is basically leftover lava from an ancient volcanic eruption and is a smooth, usually black glass. The rock cooled so quickly after the eruption—it was quenched, in fact—that it lacks the mineral crystals of granite and rhyolite, its close cousins. When struck, obsidian breaks in a way that leaves a microscopic edge sharp and durable enough that primitive hunters used it for projectile points, knives, and scrapers. Indeed, that edge is so sharp that obsidian is still used in operating rooms today: Scalpels made of obsidian are many times stronger than standard surgical steel, can be reused, and cause less tissue trauma.

The earliest Arizona residents were well aware of obsidian's value. Not only did they use it to make arrowheads and spear points, but it was a vital trading currency as well. According to some fascinating research by Dr. M. Steven Shackley at the University of California–Berkeley, Government Hill and RS Hill were both sources of obsidian for the Hohokam culture, which flourished around A.D. 1150. Recent evidence indicates that obsidian from the San Francisco volcanic fields ended up all over Arizona and as far away as the California coast.

(Note: These trails are set up for cross-country skiers and are marked in one direction only to avoid accidents and to make the most appropriate use of the topography. The trail descriptions follow the same convention, but once you're familiar with the area, you can ride them in either direction.)

8 Spring Valley Eagle Rock Loop Trail

This is a moderate 11.3-mile loop with a 1,400-foot climb on mostly solid, wide singletrack or cross-country ski trails. Motorized vehicles are prohibited in this lightly used area, and it is easily accessed just north of Parks.

Start: 6 miles north of Parks; Coconino County.
Distance: 11.3-mile loop.
Approximate riding time: 3 hours at a leisurely pace.
Total ascent: 1,400 feet.
Difficulty: Moderate, with good footing except in mud season.
Seasons: Best in late spring (after snowmelt), summer, and fall.

Water availability: Spring Valley Tank at 1.1 and 10.3 miles usually has water.
Other trail users: Hikers.
Canine compatibility: Good trail for dogs. Bring water in hot weather.
Fees and permits: None.
Facilities: None.
USGS maps: Parks.
Contact: USDA Forest Service, Kaibab National Forest, Williams Ranger District, (928) 635-2633.

Reaching the trailhead: From Flagstaff, take Interstate 40 west toward Kingman to the Parks exit (Exit 178). At the end of the ramp, go north (right). At the T-intersection with Old Route 66, go west (left). Travel 0.5 mile to the Parks General Store (which is well worth a visit), and go north (right) on Spring Valley Drive (Forest Road 141) for 6 miles. The parking area will be on your right. *DeLorme: Arizona Atlas and Gazetteer:* Page 41 A6.

Trailhead parking: There's limited parking for big rigs, but room for four to five smaller ones.

The Ride

This trail is gnarlier than the RS Hill Loop (the other loop from this trailhead), with three times the climb and proportionally more singletrack trail—plus a great view of Eagle Rock. There's a steep gravelly downhill after the one major ascent. Other than the open meadow near the Spring Valley Tank, the trail doesn't offer much in the way of views, but it's a pleasant ride through ponderosa pine with an occasional Douglas fir.

Miles and Directions

0.0   Go through the gate behind the residence and to the right of the trailhead sign. Follow the blue diamonds (singletrack) or the two-track road. If you follow the road, go around a ROAD CLOSED gate at 0.7 mile in order to bypass private property.

1.1   The road goes across a swampy meadow and below Spring Valley Tank. (If you want to water your horse, go past the lower wall of the dirt tank around to the opposite side.)

1.3   The blue-diamond singletrack trail crosses the meadow above the tank, then rejoins the road.

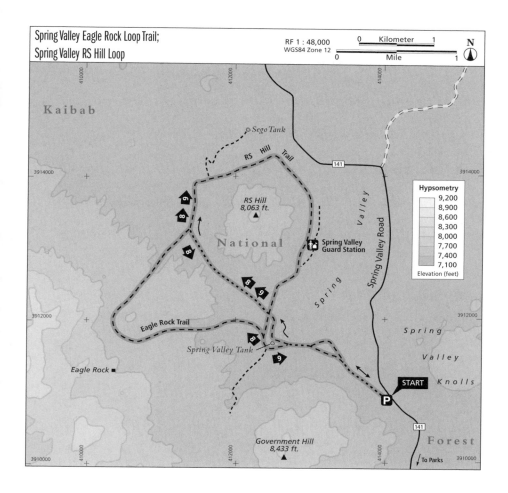

1.4 Go left, following the sign that reads RS HILL LOOP. You'll also be following blue diamonds up the hill.

1.6 Green gate and fence. (Always leave gates open or closed, as you found them.)

2.1 Top of the hill; head downhill.

2.3 The singletrack trail rejoins the road: Continue to follow the blue diamonds.

2.9 Leave the road and follow blue diamonds to the right on a singletrack trail.

4.6 Forest Service Spring Valley Work Center is on your left.

4.8 Rejoin the road.

5.4 Back at the RS HILL LOOP sign, go straight, still following blue diamonds, down the road.

5.7 Turn right at the sign that reads EAGLE ROCK LOOP, and follow red diamonds. The trail starts climbing almost immediately. **Bail-out:** Should you decide you and your horse have had enough, go straight and follow blue diamonds 1.2 miles back to the trailhead.

6.6 Gate with a ROAD CLOSED sign to prevent vehicular access; there's plenty of room for equestrians to go around.

6.7   Leave the road to follow the red diamonds (singletrack) on your left.

7.5   This is the high point for the trail (7,845 feet); it goes downhill from here. There's a fence and gate at the top of the hill.

7.8   Rejoin the two-track road.

8.3   Fence line and gate (which is usually open).

8.6   Turn right at the sign that reads RS HILL LOOP and follow the blue diamonds back up the hill. This is the most direct way back to the trailhead.

9.1   Top of the hill.

9.7   Green gate and fence.

9.8   Back at the RS HILL LOOP sign. Turn right down the road, following the blue diamonds.

10.1   Eagle Rock trail on your right—go straight. From here, the blue diamonds go left cross-country toward Spring Valley Tank.

10.3   You're now on the opposite side of Spring Valley Tank than you were at 1.1 miles.

10.6   Leave the doubletrack road and follow the blue diamonds onto singletrack.

11.2   Rejoin the doubletrack road near the trailhead.

11.3   Arrive back at the trailhead.

Options: The RS Hill Loop; other forest and logging roads traverse the area as well.

⑨ Spring Valley RS Hill Loop

This is an easy, mostly flat 6.9-mile loop on cross-country ski trails with good footing and easily accessed from Parks. Motorized vehicles are prohibited in this area, which is only lightly used by hikers and other equestrians.

See map on page 47.
Start: 6 miles north of Parks; Coconino County.
Distance: 6.9-mile loop.
Approximate riding time: 2 hours at a leisurely pace.
Total ascent: 500 feet.
Difficulty: Easy, with good footing except in mud season.
Seasons: Best in spring, summer, and fall.
Water availability: Spring Valley Tank at 1.1 and 5.9 miles.
Other trail users: Hikers.
Canine compatibility: Good trail for dogs. Bring water in hot weather.
Fees and permits: None.
Facilities: None.
USGS maps: Parks.
Contact: USDA Forest Service, Williams Ranger District office, (928) 635-2633.

Reaching the trailhead: From Flagstaff, take Interstate 40 west toward Kingman to the Parks exit (Exit 178). At the end of the ramp, go north (right). At the T-intersection with Old Route 66, go west (left). Travel 0.5 mile to the Parks General Store (which is well worth a visit), and go north (right) on Spring Valley Drive (Forest Road 141) for 6 miles. The parking area will be on your right. *DeLorme: Arizona Atlas and Gazetteer:* Page 41 A6.

Two riders pause to take in the view near the Spring Valley Work Center.

Trailhead parking: There's limited parking for big rigs, but room for four to five smaller ones.

The Ride

This is an ideal area to bring novice horses and/or riders, with nothing alarming but the occasional elk. The wide, gently graded roads and occasional singletrack trails wind their way through ponderosa pine forest and aspen meadows. There's one open meadow with a nice view of Humphreys Peak.

Miles and Directions

0.0 Go through the gate behind the house and to the right of the trailhead sign. Follow the blue diamonds (singletrack) or the two-track road. If you follow the road, go around a ROAD CLOSED gate at 0.7 mile in order to bypass private property.

1.1 The road goes across a swampy meadow and below Spring Valley Tank. (If you want to water your horse, go past the lower wall of the dirt tank around to the opposite side.)

1.3 The blue-diamond singletrack trail crosses the meadow above the tank, then rejoins the road.

1.4 Go left, following the sign that reads RS HILL LOOP. You'll also be following blue diamonds up the hill.

1.6 Green gate and fence. (Always leave gates open or closed, as you found them.)

2.1 Top of the hill: This is the high point of this loop (7,550 feet), and you'll be heading downhill from here on.

2.3 The singletrack trail rejoins the road: Continue to follow the blue diamonds.

2.9 Leave the road and follow the blue diamonds to the right on a singletrack trail.

4.6 Forest Service Spring Valley Work Center on your left.

4.8 Rejoin the road.

5.4 Back at the RS HILL LOOP sign. Go straight, still following the blue diamonds, down the road.

5.7 Go straight past the sign reading EAGLE ROCK LOOP on your right. Soon afterward, follow the blue diamonds as they go left, heading cross-country and toward Spring Valley Tank.

5.9 You're now on the opposite side of Spring Valley Tank than you were at 1.1 miles.

6.2 Leave the two-track road and follow the blue diamonds onto singletrack.

6.8 Rejoin the two-track road near the trailhead.

6.9 Arrive back at the trailhead.

Options: Eagle Rock Loop; other forest and logging roads traverse the area as well.

Central Arizona
Bradshaw Mountains

The Bradshaw Mountains are known as one of the world's most mineralized ranges, and the main character in their story is gold. Through 1959, Yavapai County ranked first in the state for gold production.

The now abandoned gold-mining industry has left a boon for equestrians: Minor (so to speak) roads crisscross the entire region, providing a rich lode for trail riding.

The day-use area at Groom Creek is located at 6,100 feet and has plenty of room for six to eight large trailers. (Kheegan is ready to get out and ride!)

The range is named for one, or maybe both, of the Bradshaw brothers. William was a miner but also an engineer and an opportunistic, hard-drinking entrepreneur who realized that the real gold was to be found in the pockets of would-be diggers. He established what became known as the Bradshaw Trail that ran from Dos Palmas, California, to the Colorado River. He then added a ferry service to get the miners across to Arizona to where gold had been found at La Paz, just south of what would eventually became Ehrenberg.

Later, in 1863, he led the first group of white men to the Black Canyon area, where they discovered ore deposits. His brother Isaac, who'd been managing the ferry, came, settled in the area, and is buried near Bradshaw Springs.

William prospered and even ran for Congress (as a Democrat in the new territory during the Civil War, he was badly beaten), but he met an unfortunate end. According to the *Los Angeles Tri-Weekly*, on December 2, 1864, he was on a "big bender" in La Paz and "pursued by ghosts. He walked deliberately into a carpenter's shop, took up a drawing knife, and with one stroke nearly severed his head from his shoulders."

The Bradshaw Ranger District encompasses the Bradshaw Range and extends beyond it, surrounding the city of Prescott. As you drive and ride through this area, you may see many dead and dying pine trees. Prescott National Forest is experiencing an epidemic of bark beetle infestation, which, as of 2005, has killed 93,000 acres of ponderosa pine. The insects (also known as the Ips, or "engraver," beetles) are always present in normal forest systems, and healthy trees can withstand their populations. However, trees stressed by prolonged drought, fire, previous insect attacks, or crowded living conditions produce a compound called turpene that the beetles can detect. Once the beetles find a potential host tree, they emit a pheromone that attracts even more of them.

The insects damage the trees in two ways. First, they essentially create a tourniquet around the tree as they feed on the inner bark, blocking the flow of nutrients from the needles to the rest of the tree. Simultaneously, they introduce a fungus that grows deeper into the stem, blocking the passage of water and nutrients from the roots.

While drought conditions persist, one way to slow the epidemic is to improve the health of the forest system through careful thinning.

10 Willow Trail/Mint Wash Loop Trail

A pleasant, easily accessed, moderate 8.5-mile trail in the Granite Basin Recreation Area, with good views, varied vegetation, and excellent footing most of the way.

Start: 9 miles west of Prescott; Yavapai County.
Distance: 8.5-mile loop.
Approximate riding time: 3.5 to 4 hours.
Total ascent: 900 feet.
Difficulty: Moderate. Most of the trail is easy, but there are several slightly technical rocky areas along Mint Wash.
Seasons: Best in late spring, summer, and fall.
Water availability: Drinking water and a water trough at the trailhead.
Other trail users: Hikers, climbers, and mountain bikers.

Canine compatibility: Leashed dogs allowed in the Cayuse day-use area, and unleashed dogs "under control" allowed in Prescott National Forest. Bring water.
Fees and permits: $2.00 day-use fee; free admittance on Wednesday.
Facilities: Pit toilet, picnic tables.
USGS maps: Iron Springs.
Contact: USDA Forest Service, Prescott National Forest, Bradshaw Ranger District, (928) 443-8000.

Reaching the trailhead: From Phoenix, take Interstate 17 north to Cordes Junction (Exit 262) and follow Arizona Highway 69 to Prescott. Stay in the right lane of AZ 69 as you enter Prescott, and follow signs for Arizona Highway 89 South. Turn right at Sheldon Street, which dead-ends at Montezuma Street. Turn right, and continue to where Willow Creek, Miller Valley, and Iron Spring Roads all intersect. Montezuma Street becomes Iron Springs Road here; continue straight through the intersection, heading out of town. From Williamson Valley Road (there is a traffic light and fire station at this intersection), stay on Iron Spring Road for 1.6 miles to Granite Basin Road (Forest Road 374). Turn right onto FR 374 and travel 2.5 miles to the Cayuse Equestrian Trailhead, which will be on your right. Cayuse is day use only, with a $2.00 day-use fee; no overnight camping. Excellent maps are available at the pay station. *DeLorme: Arizona Atlas and Gazetteer:* Page 41 D4.

    Trailhead parking: There's ample pull-through trailer parking for six to eight rigs, including goosenecks; day use only. Parking permits good for three to twelve months are also available for purchase at ranger stations and participating vendors. Equestrian groups are limited to ten animals.

The Ride

The popular Granite Basin area is only fifteen minutes from Prescott by a paved road and includes 20 miles of scenic boulder-strewn singletrack trails, a group campground, the Granite Mountain Wilderness, and the human-made Granite Basin Lake. Although the lake is only five acres and unstocked, fishing and boating (electric motors only) are permitted. Swimming is not allowed.

    The Granite Mountain area is heavily used by hikers, climbers, mountain bikers, and other equestrians, especially on weekends. Be prepared to share the trail.

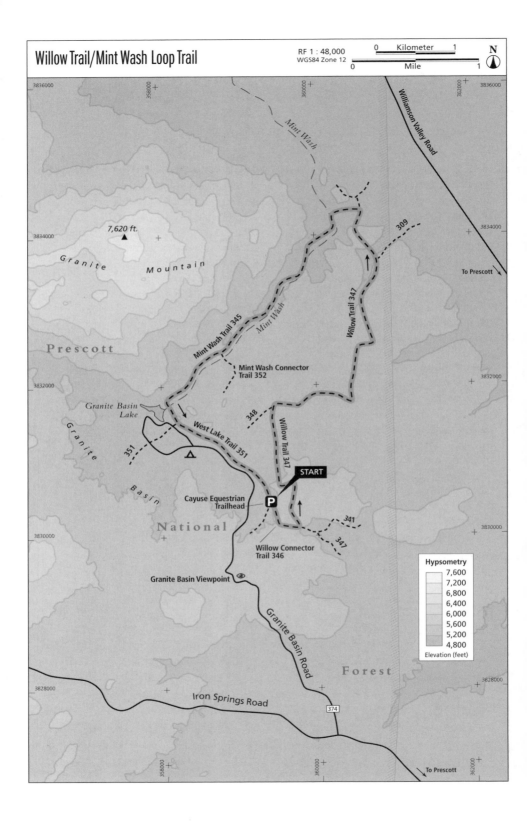

Dogs must be leashed at all times in the Cayuse day-use area. Although Prescott National Forest authorities permit dogs off-leash as long as they are "under control," this route is a long dry loop in summer until the lake at 7.5 miles. Be sure your canine friend is fit, and carry dog water. (A one-gallon ziplock bag makes an easy-to-carry collapsible dog bowl—and in a pinch your horse can drink out of it as well.)

Willow Connector Trail 346 starts out in dry woodlands with manzanita, agave, piñon-juniper, and oak scrub. As you climb, you'll get an occasional view across the town of Prescott toward Humphreys Peak. As you descend from the high point of the trail into Mint Wash, the trail becomes rockier and passes through a mixture of ponderosa pines and riparian (streamside) vegetation, including box elder and cottonwood, which are particularly lovely in fall.

Some sections of the trail, particularly the descent from the high point, may be somewhat technical on horseback—and look as if they'd be very tricky on a bike!

Miles and Directions

0.0 Head south from the southern end of the Cayuse parking lot. The trail forks almost immediately; go southeast (left) onto Willow Connector Trail 346. You'll ascend a short hill and go through a gate (you'll need to dismount if it's closed; be sure to leave it as you find it).

0.5 Intersection of Willow Connector Trail 346 and Willow Trail 347. Go northwest (a hard left) onto Willow Trail 347. The next 4 miles are gently undulating, mostly downhill trail passing through open piñon-oak-juniper woodland with occasional low scattered ponderosa pine. Prickly pear and manzanita are scattered through this woodland.

1.7 Intersection of Willow Trail 347 and Chimbly Water Trail 348. Stay on Willow Trail 347.

4.0 Intersection of Willow Trail 347 and Trail 309. Stay on Willow Trail 347, heading north. (The unnamed Trail 309 goes northeast out of the forest.) Excellent views of Granite Mountain to the west and the San Francisco Mountains to the northeast can be seen over the roofs of the subdivision.

4.5 Intersection of Willow Trail 347 and Mint Wash Trail 345. Turn west (left) onto Mint Wash Trail 345. The trail turns and heads southwest following Mint Wash, close to the boundary of Granite Mountain Wilderness. The character of the vegetation changes, becoming drier, with few ponderosa pines and fewer oaks. You'll see cottonwoods and occasional walnuts along Mint Wash, with willows and box elders as you get closer to Granite Basin Lake. This part of the loop is rockier, and you'll cross the wash a few times.

6.5 Intersection of Mint Wash Trail 345 and Mint Wash Connector 352. Stay on Mint Wash Trail 345. (Mint Wash Connector 352 is a slightly shorter route, but involves more climbing.)

7.5 Granite Basin Lake (horses are detoured away from the lake itself). Mint Wash Trail 345 passes above the lake.

7.9 Intersection of Mint Wash Trail 345 and West Lake Trail 351. Take West Lake Trail 351 east (go straight ahead; do not turn right and cross the paved road) through an open stand of ponderosa pine.

8.5 Arrive back at the Cayuse Trailhead.

Options: With some planning and a little backtracking, it's possible to do 20-plus miles in this area.

11 Wolf Creek Loop Trail

This is a scenic and moderately difficult 7.7-mile loop that starts and finishes near the Groom Creek Horse Camp, just off the Senator Highway.

Start: 6 miles south of Prescott; Yavapai County.
Distance: 7.7-mile loop.
Approximate riding time: 3 hours.
Total ascent: 1,140 feet.
Difficulty: Moderate, with a couple of short but steep, eroded, and rocky sections. The signposting is uneven: Keep alert.
Seasons: Best in late spring after snowmelt, summer, and fall.
Water availability: At some times of year, Wolf Creek at 2.6 miles and at Hassayampa Creek at about 4 miles. A horse trough at 4.9 miles is not always full.

Other trail users: Occasional hikers, mountain bikers.
Canine compatibility: Unleashed dogs "under control" are allowed.
Fees and permits: $2.00 day-use fee; free admittance on Wednesday.
Facilities: Pit toilet.
USGS maps: Groom Creek.
Contact: USDA Forest Service, Prescott National Forest, Bradshaw Ranger District, (928) 443–8000.

Reaching the trailhead: From Phoenix, take Interstate 17 north to Cordes Junction (Exit 262), and follow Arizona Highway 69 to Prescott. As you enter Prescott, the highway forks; stay to the left on Gurley Street. Remain in the left lane for 0.7 mile; at the traffic light, turn south (left) onto Mount Vernon Street. You'll drive through a lovely old neighborhood before Mount Vernon Street becomes the Senator Highway (Forest Road 52) 1 mile later; it's narrow and winding, but paved. Drive another 5.7 miles (you'll pass turnoffs to Goldwater Lake and Friendly Pines Camp) until you see signs for Groom Creek Horse Camp. *DeLorme: Arizona Atlas and Gazetteer:* Page 49 A4.

    Trailhead parking: If you plan to camp overnight, go to the horse camp, which will be on your right. For day use only, you can either park at the horse camp for $5.00 a day or use the day-use area on your left for $2.00 a day—except on Wednesday, when admittance is free. There's ample pull-through parking for six to eight large rigs. The Golden Eagle Pass is also recognized here.

The Ride

The Groom Creek Horse Camp is a pleasant, well-planned, roomy equestrian-user-only campground. There are thirty-seven pull-through sites, with a picnic table and grill at each. Water spigots are plentiful, and there are three troughs in the campground. Two corrals are available (by reservation only), and picket lines are provided in each site. Overnight camping is $10 per night; reservations are strongly recommended, particularly on weekends. For more information, call the Forest Service's Bradshaw Ranger District.

On long, difficult ascents, riders can help their horses by "tailing"—disconnecting one rein and walking behind the horse while holding the rein with one hand and the horse's tail with the other. (It's best to practice at home first!)

The trailhead is at 6,300 feet, and most of the trail passes through an open ponderosa pine forest with a scattered understory of Gambel and Emory oaks as well as manzanitas, with pockets of ponderosa pines. Although all of this trail is pleasant riding, the highlight comes about halfway along, when the trail passes above the Hassayampa River burbling its way among the boulders. This is a lovely spot for lunch (bring a tie-line with you so that your horse doesn't chew the tree bark).

Drinking any creek water without purifying it is probably a mistake, but partaking of this particular river could be especially suspect. According to Byrd Granger's *Arizona Place Names,* the Hassayampa "came to be associated with liars, more specifically, prospectors who evaded direct answers about their locations or those who bragged about how good their finds were. Such men explained their lies by saying they drank Hassayampa River water that rendered them unable to speak the truth."

Prescott National Forest authorities permit dogs off-leash as long as they are "under control." Be sure your canine friend is fit, and carry dog water. (A one-gallon ziplock bag makes an easy-to-carry collapsible dog bowl—and in a pinch your horse can drink out of it as well.)

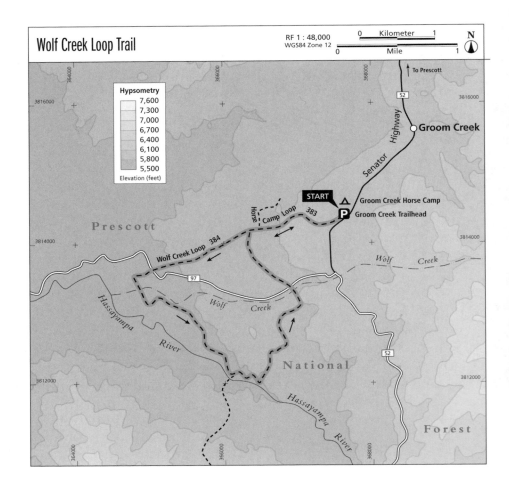

Miles and Directions

0.0 From the day-use parking area, cross the road and take Trail 383, the Horse Camp Loop Trail, just left of the campground entrance; this trail heads southwest (left).

1.0 The trail forks; go west (left).

1.1 Intersection of Horse Camp Loop Trail 383 and Wolf Creek Loop Trail 384, with a small sign that reads WOLF CREEK LOOP 5 MILES. Go straight here.

1.2 Intersection: Continue straight on Wolf Creek Loop Trail 384. (Make a mental note of this area. You'll be returning to this intersection from your left in another 5.3 miles.)

1.5 Wire gate. (Leave it as you find it.)

2.1 A gravel road comes in on your left, and you'll see a large metal culvert. Stay on the trail, and keep going straight.

2.2 Wolf Creek Loop Trail 384 intersects a gravel road (Forest Road 97, although it's not signed). Go south (left) on the road for 50 yards to where Wolf Creek Loop Trail 384 drops down to the west (right). There's no sign.

2.6 You'll cross Wolf Creek (which varies from tiny to dry) as you come into an unofficial camping area. There are no signs indicating the location of the trail: Head uphill to your left, and pick up the jeep track.

3.3 This is a rather confusing three-way intersection with no signs. Go right.

3.9 You're now in the prettiest area of this ride, where the trail passes just above the Hassayampa River. You won't be able to get your horse down to the water itself (there's a good watering spot just 0.1 mile farther), but it's a lovely place to tie your horse and stop for lunch.

4.0 Although you'll be continuing on Wolf Creek Loop Trail 384 to the left, go right to water your horse in the river. You'll see streamside vegetation including box elder, alder, and ash. Autumn temperatures turn the Virginia creeper a brilliant scarlet.

4.4 Keep alert here because it's easy to trot right by where Wolf Creek Loop Trail 384 leaves the two-wheel-drive road to take a hard turn uphill to the north (left) and dwindles to a singletrack through ponderosa pine and the occasional Douglas fir.

4.9 You'll pass a corner fence on your left with an accessible livestock trough that intermittently has water.

5.2 Wolf Creek Loop Trail 384 passes through a wire gate (leave it as you find it).

5.6 Cross over the gravel road (FR 97 again). Within a few yards, you'll pass an individual campsite labeled CAMPSITE NO. 62.

6.0 Wolf Creek Loop Trail 384 takes off from the dirt road to your left.

6.3 You're back where you started this loop. Take Horse Camp Loop Trail 383 to the east (right).

7.7 Arrive back at the trailhead parking lot.

Options: Quite a few tempting-looking Forest Service roads and trails crisscross this loop. In addition, the Groom Creek Loop Trail (approximately 9 miles) is accessible from the same trailhead.

Estrella Mountain Regional Park

T hanks to some farsighted folks in Goodyear, Avondale, and Maricopa County Parks and Recreation back in the 1940s, trail riders can still enjoy this western valley 20,000-acre gem. The park, located fifteen minutes from Interstate 10, includes two baseball fields, eight picnic ramadas (with fire rings, volleyball courts, lights, and electrical outlets for small appliances), restrooms with flush toilets (no showers), an eighteen-hole golf course, and a lighted rodeo arena with bucking and roping chutes and seating for 1,000 spectators.

But best of all, Estrella Mountain Regional Park contains 27 miles of pristine mountain and desert trails that wind through the Sierra Estrella (star mountains), arguably Arizona's most rugged, inhospitable, and lovely mountain range. For the most part the trails are superbly maintained and labeled and are an ideal mix of flat trotting areas interspersed with short, sharp dips and climbs, along with sections that meander along shady washes.

You'd be wise to call ahead or check the park Web site (www.maricopa.gov /parks/estrella/), since large groups sometimes rent the entire picnic area and campground, closing both to the general public. Even if the picnic area is closed, the trails are still available.

The park also includes 13 miles of shared-use "Competitive Track" trails, which, according to officials, are "designed to provide challenging, strenuous, and high-speed outdoor recreation . . . for cross-country runners and joggers, fast bicyclists and racers, and trotting/galloping equestrians and endurance riders." Call the park or check the Web site for information and maps for these trails, which aren't covered in this book.

Park hours are Sunday through Thursday 6:00 A.M. to 8:00 P.M., Friday and Saturday 6:00 A.M. to 10:00 P.M., 365 days a year. However, the trails close at sunset.

12 Pedersen Loop Trail

This 15.8-mile loop trail is a great workout for the well-conditioned horse-and-rider team. It's a satisfying and scenic mix of twisty singletrack and long, flat, sandy trotting stretches, along with 1,360 feet of climbing. Depending on the previous winter's rains, spring wildflowers can be phenomenal here.

Start: 8 miles south of Goodyear; Maricopa County.
Distance: 15.8-mile loop.
Approximate riding time: 4 to 5 hours.
Total ascent: 1,360 feet.
Difficulty: Moderate. The footing is good, but the long stretch of soft sand could be disheartening and stressful for a young or unfit horse.
Seasons: Best in early spring, late fall, and winter. Summer temperatures can reach 110 degrees.
Water availability: Occasional puddles after rain at 9.3 miles.

Other trail users: Occasional equestrians.
Canine compatibility: Best left at home. Dogs are only permitted in the park on a 6-foot leash.
Fees and permits: $5.00 entry fee per vehicle; waived if you camp in the park.
Facilities: Picnic area, campground, restrooms (flush toilets), ball fields, golf course.
USGS maps: Avondale SE, Avondale SW.
Contact: Estrella Mountain Regional Park, (623) 932-3811; Maricopa County Parks and Recreation Department, Headquarters Administrative Offices, (602) 506-2930.

Reaching the trailhead: From Phoenix, go west on Interstate 10 to Estrella Parkway (Exit 126). Go south 5.1 miles. *Immediately* after the bridge, turn left onto Vineyard Road (the turn is easy to miss!). You'll need to stop by the entrance booth to pick up a recent map and pay the $5.00 entry fee before getting directions to the rodeo grounds. Occasionally the road through the park is closed due to a group event. In this case, do a U-turn, using the large gravel pullout just beyond the information kiosk, and go back to Vineyard Road. Turn right and drive 1.8 miles to Indian Springs Road. Turn right, then immediately left. The trailhead and parking lot will be on your left. *DeLorme: Arizona Atlas and Gazetteer:* Page 57 B4.

Trailhead parking: The annual Goodyear rodeo is held here (usually in late February), so the gravel parking area has ample room for dozens of horse trailers. There's a $5.00 entry fee per vehicle; camping is $5.00 per night (if you camp in the park, the entry fee is waived). An annual pass is available for $75 that allows entry to all Maricopa County parks, excluding Lake Pleasant Regional Park and Spur Cross Ranch Conservation Area.

The Ride

The Pedersen Trail section of this trail is rarely used. Park officials advise all trail users to enter the Maricopa County Sheriff's Office phone number into their cell phones in case of emergency: (602) 876–1011.

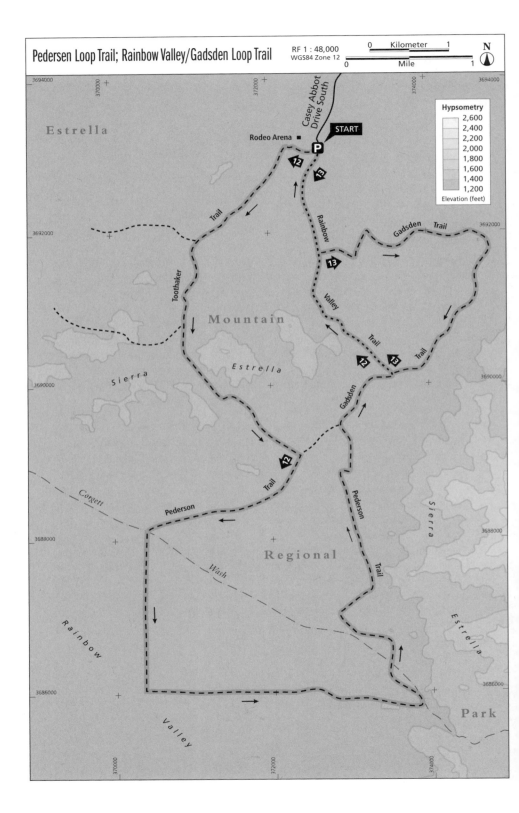

Pedersen Loop Trail; Rainbow Valley/Gadsden Loop Trail

RF 1 : 48,000
WGS84 Zone 12

Hypsometry
2,600
2,400
2,200
2,000
1,800
1,600
1,400
1,200
Elevation (feet)

START

Casey Abbot Drive South

Rodeo Arena

P

Estrella

Mountain

Estrella

Sierra

Toothaker

Trail

Rainbow

Valley

Trail

Gadsden

Trail

Gadsden

Pederson

Trail

Pederson

Trail

Corgett

Wash

Rainbow

Valley

Regional

Sierra

Estrella

Park

12 13

As you ride north on the Pedersen Trail, if you were able to see through the Sierra Estrella range, you'd be looking at the land belonging to the Gila River Indian Community. This group is actually an alliance formed in the 1800s of two tribes, the Akimel O'odham or "people of the river" (formerly known as the Pima Indians) and the Pee Posh or "people who live toward the water" (the Maricopa Indians). Both were peaceful tribes who helped anyone traveling through to or from California and who developed irrigation systems in order to farm the river bottom.

Established by Congress in 1859, the Gila River Indian Reservation was the nation's first reservation—and the only one before the Civil War. Later, in the early 1900s, increased settlement lowered the water table, and despite the assistance they had provided to white travelers, the tribes were forced to beg for enough water for their crops to survive.

The Gila River Indian Community now owns Gila River Farms (15,000 acres), three industrial parks, and three casino/resort properties. The Gila River Indian Arts and Crafts Center is at the Sacaton exit off Interstate 10, and its museum, gift shop, and restaurant are well worth a visit. The parking lot has plenty of room for horse trailers.

At the rodeo grounds trailhead, there is a portable toilet in the parking lot and a picnic area with six tables, one ramada, and a barbecue grill. There's also a water trough, which may or may not have water—it's best to bring your own, along with a bucket. Restrooms with flush toilets are available on the south side of the grandstand building, and several of the chutes surrounding the arena have water spigots, which may not always be turned on.

Miles and Directions

0.0 The trail leaves from the paved parking lot that's just north of the arena; you'll need to ride along the edge of the parking lot since horses are not permitted on the pavement. Once you get to the information kiosk, head west on the Toothaker Trail.

1.3 Intersection of the Toothaker and Dysart Trails. Go straight (south) on the Toothaker. **Bail-out:** If you go right, you'll be back at the trailhead in 2.8 miles for a total ride of 4.1 miles.

2.2 Intersection of the Toothaker and Rainbow Valley Trails. **Bail-out:** If you go right, you'll be back at the trailhead in 3.5 miles, for a total ride of 5.7 miles.

3.9 Intersection of the Toothaker and Pedersen Trails. Go right (southwest). This next section of trail is 8.2 miles, hot, flat, sandy, and rarely used. Be sure you're ready to tackle it, especially in warm weather.

6.7 Turn left (south).

9.3 Turn right down into a wash, where you'll travel for about 0.1 mile. Keep an eye out for small trail signs, which are sometimes suspended from tree branches. You'll climb back up out of the wash into a particularly dense cholla thicket.

11.3 Turn left into the wash.

12.2 Intersection of the Pedersen and Gadsden Trails. Turn right (northeast) onto the Gadsden Trail.

13.0 Intersection of the Gadsden and Rainbow Valley Trails. Go left (west). (If you want to add an extra 1.9 miles to your ride, turn right. The Gadsden Trail will rejoin the Rainbow Valley Trail. See the Rainbow Valley/Gadsden Loop for more information.)

14.5 Second intersection of the Rainbow Valley and Gadsden Trails. Go straight (north).

15.3 Intersection of the Rainbow Valley and Coldwater Trails. Turn right off the trail and onto the gravel road.

15.8 Arrive back at the trailhead.

Options: Not only can you add several loops within the park, but several four-wheel-drive tracks take off from the Pedersen Trail into state or Bureau of Land Management property. Check your proposed route with the rangers ahead of time to avoid trespassing on private or Gila River Indian Community land.

13 Rainbow Valley/Gadsden Loop Trail

This mostly easy 7.1-mile loop trail has all the advantages of the Pedersen Loop (varied, well-marked, scenic trails), without the long, hot, flat sandy stretch.

See map on page 62.
Start: 8 miles south of Goodyear; Maricopa County.
Distance: 7.1-mile loop.
Approximate riding time: 2 to 3 hours.
Total ascent: 730 feet.
Difficulty: Easy to moderate. Footing is mostly good, with about 2 miles of sandy wash and one bit of slick rock where novice horses will need to concentrate.
Seasons: Best in early spring, late fall, and winter. Summer temperatures can reach 110 degrees.
Water availability: None.

Other trail users: Hikers.
Canine compatibility: Best left at home. Dogs are only permitted in the park on a 6-foot leash.
Fees and permits: $5.00 entry fee per vehicle; waived if you camp in the park.
Facilities: Picnic area, campground, restrooms (flush toilets), ball fields, golf course.
USGS maps: Avondale SE.
Contact: Estrella Mountain Regional Park, (623) 932-3811; Maricopa County Parks and Recreation Department, Headquarters Administrative Offices, (602) 506-2930.

Reaching the trailhead: From Phoenix, go west on Interstate 10 to Estrella Parkway (Exit 126). Go south 5.1 miles. Immediately after the bridge, turn left onto Vineyard Road (the turn is easy to miss!). You'll need to stop by the entrance booth to pick up a recent map and pay the $5.00 entry fee before getting directions to the rodeo grounds. Occasionally the road through the park is closed due to a group event. In this case, do a U-turn, using the large gravel pull-out just beyond the information kiosk, and go back to Vineyard Road. Turn right and drive 1.8 miles to Indian Springs Road. Turn right, then immediately left. The trailhead and parking lot will be on your left. *DeLorme: Arizona Atlas and Gazetteer:* Page 57 B4.

    Trailhead parking: The annual Goodyear rodeo is held here (usually in late February), so the gravel parking area has ample room for dozens of horse trailers. There's a $5.00 entry fee

Estrella Mountain Regional Park is in the Sonoran/Transition Upland Zone overlooking the valley where the Gila and Salt Rivers come together. After a wet winter, it is one of the finest places in the state to see wildflowers. In February and March 2005, this area exploded into a stunning display of poppies, lupines, scorpionweed, owl clover, and brittlebush.

per vehicle; camping is $5.00 per night (if you camp, the entry fee is waived). An annual pass is available for $75 that allows entry to all Maricopa County parks, excluding Lake Pleasant Regional Park and Spur Cross Ranch Conservation Area.

The Ride

Given their proximity to Phoenix, these trails see surprisingly little use. Park officials advise all trail users to enter the Maricopa County Sheriff's Office phone number into their cell phones in case of emergency: (602) 876–1011.

If you'd ridden this trail 150 years ago, you'd be riding through northern Mexico instead of southern Arizona. Thanks to President Franklin Pierce and James Gadsden's thirst for land to run a transcontinental railroad, the United States bought 30,000 acres of what would become part of New Mexico and Arizona—for about 33 cents an acre. Before that date Estrella Mountain Regional Park—and, indeed, all of Arizona south of the Gila River—belonged to Mexico under the controversial 1848 Treaty of Guadalupe Hidalgo that ended the Mexican-American War. The treaty caused national consternation for two reasons. First, the map on which the border was based turned out to be inaccurate. Second, many antislavery Americans objected passionately to the document because they felt the United States was only buying the land as a nearby source for more slaves.

And if one suggestion for the new territory's name had been approved, we'd be living in Gadsonia, not Arizona. (Whew!)

(Note: There are two sections of the Rainbow Valley Trail: One leaves from the paved parking lot north of the arena, then merges with the Toothaker Trail. This one leaves from the trailhead at the gravel parking lot and dead-ends at the Gadsden Trail. At the rodeo grounds trailhead, there is a portable toilet in the parking lot and a picnic area with six tables, one ramada, and a barbecue grill. There's also a water trough, which may or may not have water—it's best to bring your own, along with a bucket. Restrooms with flush toilets are available on the south side of the grandstand building, and several of the chutes surrounding the arena have water spigots, which may not always be turned on.)

Miles and Directions

0.0 The Rainbow Valley Trail leaves from the trailhead west of the gravel parking lot and heads down a gravel road.

0.3 The trail leaves the gravel road to your left (south).

1.0 Intersection of the Rainbow Valley and Gadsden Trails. Take the Gadsden Trail to your left (east).

2.8 The trail bears right into a wash. You'll be in sand for the next 1.8 miles. Although markers are scarce, the occasional hoofprints, horse manure, bicycle tracks, and footprints let you know that you're on track.

3.0 The trail becomes a little faint here. Bear right.

3.6 The trail climbs up out of the wash in a rocky rut to your right. A small trail marker hung in a bush confirms the decision. Caution: Halfway up, there's a patch of smooth rock. It's safe, especially going up rather than down, but your horse will need to pay attention.

4.4 Intersection of the Gadsden and Rainbow Valley Trails. Go right (northwest).

6.1 Second intersection of the Rainbow Valley and Gadsden Trails (this intersection is where you began the Gadsden loop). Go left; you'll be able to see the rodeo grounds in the distance.

6.8 Intersection of the Rainbow Valley and Coldwater Trails. Turn right off the trail and onto the gravel road.

7.1 Arrive back at the rodeo arena parking area.

Options: Not only can you add several loops within the park, but several four-wheel-drive tracks take off from the Pedersen Trail into state or Bureau of Land Management property. Check your proposed route with the rangers ahead of time to avoid trespassing on private or Gila River Indian Community land.

Granite Dells

Once an ideal ambush site for both Indians and outlaws, the Peavine Trail became a much safer route when the Santa Fe, Prescott & Phoenix Railroad came through in 1893. More than a century later, thanks to the Rails-to-Trails program, and named by the Arizona old-timers for its twists and turns, the Peavine Trail winds its way past the towering cottonwoods of Watson Woods, along the lake's edge, and through the ancient Precambrian rock corridors of the Granite Dells themselves. Riders are treated to dramatic panoramic views toward Thumb Butte, Mingus Mountain, and the San Francisco Peaks.

The Peavine Trail is one of very few trails in this book where you're also likely to see kayakers!

14 Peavine/Iron King Trail

This almost totally flat 14-mile round trip ride is an equal-opportunity trail: It's accessible to all nonmotorized travelers and is historic, scenic, and fun.

Start: 4 miles north of Prescott; Yavapai County.

Distance: 14 miles out and back.

Approximate riding time: 3 hours.

Total ascent: None; the trail is almost completely flat.

Difficulty: Very easy.

Seasons: Any time of year, although the footing may be soft in winter.

Water availability: Depending on the season, drought, and rainfall, the edge of Watson Lake.

Other trail users: Hikers and bicyclists.

Canine compatibility: Best left at home. Dogs must be leashed at all times.

Fees and permits: None.

Facilities: None.

USGS maps: Prescott, Prescott Valley South.

Contact: Prescott Parks, Recreation and Library Department, (928) 777-1122.

Reaching the trailhead: From downtown Prescott, take Arizona Highway 89 north about 4 miles to Prescott Lakes Parkway. Cross the bridge, and turn left immediately onto Sun Dog Ranch Road. The parking area will be on your left, across from the Animal Control headquarters. *DeLorme: Arizona Atlas and Gazetteer:* Page 41 D4.

Trailhead parking: The gravel parking area has tie racks and ample space for four to five trailers.

The Ride

Despite its unfortunate (and sometimes odoriferous) beginning at the sewage plant, the Peavine/Iron King Trail is a gem lying within minutes of downtown Prescott. It begins in the riparian area of Watson Lake in the shade of huge cottonwoods, then ambles out toward the Dells with superb views of lakes and outrageously shaped granite formations. Because it's heavily used, be prepared to share the trail.

Miles and Directions

0.0 The trail takes off just past the portable toilets.

1.5 Rest area and view of the cove.

1.9 Railroad trestle over Boulder Creek.

2.6 Panoramic view.

3.0 Intersection of the Peavine and Iron King Trails. Turn left (west) onto the Iron King Trail. (As of May 2005, if you go straight, the Peavine Trail ends in another 1.2 miles, although plans are in place for the trail to continue to Chino Valley.)

3.7 Flatcar Bridge 3.

5.5 Flatcar Bridge 2.

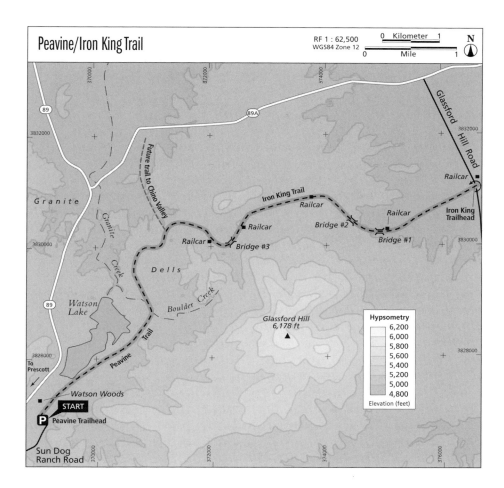

Peavine/Iron King Trail

RF 1 : 62,500
WGS84 Zone 12

0 Kilometer 1

0 Mile 1

N

Hypsometry

6,200
6,000
5,800
5,600
5,400
5,200
5,000
4,800

Elevation (feet)

6.0 Flatcar Bridge 1.

7.0 The trail goes through an underpass beneath Glassford Hill Road and ends at the Iron King Trailhead. Retrace your steps to return to the Peavine Trailhead.

14.0 Arrive back at the trailhead.

Options: An occasional very short side trail and an out-and-back trundle to the end of the Peavine Trail.

Lake Havasu

S tanding on the edge of Lake Havasu and listening to the hum and whine of powerboats, it's hard to imagine that until the 1938 construction of Parker Dam, these dry, rocky hills were desert verging on the riparian edge of the Colorado River.

But in 1968 it must have been even harder for residents to imagine Lake Havasu as the home of the London Bridge. Industrialist Robert P. McCulloch had bought the town site five years earlier at first as a motor-testing site, and then with the idea of turning it into a recreation and retirement community.

When the century-old bridge began to sink into the Thames, McCulloch bought it for $2,460,000. (The extra $60,000 was because he would turn sixty the year the bridge would be dedicated.) He had it dismantled, shipped, and reassembled, stone by stone, over an inlet in Lake Havasu City. And there it remains, a prominent and successful tourist attraction.

Fish-and-chips, anyone?

15 JJ Mine Loop Trail

This is a moderate 12-mile lollipop loop on the edge of Lake Havasu City with views of the Mohave Mountains and Lake Havasu. It's best ridden on weekdays or early on a weekend morning.

Start: The outskirts of Lake Havasu City; Mohave County.

Distance: 12-mile lollipop loop.

Approximate riding time: 3 to 4 hours.

Total ascent: 1,000 feet.

Difficulty: Moderate, due to the climb. With the exception of one washout, the footing is good.

Seasons: Best in fall, winter, and spring.

Water availability: None.

Other trail users: ATVers, target shooters, and motorbikers.

Canine compatibility: Well-conditioned dogs only. Bring water.

Fees and permits: Recreational pass required to access Arizona state lands; no permit needed for Bureau of Land Management land.

Facilities: None.

USGS maps: Lake Havasu City North.

Contact: Bureau of Land Management, Lake Havasu Field Office, (928) 505-1200 or (800) 213-2582.

Reaching the trailhead: From Parker, take Arizona Highway 95 to Lake Havasu City. Just as you reach the southern edge of town, McCulloch Boulevard comes in on your right. Turn right and drive 4.3 miles to Jamaica Avenue. Turn right onto Jamaica and go 0.7 mile to Kiowa Boulevard. Turn right again and go 1.6 miles to Bison Boulevard. Turn right onto Bison Boulevard and drive 0.7 mile to the trailhead.

From Needles or Kingman, take Interstate 40 to Exit 9 toward Lake Havasu City. Travel 16.3 miles to Palo Verde Boulevard North. Turn left and go 3.1 miles to Desert Garden Drive. Turn left and go 0.4 mile to Kiowa Boulevard. Go 0.5 mile to Bison Boulevard and turn left again. The trailhead is 0.7 mile from here. *DeLorme: Arizona Atlas and Gazetteer:* Page 46 A2.

Trailhead parking: There's room for only two or three horse trailers right at the trailhead itself, but you can drive out the dirt road 0.25 to 0.5 mile to where there are several turnouts with plenty of room to turn large rigs. Trails, washes, and four-wheel-drive tracks abound, but the downside is that this area is heavily used by ATVers, motorcyclists, and target shooters on weekends. If you're planning to ride Saturday or Sunday, be sure to go early.

The Ride

This area is a patchwork of Bureau of Land Management and state properties. No permit is needed to ride on BLM land. However, Arizona requires an annual recreation pass to access state land; this is easily obtained by calling (602) 542–4174 or going to www.land.state.az.us/programs/natural/rec_offroad_permit.htm.

Because this area is a confusing web of intersecting washes and social (unofficial) trails carved out by ATVs and motorcycles, you may encounter more turnoffs than

The area between Lake Havasu City and the Mohave Mountains is rich with trail exploration possibilities, as well as a view of the lake itself and across to the Chemehuevi Mountains of California.

are mentioned in these directions. With the Mohave Mountains to the east and the lake to the west, it's hard to get lost. When in doubt . . . enjoy the journey! (These mileages will vary, depending on where you were able to park along the road.)

Many of the miners in this area were after chrysocolla, a secondary mineral associated with copper ore. Chrysocolla is similar to turquoise but harder. Although turquoise is commonly found in the Southwest, the best specimens come from Iran. The name comes from the French *turquoise,* meaning "Turkish," because the material had passed through Turkey on its way from what was then Persia (now Iran).

The Lake Havasu City area gets hot in the summer: Temperatures are usually five to ten degrees hotter than Phoenix and can reach as high as 130 degrees. Consider both the air and the ground temperature before bringing your canine companion. Be sure your dog is fit, and carry dog water. (A one-gallon ziplock bag makes an easy-to-carry collapsible dog bowl—and in a pinch your horse can drink out of it as well.) Rain here is rare. The average rainfall in this area is 5 inches per year.

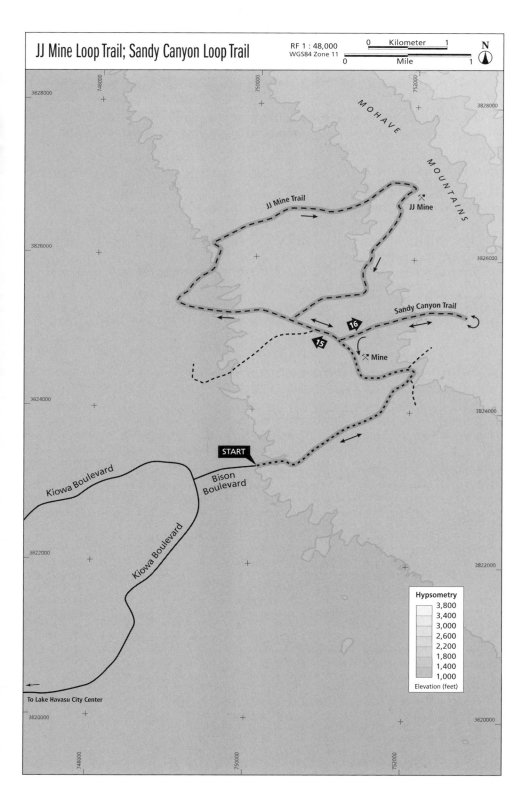

JJ Mine Loop Trail; Sandy Canyon Loop Trail

RF 1 : 48,000
WGS84 Zone 11

0 — Kilometer — 1

0 — Mile — 1

N

3828000
748000
3828000

MOHAVE

MOUNTAINS

JJ Mine Trail

JJ Mine

750000

752000

3826000
3826000

Sandy Canyon Trail

16

15

Mine

3824000
3824000

START

Kiowa Boulevard

Bison Boulevard

Kiowa Boulevard

3822000
3822000

Hypsometry

	3,800
	3,400
	3,000
	2,600
	2,200
	1,800
	1,400
	1,000

Elevation (feet)

To Lake Havasu City Center

3820000
748000
750000
752000
3820000

Miles and Directions

0.0 From the Bison Boulevard trailhead, follow the dirt road east. Be prepared to hand-walk novice horses if the trail is very busy! (This road continues on to the waterfalls.)

1.4 Intersection with Pittsburg Mine Road. Turn left (north) onto the four-wheel-drive road.

1.7 Turn left again. You'll be facing the lake. Follow the road past the mine.

4.1 Turn right (east) off the road onto a trail.

4.4 Turn left (northwest) up a wash.

5.0 Go right (northeast) onto the jeep trail.

5.9 Go right onto the power line road, and within 0.1 mile, bear left.

6.3 The road forks; go right (northeast).

6.8 Take the trail that turns off sharply to your right (southwest). If you look uphill to your left, you can see the JJ Mine.

7.1 As you reach the top of the hill, you'll be at Horseshoe Pass. (You can take the side trail to the left to avoid the washed-out area.)

7.6 Bear left.

8.0 Go right, following the wash.

9.4 The trail intersects with the four-wheel-drive road you came in on (the stick of the lollipop). Turn left (east).

10.6 Intersection with the road that leads to the waterfalls. Go right (south).

12.0 Arrive back at the trailhead.

Options: The dirt road you parked on connects to many trails and four-wheel-drive tracks.

16 Sandy Canyon Loop Trail

A gentle, mostly flat, out-and-back route ideal for a short social ride or starter ride for a young horse. It's best during the week or early on a weekend morning.

See map on page 73.
Start: The northern outskirts of Lake Havasu City; Mohave County.
Distance: 7.8 miles out and back.
Approximate riding time: 1 to 2 hours.
Total ascent: 800 feet.
Difficulty: Easy.
Seasons: Best in fall, winter, or spring.
Water availability: None.
Other trail users: ATVers, target shooters, and motorbikers.

Canine compatibility: Dogs are allowed. Bring water.
Fees and permits: Recreational pass required to access Arizona state lands; no permit needed for BLM land.
Facilities: None.
USGS maps: Lake Havasu City North.
Contact: Bureau of Land Management, Lake Havasu Field Office, (928) 505-1200 or (800) 213-2582.

Reaching the trailhead: From Parker, take Arizona Highway 95 to Lake Havasu City. Just as you reach the southern edge of town, McCulloch Boulevard comes in on your right. Turn right and drive 4.3 miles to Jamaica Avenue. Turn right onto Jamaica and go 0.7 mile to Kiowa Boulevard. Turn right again and go 1.6 miles to Bison Boulevard. Turn right onto Bison Boulevard and drive 0.7 mile to the trailhead.

From Needles or Kingman, take Interstate 40 to Exit 9 toward Lake Havasu City. Travel 16.3 miles to Palo Verde Boulevard North. Turn left and go 3.1 miles to Desert Garden Drive. Turn left and go 0.4 mile to Kiowa Boulevard. Go 0.5 mile to Bison Boulevard and turn left again. The trailhead is 0.7 mile from here. *DeLorme: Arizona Atlas and Gazetteer:* Page 46 A2.

Trailhead parking: There's room for only two or three horse trailers right at the trailhead itself, but you can drive out the dirt road 0.25 to 0.5 mile to where there are several turnouts with plenty of room to turn large rigs. Trails, washes, and four-wheel-drive tracks abound, but the downside is that this area is heavily used by ATVers, motorcyclists, and target shooters on weekends. If you're planning to ride Saturday or Sunday, be sure to go early.

The Ride

This area is a patchwork of Bureau of Land Management and state properties. No permit is needed to ride on BLM land. However, Arizona requires an annual recreation pass to access state land; this is easily obtained by calling (602) 542–4174 or going to www.land.state.az.us/programs/natural/rec_offroad_permit.htm.

Because this area is a confusing web of intersecting washes and social (unofficial) trails carved out by ATVs and motorcycles, you may encounter more turnoffs than are mentioned in these directions. With the mountains to the east and the lake to the west, it's hard to get lost. When in doubt . . . enjoy the journey! (These mileages will vary, depending on where you were able to park along the road.)

The average rainfall in this area is 5 inches per year. In a rare year of plentiful fall and winter rains, however, the desert in the Lake Havasu City area explodes into a riot of yellow brittlebush, blue scorpionweed, and bright orange poppies against the backdrop of the rugged peaks of the Chemehueve and Whipple Mountains to the west and southwest and the Mohaves to the east.

The Lake Havasu City area gets hot in summer: Temperatures are usually five to ten degrees hotter than Phoenix and can reach as high as 130 degrees. Consider both the air and the ground temperature before bringing your canine companion. Be sure your dog is fit, and carry dog water. (A one-gallon ziplock bag makes an easy-to-carry collapsible dog bowl—and in a pinch your horse can drink out of it as well.)

Miles and Directions

0.0 From the Bison Boulevard trailhead, follow the dirt road east. Hand-walk your horse if the trail is very busy! (This road continues on to the waterfalls.)

1.4 Intersection with Pittsburg Mine Road. Turn left (north) on the four-wheel-drive road.

1.7 Turn left again. You'll be facing the lake. Follow the road past the mine.

2.7 Turn right onto the trail near the wash.

3.0 Turn left up the wash.

3.4 Sandy Canyon dead-ends here. Retrace your steps, or take the time to explore more of the washes and dirt roads.

7.8 Arrive back at the trailhead.

Options: The dirt road you parked on connects to many trails and four-wheel-drive tracks.

If autumn and winter rains are plentiful, Mexican gold poppies light up the trail throughout the state below 4,500 feet. In 2001 and 2005 the flower displays were so vast they could be seen from airplanes.

17 SARA Park Trails

Special Activity and Recreation Area (SARA) Park is a Lake Havasu City–leased area that includes baseball fields, a motocross track, a shooting range, a radio-controlled airplane field, and a racetrack. It also includes hiking and mountain biking tracks, and in 2005 community members were working with the city of Lake Havasu City and the local Bureau of Land Management field office to measure trails and establish an equestrian staging area.

The SARA trails will enable riders to access the lake while viewing various remarkable natural arches, slot canyons, sandstone spires, and rock formations.

Contact the BLM's Lake Havasu Field Office for the most up-to-date information: (928) 505–1200 or (800) 213–2582.

The dramatic and rugged Aubrey Hills separate the southern edge of Lake Havasu City from the lake and are a part of SARA Park.

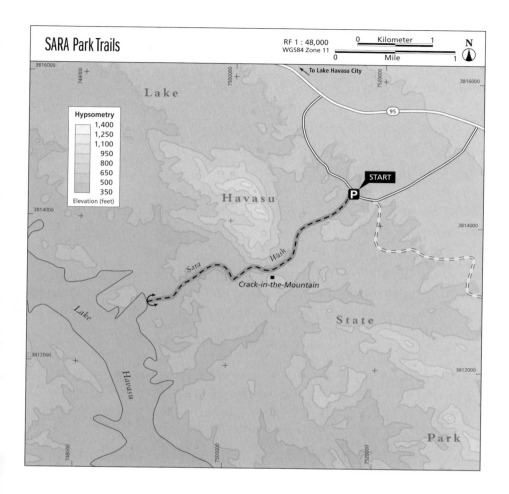

SARA Park Trails

RF 1 : 48,000
WGS84 Zone 11

Kilometer

Mile

N

Lake

To Lake Havasu City

95

START

P

Hypsometry
1,400
1,250
1,100
950
800
650
500
350
Elevation (feet)

Havasu

Sara

Wash

Crack-in-the-Mountain

State

Lake

Havasu

Park

Pinal Mountains

The first residents of this area were members of the Salado culture (named for the Rio Salida, or "salt river") that existed from A.D. 1150 through A.D. 1450 between the Salt and Gila Rivers. Some archaeologists believe them to have been a blend of cultures: the Mogollon from the south and east, Hohokam from the southwest and west, and Anasazi from the north. Whatever their origin, this group grew to be an extensive civilization, notable for polychrome pottery, baskets, and in particular for both turquoise and copper bells that they traded from Colorado to central Mexico. Their houses were pueblos, aboveground and often multistoried structures with no doors and an entrance on the roof.

No one knows exactly why the culture disappeared. Tree ring data suggest the culture was either weakened or destroyed by extensive flooding followed by a severe and prolonged drought that hit somewhere between A.D. 1400 and A.D. 1450.

Later this heavily forested range was named *Walkame,* or "pine mountains," by the Yavapai, then translated into "pine-burdened mountain" by the Apaches, and finally to *Pinal* or "stand of pine trees" by the Spanish in the 1600s.

The Pinals are particularly rich in mining history. In 1877 Hiram C. Hodge wrote in *Arizona as It Is; Or the Coming Country,* "There is no better opening for mining capital anywhere than in the Pinal Mountains, and the whole of the eastern portion of Pinal County seems to be a mass of mineral, including gold, silver, copper, lead, and iron."

One of the most massive mineral discoveries was that of the Silver King, Arizona's richest silver mine. It was discovered in 1875 by four farmers out doing a little prospecting between chores—the exact same four farmers, it turns out, who'd discovered the Globe mine two years earlier. According to Hodge, the vein was 87 feet wide by 110 feet deep. A smelter was needed, so a mill town formed at the base of Picket Post butte (so named, presumably, because soldiers were on "picket" to guard against Indians).

In 1879 the name was changed to Pinal, or sometimes Pinal City—although the name mattered less when the mine closed down and everyone left in 1888.

Pinal City is now the site of the plant research institute established by mining magnate William Boyce Thompson. It's now known as the Boyce Thompson Arboretum and well worth a visit.

18 Sixshooter Loop Trail

Although it's a relatively short loop with good footing and great views, this route does require that your horse be ready for a 1,600-foot climb.

Start: 5 miles south of Globe; Gila County.
Distance: 7-mile loop.
Approximate riding time: 2.5 to 3.5 hours.
Total ascent: 1,600 feet.
Difficulty: Moderate, with good footing and one slightly tricky creek crossing.
Seasons: Best in late spring, summer, and fall.
Water availability: Several good watering spots in spring; intermittent in summer.
Other trail users: Occasional hikers and mule riders.

Canine compatibility: Dogs "under control" are allowed. Bring water.
Fees and permits: None required.
Facilities: Picnic area with barbecue grills, pit toilet, occasional site host. Overnight camping not permitted.
USGS maps: Pinal Peak.
Contact: USDA Forest Service, Tonto National Forest, Globe Ranger District, (928) 425–6200.

Reaching the trailhead: From Phoenix, take U.S. Highway 60 to Globe. Just past milepost 251, turn left (south) onto Hill Street. Following the brown-and-white signs for Pinal Mountain Recreation Area, go across the bridge and curve left onto Jesse Hayes Road. Continue to the junction of Icehouse Canyon Road (Forest Road 112) and Sixshooter Canyon Road (FR 222). Drive 1.8 miles to where Icehouse Canyon and Kellner Canyon Roads split. Go straight on Icehouse Road (FR 112). In 1.9 miles you'll pass the DC Cattle Company on your right. There's a dirt pullout on your right in 0.2 mile. *DeLorme: Arizona Atlas and Gazetteer:* Page 59 5B and 5C.

    Trailhead parking: Technically speaking, this ride starts at the CCC (Civilian Conservation Corps) Icehouse picnic area; however, unless you're driving a small rig or are absolutely sure how many trailers are already parked there, you are best off *not* driving your trailer into the picnic area. The entrance road is narrow, and if several others have preceded you, there may not be room for you to turn around.

    Instead, park in the gravel pullout, tack up, and ride the 0.3 mile up the road to the picnic area turnoff and then the 0.3 mile to the picnic ground itself. Alternatively, you could park temporarily in the pullout and walk in to the picnic area to make sure you'll have enough room.

The Ride

The Tollroad Trail was originally an actual toll road, built in 1883, and led miners to and from the Pioneer Mine. Icehouse Canyon is named for the ice-delivery business run by Charles and Robert Bronson in the early 1900s.

    The most engaging legend about the naming of Globe is based on the (shadowy) discovery of a huge round nugget of silver with veins and scars that resembled the outlines of the Earth's continents. The less appealing, but probably more accurate, version is that the town was named for the Globe mine located on the Globe Ledge.

Riders don't even have to leave the CCC Icehouse Picnic Area to enjoy the views overlooking Globe and the Globe Hills to the north and the San Carlos Indian Reservation to the northeast.

These are quiet trails. Even on a beautiful (but windy) spring Saturday, I saw no hikers and only one group of mule riders. Be sure your canine friend is fit, and carry dog water. (A one-gallon ziplock bag makes an easy-to-carry collapsible dog bowl—and in a pinch your horse can drink out of it as well.)

Miles and Directions

0.0 Ride through the picnic area and across the flat area that's cabled off. The trailhead is at the eastern end.

0.6 Intersection with Trail Route (TR) 190, or the Check Dam Trail. Turn left down the hill.

1.7 Turn right off the road—just past a fence. (If you get to an earthen dam and gate, you've gone too far—go back.) The trail crosses the creek just after the fork and then heads back uphill.

2.2 Intersection of TR 190 and TR 200, the Tollroad Trail—turn right. (If you go left, you'll end up at the end of Sixshooter Canyon Road in 0.8 mile.)

3.0 The trail starts to ascend more steeply, although the footing is still very good. The vegetation is still a low thicket of scrub oak and manzanita, but as the elevation increases, the plants become taller and more diverse.

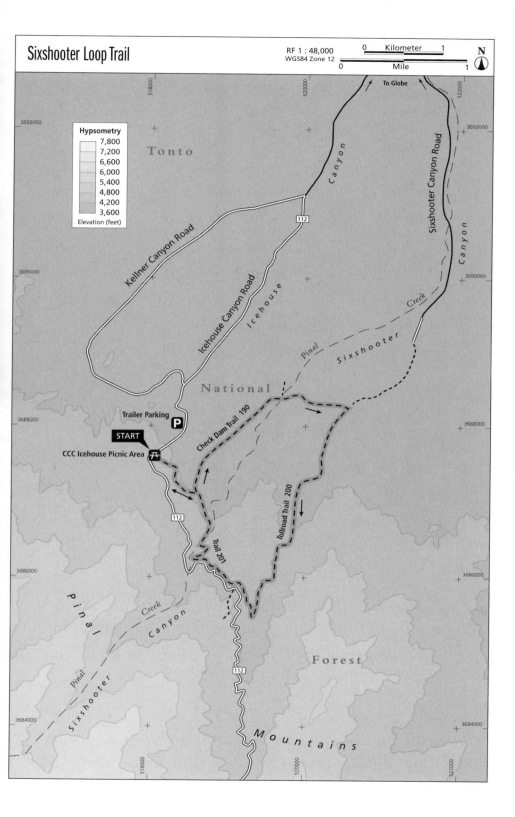

Sixshooter Loop Trail

RF 1 : 48,000
WGS84 Zone 12

0 Kilometer 1

0 Mile 1

N

Hypsometry

7,800
7,200
6,600
6,000
5,400
4,800
4,200
3,600
Elevation (feet)

To Globe

Canyon

Sixshooter Canyon Road

112

Kellner Canyon Road

Icehouse Canyon Road

Icehouse

Creek

Pinal

Sixshooter

Canyon

Tonto

National

Check Dam Trail 190

Trailer Parking

P

START

CCC Icehouse Picnic Area

112

Trail 201

Tollroad Trail 200

Forest

Pinal

Creek

Canyon

Pinal

Sixshooter

112

Mountains

3692000

3690000

3688000

3686000

3684000

518000

520000

522000

4.4 Intersection of Trails 200 and 201. Turn right (toward the road). Once you've crossed the road, you'll encounter occasional ponderosa pines.

4.9 Intersection of TR 201 and Forest Road 112. Turn right (downhill).

5.6 Intersection of FR 112 and TR 197. Turn right (downhill) onto TR 197.

6.6 Connector trail back to Icehouse parking. Turn left to retrace your steps to the trailhead.

7.0 Arrive back at the CCC Icehouse picnic area.

Options: Several very steep trails head up toward Pinal Peak. If you choose to tackle these, be sure your equine companion is in shape.

Superstition Mountains

T he scout Pauline Weaver ... the mysterious Lost Dutchman (who was actually German) ... countless explorers who never returned—rich in both legends and rugged landscapes, the Superstitions are a feast for hikers, bikers, naturalists, runners, and riders and truly deserve their own book. (One good one is Jack Carlson and Elizabeth Stewart's *Hiker's Guide to the Superstition Wilderness*.)

One story behind the name is that the valley Indians believed that anyone who dared go into the mountains would never come back alive. Another, based on Pima Indian legend, says that a great flood took place; the froth-topped waves explain the white limestone streak that stretches several miles across the range. The Spanish heard the legend and named the Superstitions *Sierra de la Espuma*—"mountains of foam."

One of these trails provides a distant big-picture view of the range, while the other just touches the edge. May they both whet your appetite for more.

(Note: Technically, the Alamo Canyon Passage belongs in the Southern Arizona section, since it's south of Arizona Highway 60. However, if you're riding the area, it makes sense to keep these together.)

19 Alamo Canyon Passage Trail

This is an easily accessed, lightly traveled, and particularly lovely 12.2-mile out-and-back route with stunning views of Picketpost Mountain and the Superstitions. Although moderate, it does include 2,100 feet of climbing with some slow going, and horses will need to be both fit and experienced.

Start: 10 miles west of Florence Junction; Pinal County.
Distance: 12.2 miles out and back.
Approximate riding time: 4 to 6 hours.
Total ascent: 2,100 feet.
Difficulty: Moderate, but your horse will need to be experienced and fit.
Seasons: Best in spring, fall, and winter.
Water availability: None.
Other trail users: Occasional through-hikers.

Canine compatibility: Dogs "under control" are allowed. Bring water.
Fees and permits: None required.
Facilities: Pit toilet, hitching rails, occasional site host.
USGS maps: Picketpost Mountain, Mineral Mountain, Teapot Mountain.
Contact: USDA Forest Service, Tonto National Forest, Globe Ranger District, (928) 402-6200.

Reaching the trailhead: From Tucson or Phoenix, drive to the Florence Junction (the intersection of U.S. 60 and Arizona Highway 79). From there, travel east on US 60 approximately 7 miles to milepost 220. Go another 0.4 mile, and turn right (south) onto Forest Road 231. The turn is very easy to miss from the west. If you do miss it, drive east on US 60 another 0.5 mile, and, immediately after crossing Queen Creek, turn left into a large gravel parking area to turn around. (This parking area is the intersection of Hewitt Station and Happy Camp Roads, as well as the trailhead for the Happy Camp Loop.)

Drive 0.3 mile on FR 231, passing the corrals and windmill, to where FR 231 comes to a T-intersection with an old asphalt road. Turn left (east) and continue 0.6 mile to the trailhead. *DeLorme: Arizona Atlas and Gazetteer:* Page 58 C3.

Trailhead parking: The official trailhead includes a designated horse trailer parking area with plenty of pull-through parking for ten to twelve large rigs. Another possibility is to park in the pullout just beyond the windmill. From there, you can walk your horse (do not try to drive your trailer across the creekbed) to a cement water trough inside a lovely old stone corral.

The Ride

This section of the Arizona Trail winds through stunning Sonoran Desert landscape, dips into the Alamo Canyon drainage, and stops with the intersection with Forest Road 4 at the high point of the ride. Views from here are magnificent in every direction. For the most part, 4-by-4 posts and rock cairns (some so huge they're works of art) make it easy to follow the trail.

Although the footing is safe, a quarter of the ride involves clattering around in a slate-bottomed creekbed. There are several short sections where dismounting and leading will be easier than riding. Several of the climbs/descents are safe, but steep.

Alamo Canyon is a stunning ride, particularly after good winter rains. Although slogging through the loose, flat rocks in the creekbed may get tiresome, the 360-degree vistas—with Picketpost Mountain to the north—are well worth the effort.

Much of the canyon rock is a smooth, reflective slate, which is attractive but also makes this feel like a hotter ride than it is. You may encounter occasional puddles in the creekbed, but both the trough at the windmill at 3.8 miles and the spring at 5.3 miles are unreliable. Be sure your canine friend is fit, and carry dog water. (A one-gallon ziplock bag makes an easy-to-carry collapsible dog bowl—and in a pinch your horse can drink out of it as well.)

Eventually the Arizona Trail will connect through the White Canyon Wilderness to an access point on Battle Axe Road between mileposts 158 and 159 on U.S. Highway 177.

Miles and Directions

0.0   The trail leaves at the south end of the parking lot. You'll be following rock cairns (some of which are large and quite artistic) and 4-by-4 wooden posts with the AZT logo.

1.8   Your horse will have already climbed 550 feet to this lovely vista point.

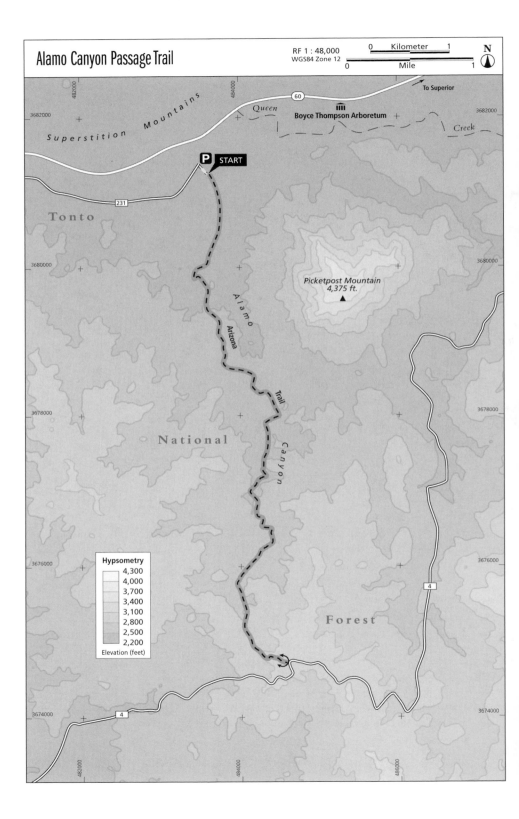

Alamo Canyon Passage Trail

RF 1 : 48,000
WGS84 Zone 12

Kilometer
Mile

N

To Superior

Superstition Mountains

Queen

Boyce Thompson Arboretum

Creek

P START

231

Tonto

Alamo

Arizona

Picketpost Mountain
4,375 ft.

Trail

National

Canyon

Forest

Hypsometry
4,300
4,000
3,700
3,400
3,100
2,800
2,500
2,200
Elevation (feet)

4

4

2.7 Just past the corral, turn right (south) to rejoin the creekbed, and follow it another mile.

3.7 Leave the wash.

4.0 This is a nice spot to stop for a break, especially if the trough has water (but don't count on it). **Bail-out:** If you have doubts about your horse's fitness, this is a good time to turn back for a total ride of 8 miles and a climb of about 1,100 feet.

5.1 Even if the creek is dry, you may encounter occasional puddles from the spring on the left (east) bank.

5.3 The creekbed narrows just before you climb out of it. The next mile is a hard climb.

6.0 Having ridden close to a fence line, you'll come to an easily opened, equestrian-friendly gate. Although the route actually finishes in another 0.1 mile at the intersection with Forest Road 4, this is a more pleasant area to stop.

6.1 Intersection with FR 4. The AZT continues on up the gravel road for another 1.5 miles before turning off.

12.2 Arrive back at the trailhead.

Options: The Arizona Trail continues on up FR 4 for another 1.5 miles and then on to Wood Canyon toward a not-yet-developed trailhead at Battle Axe Road off US 177.

20 Happy Camp Loop Trail

This 16.6-mile loop just west of Superior has a little of everything: rolling hills, steep climbs, ridgeline views, rocky creek bottoms, washes shaded by huge cottonwoods, and stretches of four-wheel-drive roads good for moving out. Your horse will need to be moderately fit to handle the 2,000-foot climb.

Start: 10 miles west of Florence Junction; Pinal County.
Distance: 16.6-mile loop.
Approximate riding time: 4 to 6 hours.
Total ascent: 2,038 feet.
Difficulty: Moderate, primarily due to the amount of climbing. Most of the footing is good, although it's rocky in places.
Seasons: Best in spring, fall, and winter.
Water availability: Usually the creek crossing at 4 miles in winter.

Other trail users: Hikers, mountain bikers, and motor vehicles on Forest Road 650.
Canine compatibility: Dogs "under control" are allowed. Bring water.
Fees and permits: None required.
Facilities: None.
USGS maps: Picketpost Mountain.
Contact: USDA Forest Service, Tonto National Forest, Globe Ranger District, (928) 402-6200.

Reaching the trailhead: From Tucson or Phoenix, drive to the Florence Junction (the intersection of U.S. Highway 60 and Arizona Highway 79). From there, travel east on US 60 approximately 9.3 miles to milepost 222. The trailhead, which is not signed, is a large gravel parking area on the north side of the highway. *DeLorme: Arizona Atlas and Gazetteer:* Page 58 C3.

County Line Riders enjoy a lunch break under one of the impressive cottonwood trees that are a favorite feature of the Happy Camp Loop Trail.

Trailhead parking: There's plenty of room for ten to twelve large rigs.

The Ride

Soon after leaving the parking area, this trail crosses the railroad line, picks up the Arizona Trail, and climbs to a ridge with particularly lovely views overlooking Potts Canyon and the Superstitions. It then drops down into Rice Water Canyon, then Whitford Canyon, where it winds in and out of the creekbed and through a forest of gigantic cottonwoods with a backdrop of redrock walls.

If the fall and winter rains have been good, the grass will be ankle high even in January, with a few early poppies, desert marigolds, and the occasional leafy ocotillo.

In wintertime the creek crossing at 4 miles is often running; in addition, Forest Road 650 wanders in and out of a wash that may run intermittently. Be sure your canine friend is fit, and carry dog water. (A one-gallon ziplock bag makes an easy-to-carry collapsible dog bowl—and in a pinch your horse can drink out of it as well.)

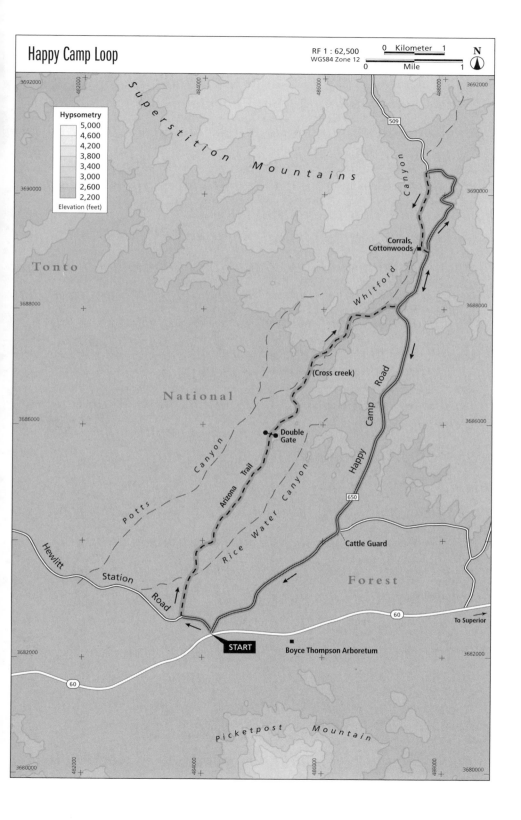

Happy Camp Loop

RF 1 : 62,500
WGS84 Zone 12

0 — Kilometer — 1

0 — Mile — 1

N

Hypsometry

Elevation (feet)
5,000
4,600
4,200
3,800
3,400
3,000
2,600
2,200

S u p e r s t i t i o n   M o u n t a i n s

Whitford Canyon

509

Corrals,
Cottonwoods

Tonto

(Cross creek)

Happy Camp Road

National

Potts Canyon

Arizona Trail

Double
Gate

Rice Water Canyon

650

Cattle Guard

Forest

Hewlitt

Station

Road

60

To Superior

START

Boyce Thompson Arboretum

P i c k e t p o s t   M o u n t a i n

60

Miles and Directions

0.0 From the parking lot, head west on Hewitt Station Road. Within a 0.5 mile, you'll see a brown hikers sign pointing to the right (east) and the Arizona Trail. (Your first challenge will be get your horse over the railroad tracks.) The trail is easy to find, marked either with carsonite signs or with clear (sometime very large!) piles of rocks.

3.0 Two wire gaps within 10 yards.

3.9 Cross over a wash; stay on the Arizona Trail.

4.1 The trail drops down into Whitford Canyon and crosses Whitford Creek, which in winter can be flowing generously. Once you climb back up out of the creek, you'll be able to look down on the corrals you'll be passing later.

9.2 Gravel road Forest Road 509. Here you'll leave the Arizona Trail (which goes straight across the road). Turn left (south).

10.3 A lovely shady lunch spot with plenty of grass, a burbling (well, sometimes) creek nearby, and safe tying places for as many as ten horses. When you leave, you can either just continue on down the road (with, unfortunately, its passenger cars, ATVs, and motorcycles) or enjoy a trail for a little longer. If you choose the latter, take the jeep track that leads southeast from the corrals. Within a few yards, you'll pick up the trail again; go right.

11.9 You'll encounter the road (FR 650), although it looks more like a sandy creekbed here. Take it to the left (east) and keep following it.

13.9 Cattle guard with a gate on the right side.

14.7 Intersection: go right (southwest).

16.6 Arrive back at the trailhead.

Options: Numerous dirt roads wind through this area.

Timber Camp Mountain

This small but appealing mountain range, which lies between Globe and the Salt River Canyon, includes an easily accessed USDA Forest Service campground and at least 20 miles of scenic trails. The existing campground is roomy, nestled in a grove of ponderosa pines, and, at 5,700 feet, a welcome respite from the lower-elevation desert areas. Its only flaw is the road noise from U.S. Highway 60. Area wildlife includes elk, javelina, jackrabbit, and deer.

A new facility, the proposed Timber Camp Recreation Site, due to open in 2006, will accommodate day use, single-family camping, group camping, a multilooped trail system, and equestrian camping. Contact the Globe Ranger District listed in Appendix B for the most recent information.

According to *Arizona Place Names* (a fascinating book written in 1935 by Will C. Barnes, one of Arizona's pioneers), the Timber Camp Mountains were named for a sawmill that was active in the area during the 1870s.

Parry's agave is prevalent in the Timber Camp area and is easily recognized by its spherical shape. Before dying, the plant produces a glorious cluster of orange-gold flowers atop a 10- to 15-foot stalk.

21 Big Loop

Even though this route is the longest of the three trails from the Timber Camp campground—and includes 1,100 feet of climbing—it's still an easy ride suitable for novice horse-and-rider teams.

Start: 25 miles north of Globe; Gila County.
Distance: 7.9-mile loop.
Approximate riding time: 2 hours.
Total ascent: 1,100 feet.
Difficulty: Easy, with some rocky footing.
Seasons: Best in April through June, and September through November.
Water availability: Small stock pond at 2.7 miles.
Other trail users: ATVers.

Canine compatibility: Dogs "under control" are allowed. Bring water.
Fees and permits: $40 per day for use of the group camping area.
Facilities: Two vault toilets, barbecue grills, tables.
USGS maps: Chrysotile.
Contact: USDA Forest Service, Tonto National Forest, Globe Ranger District, (928) 402-6200.

Reaching the trailhead: From Globe, travel north 25 miles on Arizona Highway 77/U.S. Highway 60. The Timber Camp campground will be on the left (west) side of the highway between mileposts 280 and 281. *DeLorme: Arizona Atlas and Gazetteer:* Page 59 A6.

Trailhead parking: There's ample parking for ten to twelve trailers, depending on other users. This can be a popular destination on weekends.

The Ride

This loop features superb vistas of Roosevelt Lake and its surrounding mountains, as well as the White Mountains to the north, visible from the viewpoint.

Snow and mud can make both the trails and the area around the campground impassable. During the summer be aware that parts of the trails are open and exposed and should be avoided during lightning storms. This area is quite heavily used on weekends by ATVers; the group area is often reserved for family reunions, saddle clubs, and other gatherings.

Be sure your canine friend is fit, and carry dog water since the only water on the trail is at 2.7 miles. (A one-gallon ziplock bag makes an easy-to-carry collapsible dog bowl—and in a pinch, your horse can drink out of it as well.) The small stock pond has a generally reliable amount of water for horses.

Parry's agave is particularly prevalent in this area, and if you ride here in summer, you're more than likely to see its golden flowers atop 10- to 15-foot stalks. Rounder and more compact than the Palmer's agave commonly seen at lower elevations, these specimens have teeth along the margin of their gray-green leaves as

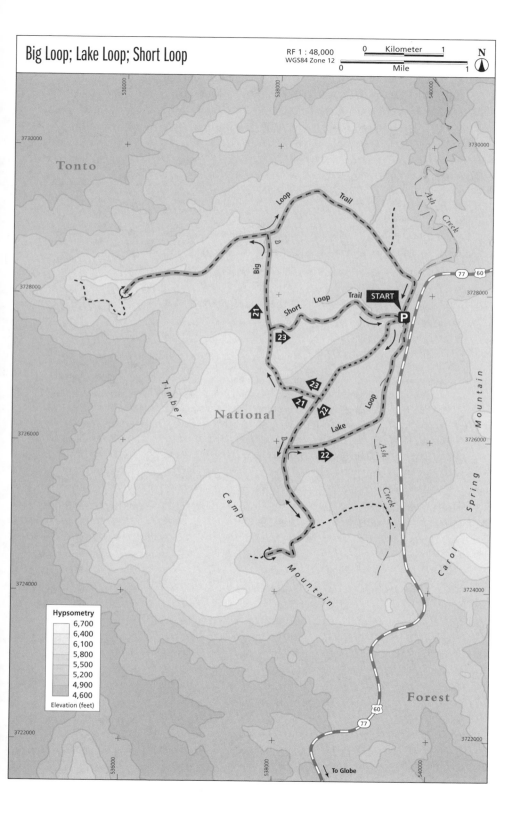

Big Loop; Lake Loop; Short Loop

RF 1 : 48,000
WGS84 Zone 12

Kilometer
Mile

N

Tonto

Ash Creek

77 60

Loop   Trail

Big

Short   Loop   Trail   START

21   P

23

National

23

21 22

Lake   Loop

22

Timber

Ash   Creek

Mountain

Spring

Carol

Camp

Mountain

Forest

60

77

To Globe

Hypsometry

	6,700
	6,400
	6,100
	5,800
	5,500
	5,200
	4,900
	4,600

Elevation (feet)

well as a contrasting dark spine on the end. Even though they're called century plants, agaves actually bloom only once at around twenty-five years before they die.

Both Edward Palmer (1829–1911) and Charles Christopher Parry (1823–1890) were botanists who were born in England but moved to the American West. Parry served as both a surgeon and a naturalist for the Mexican Boundary Survey from 1849 to 1852.

Miles and Directions

0.0 The trail takes off and heads uphill just west of the creekbed at the back of the campground and to the right of the corral.

0.6 The trail appears to fork but comes back together shortly. Take the right fork to avoid ruts.

1.0 The trail forks; go right (west). (Going left would take you on the Lake Loop.)

1.9 The trail forks again; go left. (Go right here for the Short Loop.) Parry's agave is quite common on this and the Short Loop; it starts to appear just before this fork.

2.7 Small stock pond on your right. Immediately after the pond, this trail ends at a T-intersection; turn left.

3.5 Fence and wire gate (always leave gates open or closed, as you found them). The trail heads uphill more steeply after the fence.

4.2 The trail comes to a high point (6,270 feet) on a hill with excellent views to the west of Roosevelt Lake and beyond. From here, the trail cuts downhill steeply at first and then heads west; it is slow and rocky. Your best option is to head back the way you came, allowing you to enjoy superb vistas of the White Mountains to the north.

5.7 Reach the same intersection (by the stock pond) you went through at 2.7 miles; go straight (north) here.

7.1 A minor track takes off to your left; stay straight.

7.9 Arrive back at Timber Camp, approaching from the north end of the group camping area.

Options: In addition to the two other trails described in this section, the area includes quite a few tempting jeep tracks.

22 Lake Loop

This easy 6.7-mile loop features a small lake and a perfect picnic spot with views for the humans and (sometimes) a little grass for the equines.

See map on page 95.
Start: 25 miles north of Globe; Gila County.
Distance: 6.7-mile loop.
Approximate riding time: 2 to 3 hours.
Total ascent: 400 feet.
Difficulty: Easy, with some rocky footing.
Seasons: Best in April through June, and September through November.
Water availability: Large stock pond at 1.6 miles.
Other trail users: ATVers.

Canine compatibility: Dogs "under control" are allowed. Bring water.
Fees and permits: $40 per day for use of the group camping area.
Facilities: Two vault toilets, barbecue grills, tables.
USGS maps: Chrysotile.
Contact: USDA Forest Service, Tonto National Forest, Globe Ranger District, (928) 402-6200.

Reaching the trailhead: From Globe, travel north 25 miles on Arizona Highway 77/U.S. Highway 60. The Timber Camp campground will be on the left (west) side of the highway between mileposts 280 and 281. *DeLorme: Arizona Atlas and Gazetteer:* Page 59 A6.

    Trailhead parking: There's ample parking for ten to twelve trailers, depending on other users. This can be a popular destination on weekends.

The Ride

About 2 miles into this ride, you'll begin to see microwave towers to the east atop Carol Spring Mountain. The land for this structure was acquired in 1957 by the Department of the Air Force for a radar gap filler facility, known as Globe Gap Filler M-92D. In 1961 the Department of Defense surplused the site, and it reverted to the USDA Forest Service, which leases it out for telecommunications.

This area is quite heavily used on weekends by ATVers, and the group area is often reserved for family reunions, saddle clubs, and other gatherings.

The turnaround point of this ride has a particularly lovely view and is a perfect spot for lunch or viewing the sunset. Although the end of the loop passes within a few yards of US 60, there's a fence between the trail and the highway.

Snow and mud can make both the trails and the area around the campground impassable. During the summer be aware that the trails can be exposed and should be avoided during lightning storms.

Tonto National Forest policy requires that dogs be "under control" at all times. Be sure your canine friend is fit, and carry dog water since the only water on the trail is at 1.6 miles. (A one-gallon ziplock bag makes an easy-to-carry collapsible dog bowl—and in a pinch, your horse can drink out of it as well.) The large stock pond (or small lake, depending on your point of view) has reliable water, although the edges may be muddy.

The stock pond on the Timber Camp Lake Loop is as refreshing for dogs as it is for horses.

Miles and Directions

0.0 The trail takes off and heads uphill just west of the creek at the back of the campground and to the right of the corral.

0.6 The trail forks, but rejoins shortly. Take the right fork to avoid ruts.

1.0 The trail forks; go left (east).

1.5 The trail forks; go left at the rock pile.

1.6 Stock pond (with the occasional optimistic fisherman).

2.3 The trail forks; go right (southwest). You'll be able to see radio towers and the highway to the southwest.

2.6 The trail climbs gradually to a lovely, flat open meadow near a fence and a great view toward the Pinal Mountains. This is the turnaround spot: If you go through the gate (leave all gates open or closed, as you find them), the trail heads down a treacherously steep rocky grade. Although the trail you rode in looks as if it continues on up through the woods, it soon dwindles to nothing.

3.0 Return to the intersection with the view of the radio towers. Continue to retrace your steps.

3.9 Return to the pond. Instead of going left to return to the campground, go right (east) up the hill.

5.6 The trail forks; go left (away from the highway, which is only 200 yards to your right).

6.7 Arrive back at the campground, although you'll be coming in at the southern end and well east of the creekbed.

Options: In addition to the two other trails described in this section, the area includes quite a few tempting jeep tracks.

23 Short Loop

This is a very easy 3.5-mile loop that makes a perfect short, social ride for first-timers.

See map on page 95.
Start: 25 miles north of Globe; Gila County.
Distance: 3.5-mile loop.
Approximate riding time: 1 to 2 hours of leisurely riding.
Total ascent: 500 feet.
Difficulty: Easy, with some rocky footing.
Seasons: Best in April through June, and September through November.
Water availability: Small stock pond at 2.7 miles.

Other trail users: ATVers.
Canine compatibility: Dogs "under control" are allowed. Bring water.
Fees and permits: $40 per day for use of the group camping area.
Facilities: Two vault toilets, barbecue grills, tables.
USGS maps: Chrysotile.
Contact: USDA Forest Service, Tonto National Forest, Globe Ranger District, (928) 402-6200.

Reaching the trailhead: From Globe, travel north 25 miles on Arizona Highway 77/U.S. Highway 60. The Timber Camp campground will be on the left (west) side of the highway between mileposts 280 and 281. *DeLorme: Arizona Atlas and Gazetteer:* Page 59 A6.

 Trailhead parking: There's ample parking for ten to twelve trailers, depending on other users. This can be a popular destination on weekends.

The Ride

This brief trail is ideal if you arrive late and only have a little daylight left, or if you have novice riders or equines in your group who aren't ready for a longer ride. This area is quite heavily used on weekends by ATVers; the group area is often reserved for family reunions, saddle clubs, and other gatherings.

 Tonto National Forest policy requires that dogs be "under control" at all times. Be sure your canine friend is fit, and carry dog water since the only water on the trail is at 2.7 miles. (A one-gallon ziplock bag makes an easy-to-carry collapsible dog bowl—and in a pinch your horse can drink out of it as well.) The large stock pond (or small lake, depending on your point of view) has reliable water, although the edges may be muddy.

Snow and mud can make both the trails and the area around the campground impassable. During the summer be aware that the trails can be exposed and should be avoided during lightning storms.

Miles and Directions

0.0 The trail takes off and heads uphill just west of the creek at the back of the campground and to the right of the corral.

0.6 The trail forks, but rejoins shortly. Take the right fork to avoid ruts.

1.0 The trail forks—go right (west). (Going left would take you onto the Lake Loop.)

1.9 The trail forks again—go right. (Go left here for the Big Loop.) Parry's agave is quite common on both this and the Big Loop; it starts to appear just before this fork.

3.5 Arrive back at Timber Camp, approaching from the north end of the group camping area.

Options: In addition to the two other trails described in this section, the area includes quite a few tempting jeep tracks.

White Mountains

O riginally named Sierra Blanca (the mountains are indeed topped with snow seven months of most years), the Whites are a summer mecca for desert dwellers. The seasonal appeal is nothing new—the Railroad Grade Trail where you'll be riding carried tourists from McNary to Big Lake as far back as the early 1900s.

Unlike some of Arizona's jagged, craggy, and often impassable ranges, the White Mountains are gently rounded with many well-maintained, equestrian-friendly trails. The White Mountains trail system also attracts other users and annual events, such as the Arizona White Mountain Trail Marathon, which is usually in late August, and the Benefit Tour of the White Mountains mountain bike race, which takes place in mid- to late September.

Pinetop-Lakeside was incorporated as one town in 1984. Long before that, the town next to Pinetop was known as Fairview until the resident Mormons dammed Showlow Creek in the 1880s, creating both a lake and a new name.

Interestingly, Pinetop's name has nothing to do with the local flora. Instead, it memorializes the local 1880s cavalry's favorite bartender: Walt Rigney ran the saloon and store between Camp Apache and Show Low, and according to several accounts was tall and lanky—with a good crop of standing-up fuzzy red hair.

These mountains are still home to the 15,000 members of the White Mountain Apache Tribe. The reservation, which covers 1.67 million acres (more than 2,600 square miles), lies between Pinetop-Lakeside and the trails near Springerville. Recreational opportunities for hiking, hunting, biking, backpacking, camping, and fishing abound on the reservation, as long as you have the appropriate permit. However, *you absolutely may not ride your horse on the reservation*. You are allowed to drive through the reservation on Arizona Highway 260 with your horse trailer, but if you want to do some sightseeing or picnicking on your way through, you'll need to pick up a $6.00 day-use permit—and your equine companion will need to remain in the trailer. Permits are available at Hon-Dah (the Apache phrase for "be my guest") Ski and Outdoor Sport, 787 Highway 260, Pinetop-Lakeside, AZ 85935, (928) 369–7669 or (877) 226–4868; www.hon-dah.com. This store is on the east side of the Hon-Dah Casino complex and open daily year-round.

You may see references to FAIR, for Fort Apache Indian Reservation, on various federal or government Web sites. Fort Apache was established in 1870 as Fort Ord to monitor the Apaches (who had been friendly). Not surprisingly, perhaps, the tribe usually refers to the area as the White Mountain Apache Reservation.

24 Country Club Trail

This gently rolling 4.4-mile loop right—easily accessed from Pinetop-Lakeside—winds its way through pine forests and past an aspen meadow.

Start: 5 miles east of Pinetop-Lakeside; Navajo County.
Distance: 4.4-mile loop.
Approximate riding time: 1 to 2 hours.
Total ascent: 740 feet.
Difficulty: Easy, with good footing.
Seasons: Best in summer and fall.
Water availability: None.

Other trail users: Hikers.
Canine compatibility: Dogs are allowed. Bring water.
Fees and permits: None needed.
Facilities: None.
USGS maps: Lakeside, Sponseller Mountain.
Contact: USDA Forest Service, Lakeside Ranger District, (928) 368–5111.

Reaching the trailhead: From Show Low, travel south on Arizona Highway 260 past the Lakeside Ranger Station before turning left (east) onto Buck Springs Road between mileposts 355 and 356. Go 0.6 mile and take the next left onto Sky-Hi Road, which is also Forest Road 182. Drive 2 miles through a residential area, passing the Springs Trailhead at 1 mile. The Country Club Trailhead will be on your right and is where FR 182 and Forest Road 185 intersect with the entrance to Sierra Springs Ranch. A second trailhead that has room to camp is 1.2 miles farther down FR 185; in spring, however, it may be impassable due to snow, mud, or deep ruts. Call the Forest Service before attempting it. *DeLorme: Arizona Atlas and Gazetteer:* Page 52 C3.

Trailhead parking: There's a gravel pullout with room for two to three trailers.

The Ride

The Country Club Trail is a short, easy loop—perfect for a novice horse or when you're trying to fit in a short morning ride before the afternoon thunderstorms. Close to town and frequently used by hikers, the trail winds through oak–juniper woodland interspersed with occasional aspen groves and a view over Whitcomb Springs Meadow. It also includes a short climb up Pat Mullen Mountain past some venerable granddaddy junipers.

Note that the trails may be closed into May due to snow and mud.

Miles and Directions

0.0 To ride the trail counterclockwise, start behind the information kiosk, and head east. The trail is clearly marked with blue plastic diamonds nailed to trees.

0.7 Cross over the jeep road.

Huge alligator junipers enhance the climb up Pat Mullen Mountain. The name of these venerable trees comes from their checkered scaly bark; some are hundreds of years old.

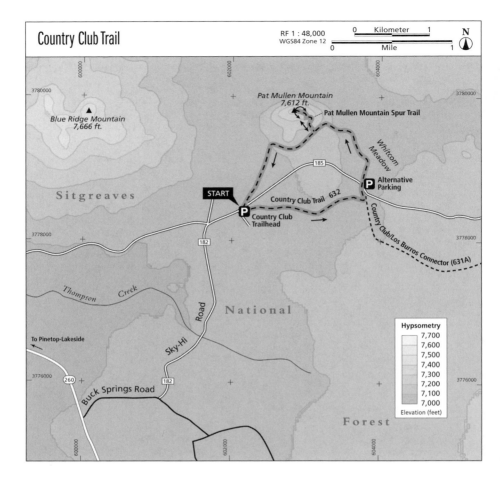

Country Club Trail

RF 1 : 48,000
WGS84 Zone 12

1.3 Intersection of the Country Club Trail 632 with the Country Club/Los Burros Connector Trail 631A. Go left.

1.5 Intersection of the Country Club Trail and FR 185 at the corrals.

1.6 Equestrian-friendly step-over gate.

1.9 Equestrian-friendly step-over gate.

2.3 Intersection of the Country Club and Pat Mullen Mountain Spur Trails. Go right, following the sign to VISTA POINT.

2.9 There's no real "Vista Point," but you will find beautiful, venerable, huge junipers. Retrace your route to the Country Club Trail.

3.4 Back to the Country Club Trail.

3.9 Equestrian-friendly step-over gate.

4.4 Arrive back at the trailhead.

Options: This trail is part of the White Mountain Trail System with access to many more miles.

25 Country Club/Los Burros Connector/Los Burros

This trail, one of the longest in the book, is also among the most beautiful. The 24.9-mile loop begins and ends at the Country Club Trailhead near Pinetop-Lakeside and extends out to Los Burros. Endurance riders will particularly enjoy this one, since the footing is good enough that a well-conditioned horse can trot much of the way.

Start: 5 miles east of Pinetop; Navajo and Apache Counties.
Distance: 24.9-mile loop.
Approximate riding time: 4 to 6 hours.
Total ascent: 2,300 feet.
Difficulty: Difficult, but only due to its length and climb. For the most part, the footing is good and the climb gradual and well graded.
Seasons: Best in summer and fall.
Water availability: None.

Other trail users: Hikers and mountain bikers.
Canine compatibility: Well-conditioned dogs only.
Fees and permits: None needed.
Facilities: None.
USGS maps: Lakeside, Sponseller Mountain, McNary, Boundary Butte.
Contact: USDA Forest Service, Lakeside Ranger District, (928) 368-5111.

Reaching the trailhead: From Show Low, travel south on Arizona Highway 260 past the Lakeside Ranger Station before turning left (east) onto Buck Springs Road between mileposts 355 and 356. Go 0.6 mile and take the next left onto Sky-Hi Road, which is also Forest Road 182. Drive 2 miles through a residential area, passing the Springs Trailhead at 1 mile. The Country Club Trailhead will be on your right and is where FR 182 and Forest Road 185 intersect with the entrance to Sierra Springs Ranch. *DeLorme: Arizona Atlas and Gazetteer:* Page 52 C3.
    Trailhead parking: There's a gravel pullout with room for two or three trailers.

The Ride

This is a long but beautiful and not-too-strenuous ride if your horse is well conditioned; however, it's too long of a day for all but the most fit of canine companions. The trail starts in a low-elevation ponderosa pine forest (7,100 feet) and climbs slowly and gradually to moist, higher-altitude forest of Douglas fir, aspen, and white pine (8,200 feet). You'll pass through high-altitude meadows, groves of quaking aspen, and forests of ponderosa pine on the Los Burros Trail. The farther you are from Pinetop, the less likely you are to see other trail users, especially during the week. You may be fortunate enough to see wild turkeys or elk, and in May irises edge many of the marshes.

Note that the trails in this area may be closed due to snow and mud into May.

Combining the Country Club and Los Burros Trails makes for a long—but lovely—day. Although you're more likely to see elk than humans, mountain bikers and hikers also use the trail.

Miles and Directions

0.0 Take Country Club Trail 632 east from behind the information kiosk. The trail is a narrow singletrack, clearly marked with plastic White Mountain Trail System (WMTS) blue-diamond signs.

1.3 Intersection of Country Club Trail 632 with Country Club/Los Burros Connector Trail 631A. Take the connector trail to the right (south).

2.7 The trail leaves the road; turn right as it follows an old logging road (the turn is well marked with WMTS blue diamonds).

3.7 Fence with a wire gate; always leave gates open or closed, as you found them.

5.7 The trail crosses Forest Road 271.

7.1 Fence with a wire gate.

7.7 The trail crosses Forest Road 224.

8.4 Fence with a wire gate.

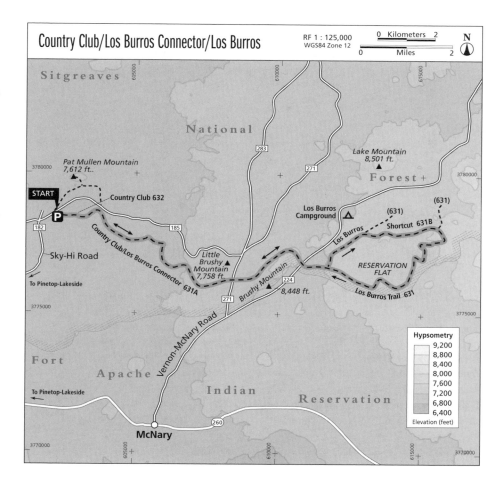

Country Club/Los Burros Connector/Los Burros

RF 1 : 125,000
WGS84 Zone 12

0 Kilometers 2

0 Miles 2

N

Sitgreaves

National

283

271

Pat Mullen Mountain
7,612 ft..

Lake Mountain
8,501 ft.

Forest +

3780000

3780000

START

Country Club 632

Los Burros
Campground

(631)

(631)

P

182

185

Shortcut 631B

Sky-Hi Road

Country Club/Los Burros Connector 631A

Little
Brushy
Mountain
7,758 ft.

RESERVATION
FLAT

To Pinetop-Lakeside

Brushy Mountain

224

Los Burros Trail 631

271

8,448 ft.

3775000

3775000

Hypsometry
9,200
8,800
8,400
8,000
7,600
7,200
6,800
6,400
Elevation (feet)

Fort

Apache

Indian

To Pinetop-Lakeside

Reservation

Vernon-McNary Road

260

McNary

3770000

3770000

8.6 Intersection of Country Club/Los Burros Connector Trail 631A with Los Burros Trail 631; Trail 631A ends here. Go left (north) onto Los Burros Trail 631. So far you've climbed 940 feet. **Bail-out:** Should you decide that you and/or your horse don't need to do the extra loop, you can retrace your steps from here to the Country Club Trailhead for a total ride of 17.2 miles.

9.6 Turn right to take the shortcut Los Burros Trail 631B. The Los Burros campground and trailhead are to your left.

10.1 Begin a sharp climb for 0.3 mile through aspen, Douglas fir, and white pine to the high point on a ridge.

11.4 Intersection of Los Burros Trail 631B with Los Burros Trail 631. Continue straight; do not take the northern part of the Los Burros Trail, which is back to your left.

11.7 Gradual ascent to the high point of the trail (8,260 feet) through a forest of tall ponderosa pine.

16.3 Intersection of the short loop and Country Club/Los Burros Connector 631A. Head straight to retrace your steps to the Country Club Trailhead. By now you've climbed 2,260 feet, and the remaining 8.6 miles are all a gradual downhill stretch.

17.2 The trail crosses FR 224.

19.2 The trail crosses FR 271.

23.6 Intersection of Country Club/Los Burros Connector Trail 631A with Country Club Trail 632. Turn left to return to the trailhead.

24.9 Arrive back at the Country Club Trailhead.

Options: From the Country Club Trailhead, you can head south toward the Springs Trail. You can also choose to do the entire Los Burros loop instead of taking the shortcut.

26 Pole Knoll/Squirrel Spring Loop Trail

A moderate 12.1-mile out-and-back route that crosses from the Pole Knoll Recreation Area to the Squirrel Spring Recreation Area. The trail is easily accessed from Arizona Highway 260 approximately 12 miles west of Eagar.

Start: 30 miles east of Pinetop-Lakeside; Apache County.

Distance: 12.1-mile loop.

Approximate riding time: 3 to 4 hours.

Total ascent: 970 feet.

Difficulty: Moderate. Although most of the terrain is easy, parts of the trail are rocky and slow going.

Seasons: Best in late spring, summer, and fall.

Water availability: Hall Creek crosses the trail at 3.5 and 7.3 miles.

Other trail users: Very few.

Canine compatibility: Dogs must be leashed in the parking lot and picnic area, allowed off-leash elsewhere.

Fees and permits: None.

Facilities: Four picnic shelters with grills, vault toilet; no camping or fires outside grills allowed.

USGS maps: Greens Peak.

Contact: USDA Forest Service, Springerville Ranger District, (928) 333-4372.

Reaching the trailhead: From the Eagar traffic light, travel west approximately 12 miles on AZ 260. The trailhead will be on your left between mileposts 383 and 384.

From Show Low, go through Pinetop-Lakeside to the intersection of AZ 260 and Arizona Highway 73 at Hon-Dah. Travel another 25.6 miles; the trailhead will be on your right between mileposts 383 and 384. DeLorme: Arizona Atlas and Gazetteer: Page 53 C4.

Trailhead parking: There's a paved parking lot with room for five or six trailers.

The Ride

This trail features magnificent ponderosa and aspen areas, as well as deep spruce–fir forests and vistas stretching to the snow–topped Mount Baldy.

Parts of this trail are very open and exposed with no shelter from lightning. Plan your ride carefully, especially during summer.

If you bring a canine companion, keep in mind that this region is one in which

Although the Pole Knoll Recreation Area is designed for cross-country skiers, the trails are ideal for equestrian use.

the endangered Mexican gray wolf has been reintroduced. Although wolves are not aggressive toward humans, they may regard your dog as a territorial threat—or lunch. Be prepared to keep your dog in your tent or vehicle if wolves approach your parking area; should a curious wolf approach you on the trail, dismount and leash your dog. Mexican wolves are protected as an endangered species, so you may not kill or injure a wolf that attacks your pet unless human life is threatened as well; however, you may harass a bothersome wolf in any way that doesn't injure it (banging pots together, throwing objects, shouting, and the like). The penalty for killing a Mexican gray wolf can be up to $25,000 and/or six months in jail or a civil penalty of up to $25,000. If you kill or injure a wolf in defense of human life, you must report the incident within twenty-four hours by calling (888) 459–WOLF (9653).

Miles and Directions

0.0   Head southwest on the Pole Knoll Loop Trail, which leaves directly behind the picnic shelters and information kiosk. (You'll be doing the loop in a counterclockwise direction.)

0.1   Almost immediately the Redtail Trail goes off to the left (southeast). Stay on the Pole Knoll Loop Trail.

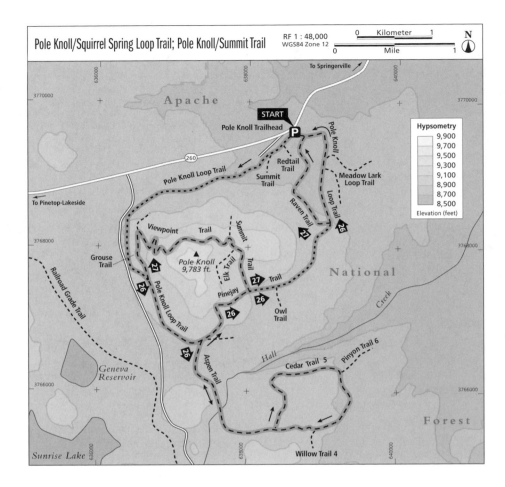

Pole Knoll/Squirrel Spring Loop Trail; Pole Knoll/Summit Trail

RF 1 : 48,000
WGS84 Zone 12

Hypsometry

| | 9,900 |
| 9,700 |
| 9,500 |
| 9,300 |
| 9,100 |
| 8,900 |
| 8,700 |
| 8,500 |

Elevation (feet)

0.2   Intersection of the Pole Knoll Loop and Summit Trails. Remain on the Pole Knoll Loop Trail.

0.4   The trail seems to fork; go left, continuing to follow the blue diamonds.

1.2   Even though turning uphill on the jeep trail seems like the logical route, cross straight over it and into the grass, heading for the next blue diamond. You won't be on a trail but will be following blue diamonds as you travel cross-country around the base of the knoll, with the gravel road on your right.

1.5   Continue following blue diamonds as you pick up a faint trail. (Since you're only a few yards from the gravel road, which has almost no traffic, you may prefer the road to slowly picking your way through the rocks and grass tufts.)

2.0   At a large rock pile, the trail veers away from the road and heads uphill on an old roadbed.

2.2   Intersection of the Pole Knoll Loop and Grouse Trails. Stay on the Pole Knoll Loop, which heads generally south.

2.5   The old roadbed becomes less rocky, making for easier progress.

2.8   The Aspen Trail heads off to the right (south). Follow it cross-country.

3.1 The Aspen Trail merges with a dirt road and reenters the forest. The trail goes over a low saddle and downhill.

3.4 Leave the dirt road and head cross-country, following blue diamonds.

3.5 Cross Hall Creek and head uphill.

3.8 Turn left following the sign TRAILS 1-6. You're back in forest again: ponderosa pine, aspen, and spruce.

3.9 Follow a dirt jeep track to the left and the TRAILS 1-6 sign.

4.2 At a T-intersection, go left. The trail here is wide and flat with good footing. (On the Forest Service map, at this point you are beginning the Cedar Trail loop, which is Trail 5. However, you may only see one sign that says CEDAR TRAIL.)

5.6 The trail forks—go straight ahead, not left. (Heading left here would put you on Pinyon Trail 6, which is a long trail that eventually reaches Arizona Highway 373.)

6.1 At a trail intersection, go right. (A left here would put you on Willow Trail 4, which is a good alternative if you wish to add another mile and to connect to other trails in the Squirrel Spring Recreation Area. Consult the Forest Service map for more details.)

6.6 You're back at same point as 4.2 miles. Go straight, following the sign to the Pole Knoll trails.

6.9 Take the trail to your right, following the POLE KNOLL TRAILS sign.

7.0 Turn right.

7.3 Cross Hall Creek.

7.7 Leave the dirt track and turn to your right, following blue diamonds cross-country and back to Pole Knoll.

8.0 Rejoin the Pole Knoll Loop Trail, heading gradually uphill away from the old roadbed (to the northeast) following blue diamonds. This becomes the Pinejay Trail.

8.2 Reenter forest.

8.6 Intersection (with a sign) of the Pinejay and Elk Trails. Stay on Pinejay (straight).

8.8 Intersection of the Pinejay and Summit Trails. Continue on Pinejay (straight ahead).

9.2 Intersection of the Pinejay and Owl Trails; follow Pinejay straight ahead.

10.4 Intersection of the Pinejay, Raven, and Pine Knoll Loop Trails. Go right onto the Pine Knoll Loop (not Raven).

11.0 Intersection of the Pine Knoll Loop and Meadow Lark Trails. Stay on the Pine Knoll Loop (straight ahead).

11.1 Intersection (again) of the Pine Knoll Loop and Meadow Lark Trails. Stay straight on Pine Knoll.

11.6 Intersection of the Pine Knoll Loop and Raven Trails. Continue straight on the Pine Knoll Loop.

11.7 Gate to the Pole Knoll Trailhead. Continue following blue diamonds as the trail first parallels the road, then veers slightly away from it until you approach the trailhead itself.

12.1 Arrive back at the trailhead.

Options: Several other combinations of trails are possible once you reach Squirrel Spring Recreation Area. The Cedar Trail Loop is the shortest; at least 20 more miles of trails are available.

27 Pole Knoll/Summit Trail

This scenic and moderate 7.6-mile loop winds its way around the base of Pole Knoll itself, then climbs about 800 feet to near the top, and drops back down again.

See map on page 110.
Start: 30 miles east of Pinetop-Lakeside; Apache County.
Distance: 7.6-mile loop.
Approximate riding time: 2 to 3 hours.
Total ascent: 820 feet.
Difficulty: Moderate. Although most of the terrain is easy, parts of the trail are rocky and slow going.
Seasons: Best in late spring, summer, and fall.
Water availability: None.

Other trail users: Not likely.
Canine compatibility: Dogs must be leashed in the parking lot and picnic area, allowed off-leash elsewhere.
Fees and permits: None.
Facilities: Four picnic shelters with grills, vault toilet; no camping or fires outside grills allowed.
USGS maps: Greens Peak, Greer.
Contact: USDA Forest Service, Springerville Ranger District, (928) 333-4372.

Reaching the trailhead: From the Eagar traffic light, travel west approximately 12 miles on Arizona Highway 260. The trailhead will be on your left between mileposts 383 and 384.

From Show Low, go through Pinetop-Lakeside, to the intersection of Arizona Highway 260 and Arizona Highway 73 at Hon-Dah. Travel another 25.6 miles; the trailhead will be on your right between mileposts 383 and 384. *DeLorme: Arizona Atlas and Gazetteer:* Page 53 C4.

Trailhead parking: There's a paved parking lot with room for five or six trailers.

The Ride

As you follow the trail around the knoll, you'll pass through various habitats depending on what side of the knoll you're on: open bunchgrass at the west- and south-facing aspects; then some oak and mixed conifers on the east; and spruce, fir, and aspen at the top and on the north-facing slopes.

To the southwest you can see Mount Baldy (often snow covered) and Sunrise Lake, while Greens Peak is the dominant feature to the north.

If you bring a canine companion, keep in mind that this region is one in which the endangered Mexican gray wolf has been reintroduced. Although wolves are not aggressive toward humans, they may regard your dog as a territorial threat—or lunch. Be prepared to keep your dog in your tent or vehicle if wolves approach your parking area; should a curious wolf approach you on the trail, dismount and leash your dog. Mexican wolves are protected as an endangered species, so you may not kill or injure a wolf that attacks your pet unless human life is threatened as well; however, you may harass a bothersome wolf in any way that doesn't injure it (banging pots together, throwing objects, shouting, and the like). The penalty for killing a

Looking across the Geneva Reservoir from Viewpoint Trail in the Pine Knoll Recreation Area. In many years snow blankets Mount Baldy as late as early June.

Mexican gray wolf can be up to $25,000 and/or six months in jail or a civil penalty of up to $25,000. If you kill or injure a wolf in defense of human life, you must report the incident within twenty-four hours by calling (888) 459–WOLF (9653).

Miles and Directions

0.0   Head southwest on the Pole Knoll Loop Trail, which leaves directly behind the picnic shelters and information kiosk. (You'll be doing the loop in a counterclockwise direction.)

0.1   Almost immediately the Redtail Trail goes off to the left (southeast). Stay on the Pole Knoll Loop Trail.

0.2   Intersection of the Pole Knoll Loop and Summit Trails. Remain on the Pole Knoll Loop Trail.

0.4   The trail seems to fork; go left, continuing to follow the blue diamonds.

1.2   Even though turning uphill on the jeep trail seems like the logical route, cross straight over it and into the grass, heading for the next blue diamond. You won't be on a trail but will be following blue diamonds as you travel cross-country around the base of the knoll, with the gravel road on your right.

1.5   Continue following blue diamonds as you pick up a faint trail. (Since you're only a few yards from the gravel road, which has almost no traffic, you may prefer the road to slowly picking your way through the rocks and tussocks of bunchgrass.)

2.0   At a large rock pile, the trail veers away from the road and heads uphill on an old roadbed.

2.2   Intersection of the Pole Knoll Loop and Grouse Trails. Take the Grouse Trail turnoff to the left (north). This section is slow going: There's no discernible trail. Still, the blue diamonds are easy to follow as you head cross-country first through open grasslands, then through thick spruce forest.

2.8   Intersection of the Grouse and Viewpoint Trails. Take the Viewpoint Trail uphill to the right (southeast). Although it's labeled MOST DIFFICULT for cross-country skiers, the trail is well defined and gently graded. It skirts the top of the knoll, so the best views are at about 3.3 miles, shortly after the switchbacks.

4.1   Intersection of the Viewpoint and Summit Trails. Take the Summit Trail downhill to the left (east), and keep bearing left on the jeep road.

4.5   Intersection of the Summit and Elk Trails. Stay on Summit (the jeep trail).

4.8   Intersection of the Summit and Pinejay Trails. Go left (east) onto Pinejay. This is a flat, easy trail that winds its way through open ponderosa forest. (Keep an eye out for elk!)

5.1   Intersection of the Pinejay and Owl Trails. Remain on Pinejay.

5.8   Intersection of the Pinejay, Pole Knoll Loop, and Raven Trails. Go left (northwest) and slightly downhill onto Raven.

6.7   Intersection of the Raven and Osprey Trails. Stay on Raven.

6.9   Intersection of the Raven and Pole Knoll Loop Trails. Go left onto Pole Knoll Loop toward the trailhead (you'll be able to hear the road noise from AZ 260).

7.1   Gate to the Pole Knoll Trailhead. Continue following blue diamonds as the trail at first parallels the road, then veers slightly away from it until you approach the trailhead itself.

7.6   Arrive back at the trailhead.

Options: Several other combinations of trails are possible, or you can connect to the Squirrel Spring Recreation Area (see Pole Knoll/Squirrel Spring Loop Trail).

28 Railroad Grade Trail/Big Lake

Once you've bumped your way over several miles of dirt road to the campground, this is a very easy, gently rolling 11-mile round trip through mostly open bunchgrass meadows.

Start: Approximately 27 miles west of Springerville; Apache County.
Distance: 11 miles out and back.
Approximate riding time: 3 to 4 hours.
Total ascent: 650 feet.
Difficulty: Very easy, with no climbs and excellent footing.
Seasons: Best from mid- to late May through October.
Water availability: Trailhead stream and Big Lake.

Other trail users: Hikers.
Canine compatibility: Dogs must be leashed in the campground.
Fees and permits: None needed.
Facilities: Heavy-duty wooden 10-by-10 corrals, vault toilet.
USGS maps: Big Lake North.
Contact: USDA Forest Service, Springerville Ranger District, (928) 333-4372.

Reaching the trailhead: The trailhead is the Gabaldon Campground, which is only for those camping with livestock. To get there from Springerville, travel west approximately 27 miles, turning south onto Arizona Highway 273 between mileposts 377 and 378.

From Show Low, go through Pinetop-Lakeside to the intersection of Arizona Highway 260 and Arizona Highway 73 at Hon-Dah. Travel another 20 miles to AZ 273, which will take off to the south between mileposts 377 and 378.

Once you're on AZ 273, go 3.7 miles to Gabaldon Campground, which will be on your right between mileposts 389 and 390. The road alternates between pavement and rough gravel, with sections of very slow washboard. *DeLorme: Arizona Atlas and Gazetteer:* Page 53 5D.

Trailhead parking: Gabaldon Campground, available on a no-fee, first-come, first-served basis, has five designated camping sites. Sites 4 and 5 are only for small trailers; sites 2 and 3 are together and have room for larger trailers (limit 16 feet). Site 1 has no corral but has turnaround room for one large trailer with a HiTie or portable corral. The campground was named for Juan Gabaldon, a Forest Service employee who worked on the area's trails for many years.

The Ride

The easy and scenic Railroad Grade Trail is part of the Rails-to-Trails program that converts unused old railroad beds to hiking, biking, and horseback-riding trails. This particular trail runs along a historic railroad route that was used for hauling logs from the national forest and the White Mountain Apache Reservation, as well as carrying tourists. The cinder bed makes the footing reliable and the trail very easy to see and follow.

The trail to Big Lake curves among sweeping vistas of mountain bunchgrass meadows. Elk and pronghorn are common sights.

For much of this route, the Railroad Grade Trail is in sight of AZ 273, which can be very busy, particularly on holiday weekends. The trails and roads may be impassable (or even closed) in early spring due to snow and mud.

Insect repellent is strongly recommended for both you and your equine—the mosquitoes can be particularly bloodthirsty in May. Although thunderstorms can happen anytime during spring, summer, or fall, plan your ride especially carefully in summer as this route is completely open and has no protection or shelter from lightning.

If you bring a canine companion, keep in mind that this region is one in which the endangered Mexican gray wolf has been reintroduced. Although wolves are not aggressive toward humans, they may regard your dog as a territorial threat—or lunch. Be prepared to keep your dog in your tent or vehicle if wolves approach your parking area; should a curious wolf approach you on the trail, dismount and leash your dog. Mexican wolves are protected as an endangered species, so you may not kill or injure a wolf that attacks your pet unless human life is threatened as well;

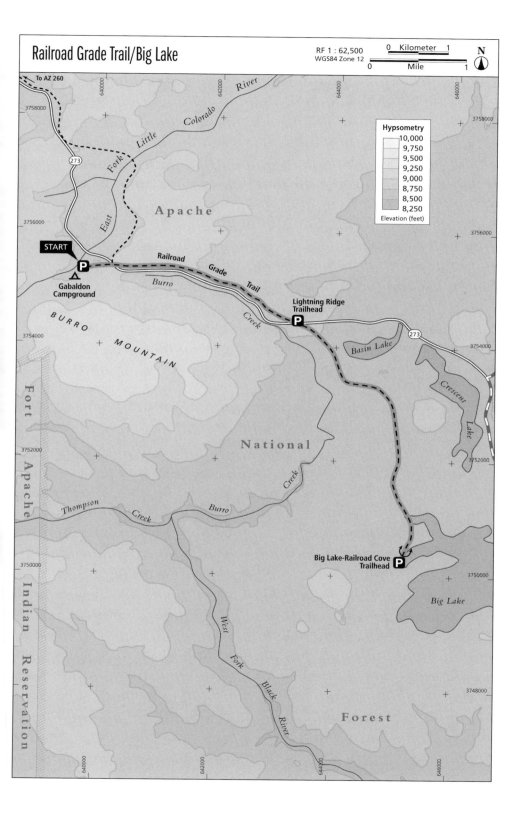

however, you may harass a bothersome wolf in any way that doesn't injure it (banging pots together, throwing objects, shouting, and the like). The penalty for killing a Mexican gray wolf can be up to $25,000 and/or six months in jail or a civil penalty of up to $25,000. If you kill or injure a wolf in defense of human life, you must report the incident within twenty-four hours by calling (888) 459–WOLF (9653).

Miles and Directions

0.0 Ride out the campground driveway, cross AZ 273, and turn right (south) onto the Railroad Grade Trail toward Big Lake and Railroad Cove.

0.1 This is the high point for this trail, which from here descends gradually through a spruce-aspen forest.

2.3 Lightning Ridge Trailhead, which has a vault toilet. The trail crosses the road at this point and heads through bunchgrass meadows.

2.8 First of five gates between Lightning Ridge and Railroad Cove. You'll also pass Basin Lake and, in the distance, Crescent Lake, both to the east.

5.5 Railroad Cove and the southernmost end of the Railroad Grade Trail. The trailhead has a vault toilet and access to the lake to water your horse. Retrace your steps toward Lightning Ridge and the campground.

8.7 Lightning Ridge Trailhead.

11.0 Turn left where the trail comes close to AZ 273 to return to the campground.

Options: Although the two routes featured start from Gabaldon Campground, you could instead day-park at the northernmost trailhead, which is right on AZ 260 between mileposts 379 and 380. From there, you could do an out-and-back ride for as much of the 21-mile Railroad Grade Trail as you wanted. The trailhead is a gravel pullout large enough for five or six trailers with plenty of room to turn around.

29 Railroad Grade Trail/Trestle Bridge

Because this trail is an old railbed, it's a gradual grade with good footing, resulting in a very easy 14.2-mile round-trip ride.

Start: Approximately 27 miles west of Springerville; Apache County.
Distance: 14.2 miles out and back.
Approximate riding time: 4 to 5 hours.
Total ascent: 550 feet.
Difficulty: Very easy, with no climbs and excellent footing.
Seasons: Best from mid- to late May through October.
Water availability: Trailhead stream and creek crossing at 2.5 and 11.7 miles.

Other trail users: Hikers.
Canine compatibility: Dogs must be leashed in the campground.
Fees and permits: None.
Facilities: Heavy-duty wooden 10-by-10 corrals, vault toilet.
USGS maps: Big Lake North, Mount Baldy.
Contact: USDA Forest Service, Springerville Ranger District, (928) 333-4372.

Reaching the trailhead: The trailhead is the Gabaldon Campground, which is only for those camping with livestock. To get there from Springerville, travel west approximately 27 miles, turning south onto Arizona Highway 273 between mileposts 377 and 378.

From Show Low, go through Pinetop-Lakeside to the intersection of Arizona Highway 260 and Arizona Highway 73 at Hon-Dah. Travel another 20 miles to AZ 273, which will take off to the south between mileposts 377 and 378.

Once you're on AZ 273, go 3.7 miles to Gabaldon Campground, which will be on your right between mileposts 389 and 390. The road alternates between pavement and rough gravel, with sections of very slow washboard. *DeLorme: Arizona Atlas and Gazetteer: Page 53 5D.*

Trailhead parking: Gabaldon Campground, available on a no-fee, first-come, first-served basis, has five designated camping sites. Sites 4 and 5 are only for small trailers; sites 2 and 3 are together and have room for larger trailers (limit 16 feet). Site 1 has no corral but has turn-around room for one large trailer with a HiTie or portable corral attached to its side. The campground was named for Juan Gabaldon, a Forest Service employee who worked on the area's trails for many years.

The Ride

The wide-open vistas here are lovely, but the aspen, ponderosa pine, and Engelmann spruce forest between crossing AZ 273 and the Mount Baldy Wilderness Trailhead is particularly glorious.

Even if you don't see anyone else on the trail, you're very likely to see many vehicles heading to and from the lake since you'll be traveling parallel to the road. Traffic may be particularly heavy on summer weekends.

This sturdy horse-safe bridge is a re-created version of the 80-foot trestle bridges typically used around 1900. Whenever possible, bridges were made of dirt and culverts to save money.

The trails and roads may be impassable (or even closed) in early spring due to snow and mud. Thunderstorms can happen anytime during spring, summer, or fall, so plan your ride especially carefully in summer, as this route is completely open and has no protection or shelter from lightning. Insect repellent is strongly recommended for both you and your equine—the mosquitoes can be particularly blood-thirsty in May.

If you bring a canine companion, keep in mind that this region is one in which the endangered Mexican gray wolf has been reintroduced. Although wolves are not aggressive toward humans, they may regard your dog as a territorial threat—or lunch. Be prepared to keep your dog in your tent or vehicle if wolves approach your parking area; should a curious wolf approach you on the trail, dismount and leash your dog. Mexican wolves are protected as an endangered species, so you may not kill or injure a wolf that attacks your pet unless human life is threatened as well; however, you may harass a bothersome wolf in any way that doesn't injure it (banging pots together, throwing objects, shouting, and the like). The penalty for killing a

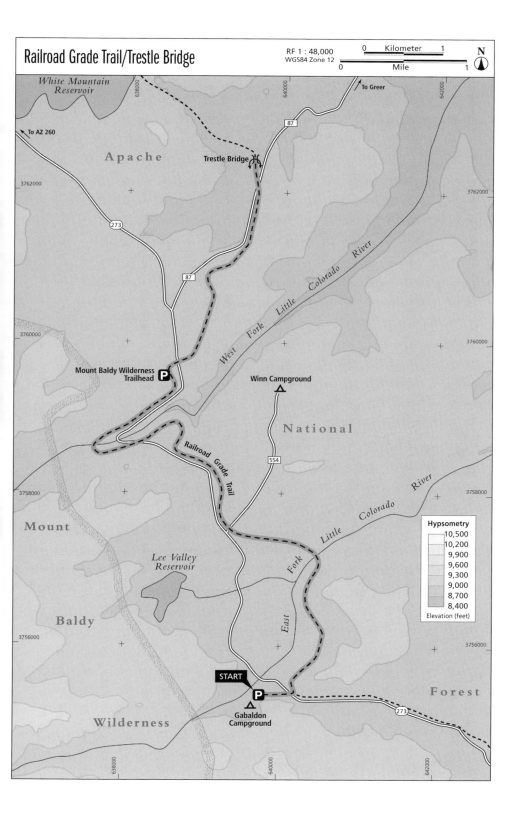

Railroad Grade Trail/Trestle Bridge

RF 1 : 48,000
WGS84 Zone 12

Kilometer
Mile

N

White Mountain Reservoir

To Greer

87

To AZ 260

Apache

Trestle Bridge

273

87

West Fork Little Colorado River

Mount Baldy Wilderness Trailhead

P

Winn Campground

National

554

Railroad Grade Trail

Mount

Lee Valley Reservoir

Fork Little Colorado River

Hypsometry
10,500
10,200
9,900
9,600
9,300
9,000
8,700
8,400
Elevation (feet)

Baldy

East

START

P

Gabaldon Campground

273

Forest

Wilderness

Mexican gray wolf can be up to $25,000 and/or six months in jail or a civil penalty of up to $25,000. If you kill or injure a wolf in defense of human life, you must report the incident within twenty-four hours by calling (888) 459–WOLF (9653).

Miles and Directions

0.0 Ride out the campground driveway, cross AZ 273, and turn left (north) onto the Railroad Grade Trail.

1.1 Equestrian-friendly gate next to a pedestrian-width cattle guard.

2.0 Reach a gate and cross Forest Road 554, which leads to Winn Campground.

2.5 Cross a creek, which is actually the west fork of the Little Colorado (you crossed the east fork about a mile ago). Negotiate the crossing carefully, as the rocks are round and somewhat slick.

3.7 The trail crosses AZ 273.

4.8 Mount Baldy Wilderness Trailhead (vault toilet).

5.4 The trail crosses AZ 273 again.

7.1 The trail crosses Forest Road 87 at the trestle bridge. This is the turnaround point, unless you choose to ride another 5 miles to the Railroad Grade Trailhead (the northernmost trailhead, which is on AZ 260). Retrace your steps to the trailhead.

8.8 The trail crosses AZ 273.

9.4 Mount Baldy Wilderness Trailhead.

10.5 The trail crosses AZ 273.

11.7 West fork of the Little Colorado. Cross with care.

12.2 Reach a gate and cross FR 554, which leads to Winn Campground.

13.1 Gate.

14.2 Turn right off the Railroad Grade Trail to return to Gabaldon Campground.

Options: Although the two routes featured start from Gabaldon Campground, you could instead day-park at the northernmost trailhead, which is right on AZ 260 between mileposts 379 and 380. From there, you could do an out-and-back ride for as much of the 21-mile Railroad Grade Trail as you wanted. The trailhead is a gravel pullout large enough for five or six trailers with plenty of room to turn around.

In addition, to ride up Mount Baldy, you could pick up East Baldy Trail 95 at the Mount Baldy Wilderness Trailhead. (The peak of the mountain is on White Mountain Apache tribal land and closed to the public.)

Southern Arizona
Chiricahua Mountains

Volcanoes, erosion, and the Apaches are the main players in the story of the Chiricahua Mountains.

Starting somewhere around twenty-seven million years ago, a series of volcanoes centered in this range spewed out molten ash and pumice in a layer 2,000 feet deep and covering close to 1,200 square miles. The hot ash flow then solidified into what geologists call a welded tuff. Carved by wind and water, the dramatic spires, hoodoos, and towers that top the Chiricahuas are the weathered remnants of that fiery time.

Known as a sky island in a sea of desert, the Chiricahuas (pronounced *cher-EE-kah-was*) cover an area that's 20 by 40 miles and include several peaks more than 9,000 feet tall. The range also marks a crossroads of the plant and animal zones usually found in the Rockies and Mexico's Sierra Madre (on a north–south axis) and those of the Sonoran and Chihuahuan Deserts (east–west). The Chiricahuas' location on that biotic intersection results in a remarkable diversity among both plants and animals. More than 300 species of birds—almost half of those found throughout the United States—can be found here, along with the southernmost occurrence of spruce forests and northernmost occurrence of Mexican species such as the parrotlike elegant trogon.

The name of the range comes from an Apache word meaning "great mountain." The Chiricahua Apaches who roamed throughout southeastern Arizona, southwestern New Mexico, and into the Sierra Madre also called this area "land of the stand-up rocks"—any barefoot horse will agree and wish for shoes, pads, and/or Easyboots.

Although Cochise, perhaps the best-known Chiricahua Apache chief, made his later headquarters in a nearby Dragoons Mountain stronghold, recent evidence shows that he also spent time in Rucker Canyon in the 1860s.

In 1872 the Chiricahua Apaches were granted their own reservation, which covered most of southeastern Arizona south of Fort Bowie. But once Custer was defeated at Little Big Horn four years later, the policy was suddenly revoked, and the tribe was sent to the San Carlos Indian Reservation. In 1886 Geronimo, the last

Apache leader, surrendered and all the Chiricahua Apaches were shipped to the swamps of Florida.

Years later, one descendant remembered: "Ours were a mountain people, and moreover a dry land people. We were accustomed to dry heat, but in Florida the dampness and mosquitoes took toll of us until it seemed that none would be left. Perhaps we were taken to Florida for that purpose; from our point of view, shooting would have been much less cruel."

From there, the survivors were sent to Mount Vernon, Alabama, and in 1894 to Fort Sill, Oklahoma. Finally, in 1914, the 271 remaining Chiricahua Apaches were told they were no longer considered prisoners of war and could choose between accepting farm allotments in Fort Sill and sharing reservation space with the Mescalero Apaches in New Mexico. Eighty-four chose to remain in Oklahoma.

30 Blacksmith Mine Trail

This 7.4-mile out-and-back route is a good one for moderately fit but still-novice horses. All of it is on rocky four-wheel-drive jeep tracks, and it ends at a lookout point with breathtaking views across the San Simon Valley and into New Mexico.

Start: 40 miles southeast of Willcox; Cochise County.

Distance: 7.4 miles out and back.

Approximate riding time: 3 to 4 hours.

Total ascent: 1,300 feet.

Difficulty: Moderate, due to the climb. The footing is rocky in places, but good throughout most of the trail.

Seasons: Best in spring and fall.

Water availability: Water tanks at 0.9 mile and 1.6 miles.

Other trail users: Hikers and ATVers.

Canine compatibility: Best left at home.

Fees and permits: None.

Facilities: None.

USGS maps: Rustler Park.

Contact: USDA Forest Service, Coronado National Forest, Douglas Ranger District, (520) 364-3468.

Reaching the trailhead: From Tucson, take Interstate 10 to Exit 336 (Willcox), and proceed east on Business I-10 to Willcox. This road becomes Haslett Street; follow it 3.5 miles to a traffic light. Turn right at the traffic light onto Arizona Highway 186, following the sign to Chiricahua National Monument.

From New Mexico, take Interstate 10 west to Exit 344 (Willcox), and proceed west on Business I-10 to Willcox. This road becomes Haslett Street; follow it for 5 miles to a traffic light. Turn left at the light onto AZ 186, following the sign to Chiricahua National Monument.

Follow AZ 186 south for 31 miles and turn left (east) onto Arizona Highway 181, still following signs to Chiricahua National Monument. After 3 miles, turn right onto a gravel road (Forest Road 42, also called Pinery Canyon Road) immediately after a sign to CORONADO NATIONAL FOREST RECREATION AREAS. (If you reach the entrance to Chiricahua National Monument, you've gone too far.) Follow FR 42 for 5.5 miles to North Fork; the trailhead parking will be on your right. *DeLorme: Arizona Atlas and Gazetteer:* Page 75 A5.

Trailhead parking: There's plenty of room for numerous trailers.

The Ride

The trail climbs from a riparian (streamside) piñon-oak habitat to shady pines as you approach the top. Bring your camera for the views on this one!

FR 42 can be impassable for trailers due to mud and snow in winter. During the week, chances are good you'll have the Hands Pass trail to yourself, but hunting season brings trucks and ATVs bristling with guns. June and early July are hot; once the monsoon storms start up in early to mid-July, you'll need to plan your ride carefully to avoid the exposed ridges.

Drawn by advertisements from the Southern Pacific Railway, eighteen-year-old John Hands arrived in New York alone in 1884, having immigrated from England.

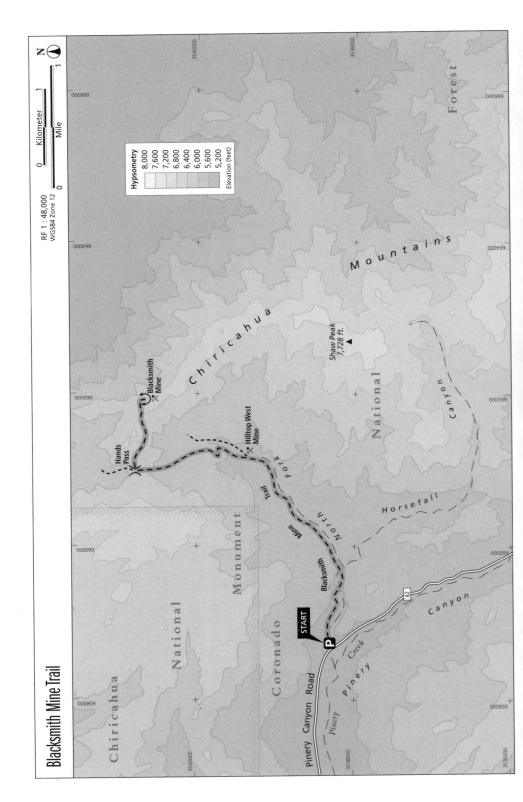

Blacksmith Mine Trail

RF 1 : 48,000
WGS84 Zone 12

Hypsometry
8,000
7,600
7,200
6,800
6,400
6,000
5,600
5,200
Elevation (feet)

N

Kilometer
Mile

Chiricahua National Monument

Coronado National Forest

Chiricahua Mountains

Pinery Canyon Road

Pinery Creek

Pinery Canyon

START

P

42

Blacksmith Mine Trail

North Fork

Horsefall

Canyon

Shaw Peak 7,728 ft.

Hilltop West Mine

Hands Pass

Blacksmith Mine

The view from Blacksmith Mine sweeps from East Whitetail Canyon, with its distinctive Split Rock and Nippers formations, across the San Simon Valley and into the Peloncillo Mountains of New Mexico. Photo by Hedley Bond

He worked his way across the country, settled in Arizona, and by 1888 had persuaded his brothers Frank and Alfred to join him. John homesteaded the Rest-a-Bit Ranch in Pinery Canyon in the 1890s. Sadly, ten years after Geronimo's final surrender, Alfred had the misfortune to be the victim of the last Apache slaying in Arizona. According to family members, he was "a studious boy" and was doing his algebra homework on March 28, 1896, when attacked and killed by a renegade band of Apaches.

John later became an amateur archaeologist, miner, cattleman, photographer, and conservationist. Pinnacle Peaks—as he referred to what is now Chiricahua National Monument—was part of his grazing allotment from the forest reserve. Incensed that the area appeared on his bill, Hands took photographs of the Pinnacles and sent them to the Forest Service, saying that if *they* could find a blade of grass in the rocky wonderland, he'd be happy to pay the fee.

Apparently he and the authorities must have come to an agreement because John Hands worked tirelessly to publicize the scenic rock wonder. He also used dynamite and shovels to build a trail from Pinery Canyon to Inspiration Point, with $200 provided by the Forest Service.

Miles and Directions

0.0 The trailhead is across the road. Follow the jeep road eastward.

0.9 Water tank on your left near an abandoned shack.

1.6 Cattle guard (leave all gates as you found them) and water tank.

2.0 The turnoff to the Hilltop West mine goes to your right; continue on to the left.

3.0 Hands Pass. Turn right (east) and follow the jeep road to Blacksmith Mine (there is no sign). The wire gate at the top of the pass is usually closed; leave it as you find it. If you continue on straight down the hill about 100 yards, you'll have a great view of the mountain-size rock formation known as Cochise Head. (Continuing straight would take you down a long rocky stretch and eventually lead to private property in Whitetail Canyon where there is no room for trailer parking.)

3.7 Blacksmith Mine. This is your turnaround point; retrace your steps.

7.4 Arrive back at the trailhead.

Options: One side trip is to check out the West Hilltop Mine, site of the town of Hilltop, established by Frank and John Hands. Eventually, around 1917, a tunnel was dug through to the other side to help in mine management. Today water from that tunnel feeds the Colibri Vineyard and Winery (the red roof you can see from the Blacksmith Mine).

(Note: On the Forest Service map, it appears as if you could take the Lime Trail over to Jhus Horse Saddle and then drop back down to North Fork—*do not* be tempted by this seemingly innocuous loop. Several segments of the Lime Trail are too narrow for horses; other parts of it traverse extremely slick, skinny, steep stretches of limestone with drop-offs that end many hundreds of feet below. In short, don't even think about it.)

31 Cottonwood Canyon Trail

Although it includes about 1,000 feet of climbing, this 11.8-mile out-and-back trail is only moderately difficult, with good footing and a variety of scenery. Hauling a horse trailer into Rucker Canyon is a long, slow proposition—and not an easy task—but once you get there you'll likely have the place to yourself.

Start: 35 miles north of Douglas; Cochise County.
Distance: 11.8 miles out and back.
Approximate riding time: 3 to 4 hours.
Total ascent: 1,030 feet.
Difficulty: Moderate. Although this trail is very rocky in places—the trail is the creekbed—and has one steep climb, there's nothing tricky or dangerous on it.
Seasons: Best in spring and fall, but ridable all year, if the road is negotiable.
Water availability: None in dry seasons, creek crossings at other times.

Other trail users: Rare except during hunting season.
Canine compatibility: Best left at home.
Fees and permits: None. Dispersed camping is permitted for up to two weeks.
Facilities: None. A corral is available for public use unless the rancher who has leased the land in this area for grazing needs it.
USGS maps: Chiricahua Peak, Swede Peak.
Contact: USDA Forest Service, Coronado National Forest, Douglas Ranger District, (520) 364-3468.

Reaching the trailhead: (Note: Rucker Canyon Road is rarely maintained and can be impassable due to mud during both winter and summer rains.)

From New Mexico, take Interstate 10 west to the Road Forks exit (Exit 5) just east of the Arizona state line. Drive south 30 miles on Arizona Highway 80 to Rodeo, New Mexico. You'll reenter Arizona as you drive another 20.8 miles to Rucker Canyon Road. The turnoff to your right will be between mileposts 396 and 397. Go 6.8 miles to the Coronado National Forest boundary. After another 7.6 miles of very slow, bumpy, narrow dirt road (which will seem like 17.6), you'll see the sign for the Cottonwood Canyon Trail; this is the trail you'll be riding, but keep driving another 0.9 mile to the parking area, which will be on your right and just past Camp Rucker.

From Tucson, take I-10 to Benson (Exit 303) to AZ 80. Continue on AZ 80 to Douglas (about 70 miles). From Douglas, although taking Leslie Canyon Road may be shorter, you'll save time by driving north on AZ 80, then northwest on Rucker Canyon Road. The turnoff will be to your left between mileposts 396 and 397. From this point, follow the directions above. *DeLorme: Arizona Atlas and Gazetteer:* Page 75 B5.

Trailhead parking: A large flat field with plenty of room for a dozen large rigs.

The Ride

The views and, in wet seasons, the burbling creeks make this trail a treat, especially in late February and early March when the manzanita is in full flower. In years of ample rainfall, Cottonwood Creek is likely to be flowing at the beginning of your ride, and you'll encounter many creek crossings as you approach the turnaround point. Once you're back in camp and your trusty mount is settled in with hay and

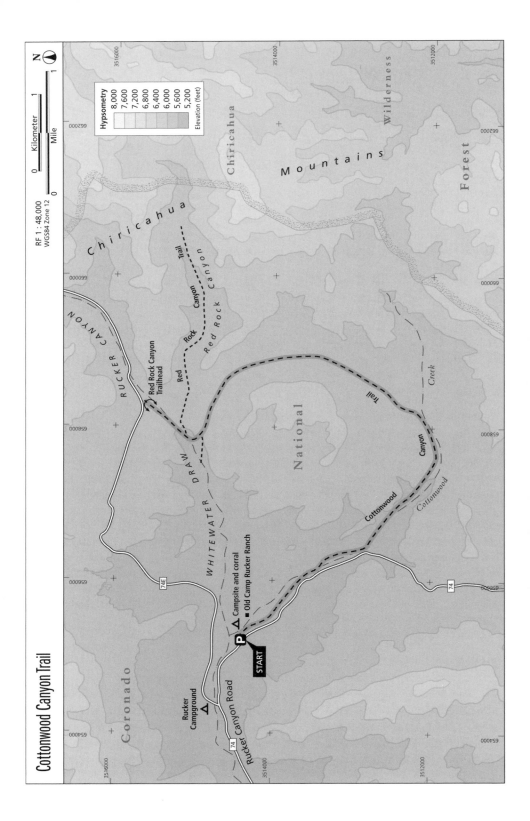

Cottonwood Canyon Trail

RF 1 : 48,000
WGS84 Zone 12

N

Hypsometry
8,000
7,600
7,200
6,800
6,400
6,000
5,600
5,200
Elevation (feet)

Kilometer
Mile

Chiricahua

RUCKER CANYON

Red Rock Canyon Trailhead

Red Rock Canyon Trail

Red Rock Canyon

Chiricahua

Chiricahua

Mountains

WHITEWATER DRAW

Coronado

National

Wilderness

Forest

Rucker Campground

74E

Campsite and corral

Old Camp Rucker Ranch

P

START

Rucker Canyon Road

74

74

Cottonwood Canyon Trail

Cottonwood Canyon

Cottonwood Creek

3516000

3514000

3512000

654000

656000

658000

660000

662000

654000

658000

660000

662000

water, take a walk through Arizona's pioneer history. The driveway immediately south of the trailhead leads to Old Camp Rucker, which is unsigned but open to the public. The gate is usually locked, but go through the pedestrian walk-through and follow the road for a few hundred yards to what's left of the 1880s military post.

As you cross the creek, imagine it in flood in July 1878 as a young soldier named Austin Henely attempted to cross on horseback. The raging creek swept him underwater, and his Detroit-born West Point buddy, John Anthony Rucker, tried to rescue him. Both were drowned, and the name of the White River was changed in Rucker's honor.

At least, that's one version of the story that appeared in newspapers at the time. You could also choose to believe the White Mountain Apache scout John Rope, who was with Henely and Rucker when they died. His version was that he and the two officers waited out the storm in the fort's saloon with a couple of military suppliers. Then the two civilians and Rope crossed the creek safely. Henely and Rucker, however, plunged in side by side instead of one in front of the other. The current knocked the two horses against each other, and both men fell off and drowned.

Both men were buried at first at the Fort Bowie cemetery. Rucker, son of a major general, was then moved near his father's grave site in Arlington National Cemetery, and Henely was moved to the San Francisco National Cemetery.

Later the post became a ranch owned by Charlie and Mary Rak (for an additional treat, read Mary Rak's *A Cowman's Wife*, the account of how she learned to ranch). Old Camp Rucker is now maintained by the Forest Service, and the volunteer program called Passport in Time has renovated the barn and other buildings. Interpretive signs describe where the bakery was and how the soldiers used the heliograph to send messages during the Apache wars.

Miles and Directions

0.0 From the trailhead, head back out to the road and go left (south).

0.7 Go left on the jeep track at the sign for Cottonwood Canyon.

0.8 Intersection; go right (southeast). The jeep track meanders gradually uphill before becoming a steep, rocky climb for about 0.5 mile.

3.3 Wire gap—very tight! (Always leave gates open or closed, as you found them.)

4.1 Huge dirt tank, which can be full of water in wet years.

5.0 Intersection of the jeep track and the creek. Bear left (west).

5.3 Intersection with a lightly used four-wheel-drive road on your left. Don't take it; remain to the right (northeasterly).

5.4 Intersection with the Red Rock Canyon Trail. Resist it, heading straight toward the creek, pausing to notice the handsome Arizona cypress on your left. Cross the stream and immediately go right.

5.9 Reach the Red Rock Canyon Trailhead; a lovely shady spot with plenty of room to tie your horse for a picnic lunch. Retrace your steps.

11.8 Arrive back at the trailhead.

Options: At the sign where you went straight to the Red Rock Trailhead, turn right and follow the sign for Red Rock Canyon. The trail is a four-wheel-drive road that dips in and out of the creek.

32 Cub Canyon Trail

This 13.8-mile out-and-back route is an adventure best attempted with experienced horses and riders. Once you've arrived (hauling your trailer into Rucker Canyon is a slow, bumpy process), the trail starts out well, but seems to have been a victim of maintenance cutbacks. Take clippers with you, and be prepared to get off and do some bushwhacking while leading your horse. It is possible to get through the scrubby part, and the views of Cub Canyon are worth the effort.

Start: 35 miles north of Douglas; Cochise County.

Distance: 13.8 miles out and back.

Approximate riding time: 4 to 5 hours, depending on the trail condition.

Total ascent: 1,600 feet.

Difficulty: Challenging. There will be some scrub bashing involved, but most of the footing is good.

Seasons: Best in spring and fall.

Water availability: Sycamore Springs, 3.9 miles.

Other trail users: Unlikely.

Canine compatibility: Best left at home.

Fees and permits: None. Dispersed camping is permitted for up to two weeks.

Facilities: None. A corral is available for public use unless the rancher who has leased the land in this area for grazing needs it.

USGS maps: Stanford Canyon West, Chiricahua Peak East.

Contact: USDA Forest Service, Coronado National Forest, Douglas Ranger District, (520) 364-3468.

Reaching the trailhead: (Note: Rucker Canyon Road is rarely maintained and can be impassable due to mud during both winter and summer rains.)

From New Mexico, take Interstate 10 west to the Road Forks exit (Exit 5) just east of the Arizona state line. Drive south 30 miles on Arizona Highway 80 to Rodeo, New Mexico. You'll reenter Arizona as you drive another 20.8 miles to Rucker Canyon Road. The turnoff to your right will be between mileposts 396 and 397. Go 6.8 miles to the Coronado National Forest boundary. After another 7.6 miles of very slow, bumpy, narrow dirt road (it'll seem like 17.6), you'll see the sign for the Cottonwood Canyon Trail; this is the trail you'll be taking, but keep driving another 0.9 mile to the parking area, which will be on your right and just past Camp Rucker.

From Tucson, take I-10 to Benson (Exit 303) to AZ 80. Continue on AZ 80 to Douglas (about 70 miles). From Douglas, although taking Leslie Canyon Road may be shorter, you'll save time by driving north on AZ 80, then northwest on Rucker Canyon Road. The turnoff will be to your left between mileposts 396 and 397. From this point, follow the directions above. *DeLorme: Arizona Atlas and Gazetteer:* Page 75 B5.

Trailhead parking: A large flat field with plenty of room for a dozen large rigs.

Turtle Mountain lies between Rucker Canyon and the main ridge of the Chiricahuas. Recent evidence suggests that Cochise used the area between Red Rock Canyon and Turtle Mountain as his hideout during the 1860s.

The Ride

This trail offers a gradual climb through oak-juniper woodland with taller forests of Douglas fir and ponderosa pine in Cub Canyon. The canyon features lovely views of dramatic cliffs composed of lichen-covered orange welded tuff.

For about a mile after you reach Sycamore Spring, the trail becomes less distinct until it is so overgrown that it's almost imperceptible. You will climb a hill, top a ridge, head across a slope, and then head uphill toward a saddle, more or less following a gully.

As you climb, you will be rewarded with superb views to the east. The last half of the trip to the saddle will be slow—it's best tackled on foot, leading your horse. (By the time you reach the saddle, you will have climbed 1,300 feet.) You'll be returning this way, so mark your way with ribbon and/or carry some clippers. Although this little-used trail is very exposed and hot in summer, there's occasional snow in winter.

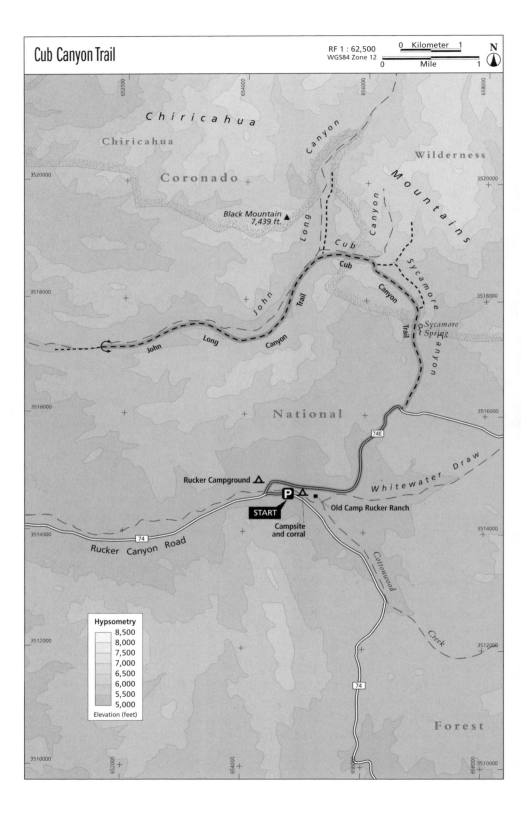

The Rucker Canyon area has many tempting four-wheel-drive tracks and trails, but this particular trail has limited turnoffs.

Although the Chiricahua Apache leader Cochise is known to have spent his later years in the Dragoons, recent research has revealed that Rucker Canyon was one of his frequently used strongholds. The area you'll be riding through (between Red Rock Canyon and Turtle Mountain) isn't far from the site of an October 20, 1869, battle between the U.S. cavalry and Cochise's troops, known as the Campaign of Rocky Mesa. Despite eighteen wounded Apaches and two dead soldiers, neither side could claim a victory. Ironically, thirty-one Medals of Honor were awarded for that day's events—the largest number of medals awarded in any single battle during the Indian wars.

It wasn't until three years later—on October 12, 1872—that Cochise declared peace between the Chiricahua Apaches and the white man.

Miles and Directions

0.0 From the trailhead, head out to the road (Forest Road 74), and turn right (northwest).

0.6 Intersection of FR 74 and FR 74E. Turn right (north) onto FR 74E.

0.8 Campground on your left after you cross a creek. Continue on FR 74E.

3.0 Turn left off the road onto a jeep track. This turnoff comes immediately after a cattle guard.

3.6 Trail intersection with a sign. Go left toward Sycamore Spring and Turtle Mountain.

3.9 Sycamore Spring. There is good water here most of the year.

5.0 Arrive at the saddle. There is a fence here with a wire gate; a recently cleared trail heads downhill to Cub Canyon.

5.2 Reach the base of Cub Canyon by the creek. Magnificent yellow-orange welded tuff rock formations tower above you here.

5.8 Signpost: Long Canyon Trail goes up to the right. Go left, down John Long Canyon.

5.9 First of three creek crossings. Good source of water in spring and early fall.

6.9 Fence with a gate. This is a good point to turn around and retrace your steps to Rucker Road and the campground. The road continues down John Long Canyon another 3.4 miles before reaching a ranch house; you'll have 8 more miles to travel after that before getting back to the campground.

13.8 Arrive back at the campground.

33 Horsefall/Barfoot Loop Trail

This route, a 15.6-mile loop with more than 3,000 feet of climbing, is among the most challenging rides in the book. It's also one of the loveliest as it ranges from deep woodlands to shaded creek bottoms, pine-forested slopes, and rocky mountaintops with views extending many miles.

Start: 40 miles southeast of Willcox; Cochise County.
Distance: 15.6-mile loop.
Approximate riding time: 4 to 6 hours.
Total ascent: 3,150 feet.
Difficulty: Difficult, due to the amount of climbing and several areas where the trail is narrow.
Seasons: Best in fall and late spring.

Water availability: Iron Spring at 2 miles and the creek crossing at 11 miles.
Other trail users: Hunters.
Canine compatibility: Best left at home.
Fees and permits: None.
Facilities: None.
USGS maps: Rustler Park.
Contact: USDA Forest Service, Coronado National Forest, Douglas Ranger District, (520) 364-3468.

Reaching the trailhead: From Tucson, take Interstate 10 to Exit 336 (Willcox) and proceed east on Business I-10 to Willcox. This road becomes Haslett Street; follow it 3.5 miles to a traffic light. Turn right at the traffic light onto Arizona Highway 186, following the sign to Chiricahua National Monument.

From New Mexico, take I-10 west to Exit 344 (Willcox), and proceed west on Business I-10 to Willcox. This road becomes Haslett Street; follow it for 5 miles to a traffic light. Turn left at the light onto AZ 186, following the sign to Chiricahua National Monument.

Follow AZ 186 south for 31 miles and turn left onto Arizona Highway 181, still following signs to Chiricahua National Monument. After 3 miles, turn right onto a gravel road (Forest Road 42, also called Pinery Canyon Road) immediately after a sign reading CORONADO NATIONAL FOREST RECREATION AREAS. (If you reach the entrance to Chiricahua National Monument, you've gone too far.) Follow FR 42 for 5.5 miles to North Fork. This area is the trailhead for the Blacksmith Mine Trail; if you're tired of bumping along on dirt roads, you could park or camp here and ride the remaining 1.7 miles to the Horsefall Trailhead. Otherwise, drive on for another 1.7 miles (7.2 miles from AZ 181) to the intersection of FR 42 and the road to the United Methodist Pine Canyon Camp, which goes off to your right. The trailhead parking will be on your left. *DeLorme: Arizona Atlas and Gazetteer:* Page 75 A5.

Trailhead parking: There's plenty of room for numerous trailers.

The Ride

The ride starts in the canyon that was the "pinery"—or source of lumber—for the 1862 construction of Fort Bowie in Apache Pass. By 1900 timber production in New Mexico and Arizona had already reached 67 million board feet, and it was clear that something needed to be done to protect the Southwest's forests. Congress thus

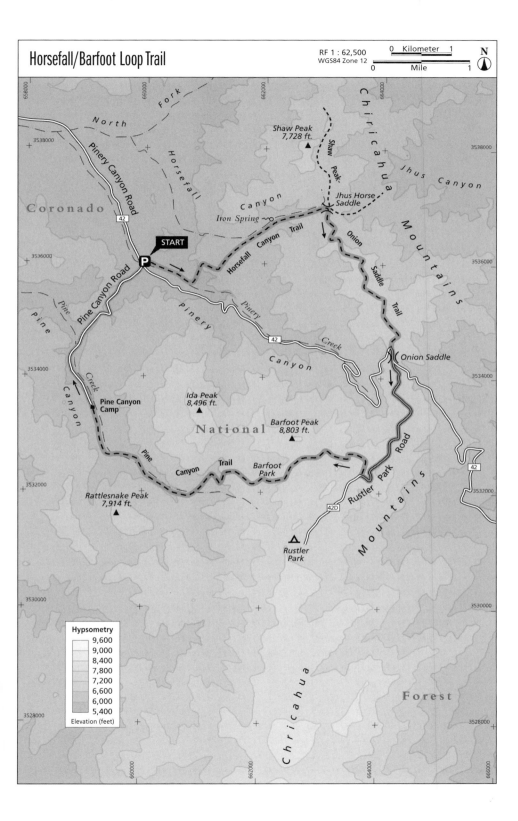

Horsefall/Barfoot Loop Trail

RF 1 : 62,500
WGS84 Zone 12

0   Kilometer   1

0   Mile   1

N

Hypsometry

9,600
9,000
8,400
7,800
7,200
6,600
6,000
5,400

Elevation (feet)

authorized the president to designate areas of forested public domain as reserves, and in July of that year the Chiricahua Forest Reserve was established. In 1908 Chiricahua and Peloncillo National Forests were merged into Chiricahua National Forest while Mount Graham, Apache, Tonto, and Pinal National Forests were consolidated into the Crook National Forest. In 1917 the Chiricahua Mountains made their last bureaucratic move to the Coronado National Forest, and the Crook National Forest name was abolished in 1953.

Three miles into the ride, you'll see signs for Jhus Canyon—a persistent misspelling. Juh (generally pronounced *who*) was an Apache warrior and a cousin of Geronimo's. Although he died from injuries related to a fall from a horse in Mexico in 1883, the name of Horsefall Canyon apparently comes from a spill taken by a forest ranger's horse many years later.

If you ride this trail during the week, you're unlikely to see anyone else. Deer-hunting season is another story, however. The Chiricahuas attract many hunters, and you'll need to ride with caution.

Heavy snow may make the trail (and even the road to the trailhead) impassable in winter. Since several miles of the trail are high and exposed, plan your ride carefully in July and August to avoid being on ridgetops in lightning storms.

Miles and Directions

0.0 The trail begins about 50 yards below the parking area on the opposite side of Pinery Road and is marked by a brown Forest Service sign that reads PINERY-HORSEFALL TRAIL.

0.7 The trail heads uphill and away from the creek, and the vegetation changes from tall pine and oaks by the creek to a lower open woodland of oak and juniper with scattered yucca and agave.

1.2 Wire gate (always leave gates open or closed, as you found them). Excellent views of Pinery Canyon.

1.8 Soon after going over a low ridge, you'll be riding next to the usually dry Horsefall Creek with ponderosa pine, occasional Douglas fir, and box elder. In late spring and summer, lupines are plentiful.

2.0 Iron Spring. A sign on large ponderosa pine points out this reliable water in a cement tank to left of the trail. Continue on above the tank, and head across the creek and uphill.

3.1 Jhus Horse Saddle. The last 0.5 mile to this 7,100-foot saddle is a gradual but significant climb through ponderosa pine and Douglas fir. Excellent views of Shaw Peak to the north. Bear right at the saddle, taking the (signed) trail to Onion Saddle. Do not go left; both options (Shaw Peak and Jhus Canyon) include areas that can be treacherously steep and narrow for horses. Below this saddle Gambel oak—a winter deciduous oak—begins to appear.

3.5 After a good climb with switchbacks, watch for panoramic views to east and west along the trail to Onion Saddle.

5.1 Reach the high point of the trail before Onion Saddle (7,920 feet). Onion Peak is to the east. The trail goes downhill to Onion Saddle from here.

5.4   The trail widens into a jeep road; follow this road straight (south) to Onion Saddle.

5.9   Onion Saddle. From here, follow the gravel road uphill (south) 2.1 miles toward Rustler Park through a ponderosa pine–Douglas fir forest. The striking vistas to the east are worth the hard, hot road. **Bail-out:** This route still has a considerable climb to go, plus a slow rocky descent. If you decide this is more challenge than you and/or your horse are ready for, you can return to the trailhead more directly from Onion Saddle by going around the cattle guard and heading down the gravel road to your right toward Willcox. It's 4.9 miles to the trailhead, for a total ride of 10.8 miles. This road is narrow, so beware of vehicles, especially on weekends. If you've chosen to do this ride in winter, be aware that the road can be extremely icy.

8.0   Turn right at the stop sign, following signs to Barfoot Park (Forest Road 357). You will climb briefly to the high point for this trail (8,370 feet) before passing through an impressive forest of large Douglas fir and dropping down to Barfoot Park.

9.0   Barfoot Park is a particularly nice spot to stop for lunch since it has picnic tables scattered among ponderosa pines. Follow the road, which soon becomes a jeep track through the park, heading downhill for 4 miles; it is well graded with mostly good footing, but rocky in some places.

10.2   Another trail goes off to your right; stay left.

10.9   First creek crossing. There is usually water here and below.

11.5   The trail follows the rocky creekbed and is slow going.

12.8   Water tank behind Pine Canyon Camp, with a sign that reads ENTERING PINE CANYON CAMP.

13.1   Reach Pine Canyon Camp. Follow the gravel road through the camp and up a short climb to a low saddle before dropping back down to Pinery Road.

15.6   The road ends at Pinery Canyon Road opposite the trailhead.

Options: Instead of turning right at the stop sign for Barfoot Park, you can add miles by riding up to the meadow at Rustler Park and on toward the Crest Trail.

(Note: On the Forest Service map, it appears as if you could take the Lime Trail from Jhus Horse Saddle across Shaw Peak and then drop back down to North Fork from the Hands Pass Trail—*do not* be tempted by this seemingly innocuous loop. Several segments of the Lime Trail are too narrow for horses; other parts of it traverse extremely slick, skinny, steep stretches of limestone with drop-offs that end many hundreds of feet below. In short, don't even think about it.)

Huachuca Mountains

F rom sabers to satellites" is the catchy slogan listed on Fort Huachuca's Web site. In actuality, the military literature indicates that soldiers often left their sabers back at the barracks since they rattled too loudly for sneak attacks.

Camp Huachuca (pronounced *hwa-CHOO-kah*) was established in March 1877 to help find and defeat Geronimo; it was one of seventy military encampments. The garrison's position at the base of the Huachucas was ideal for watching both the San Pedro and Santa Cruz Valleys as well as a providing an opportunity to block the Apaches' route in and out of Mexico.

One frequent duty for early soldiers was stringing telegraph wires so that the various garrisons could communicate with one another. When the Indians simply cut the wires, the army devised a system of heliographs in which they used the sun's reflection in mirrors to send signals from one mountaintop to another across the Southwest.

With Geronimo's surrender in 1886, most of the other military camps closed, but Fort Huachuca remained open, partly because its location at 4,600 feet on the lower slopes of the mountains was so much healthier than the malaria-ridden lowlands. The soldiers now patrolled the Mexican border, and in 1916 the last horse cavalry maneuver went after Pancho Villa (unsuccessfully).

The all-black Twenty-fourth and Twenty-fifth Infantry Regiments, as well as the Ninth Cavalry, had served at Fort Huachuca in the 1890s. In 1913 the Tenth Cavalry—also known as the Buffalo Soldiers—joined the fort. The nickname (originally "Wild Buffaloes," referring to the soldiers' hair) had been respectfully applied to them in 1867 by the Cheyenne Indians. Eventually the name was used for any black regiment, all of which served at Fort Huachuca at one time or another.

It wasn't until the Korean War in 1949 that black soldiers were allowed to join white regiments.

Heliographs gave way to electronics when Fort Huachuca became the U.S. Army Proving Ground to test communications equipment. That thread continues today: Supporting 11,000 people, the post is operated by the U.S. Army Intelligence Center and Fort Huachuca.

The Huachuca Mountains themselves (from the Chiricahua Apache word for "place of thunder") are one in a "sky island" archipelago, a complex of twenty-seven mountain ranges that stretches from subtropical Mexico to the Rockies. Many a miner has tried his luck in these particular hills, leaving plentiful evidence of searches for gold, silver, zinc, and tungsten. A quartzite-bearing cliff called Carr Reef runs along the eastern edge.

The southernmost tip of the Huachuca Mountains dips into Mexico, providing a frequently used corridor for illegal smuggling of both drugs and humans. Be aware that you're likely to run into people who have interests other than enjoying the trail. Coronado National Forest has issued the following advisory for forest visitors traveling in areas along the approximately 60 miles of common boundary, south of Sierra Vista and west of Nogales:

- Always Know Your Location:
  - Be able to describe where you are. Check your map.
  - Let others know your expected travel route, destination and times.
- Use Caution on Backcountry Roads & Trails
  - Avoid hiking or camping in areas of major border activity.
  - Stay on designated trails. Avoid "unofficial" trails.
  - Keep vehicle locked. Hide valuables from sight.
  - Unattended vehicles may be damaged or stolen.
  - Do not pick up hitchhikers.
  - High speed smuggling traffic and law enforcement pursuits may occur.
- Avoid Suspicious Items and Materials
  - Do not touch any unknown or suspicious material. Leave the area immediately. Contact the nearest law enforcement agency.
- Do not attempt to intercede if you witness illegal activity.
  - Leave the area immediately.
  - Contact the nearest law enforcement agency with descriptions of persons, vehicles, date/time, location and other pertinent information.
- In case of emergency, dial 911. (Cellular phone connections inside the United States may be affected by Mexican connections. Cellular "dead spots" exist in areas throughout the Coronado National Forest.)
  - Cochise County Sheriff's Office: 520–432–9500
  - Santa Cruz County Sheriff's Office: 520–761–7869
  - Arizona Dept. of Public Safety: 520–746–4500
  - US Border Patrol: 520–407–2300
  - Coronado National Forest: 520–388–8300

34 Brown Canyon Loop Trail

This moderate 6.4-mile loop is easily accessed from Sierra Vista and provides lovely views over the grasslands and surrounding mountain ranges. It's worth calling ahead as some of this trail is on the Fort Huachuca Military Reservation, which may be closed during national security alerts.

Start: Southwest of Sierra Vista; Cochise County.
Distance: 6.4-mile loop.
Approximate riding time: 2 hours.
Total ascent: 1,000 feet.
Difficulty: Moderate.
Seasons: Best in spring, summer, and fall.
Water availability: Water trough at 5.5 miles.

Other trail users: Hikers and mountain bikers.
Canine compatibility: Best left at home.
Fees and permits: None needed.
Facilities: None.
USGS maps: Miller Peak.
Contact: USDA Forest Service, Coronado National Forest, Sierra Vista Ranger District, (520) 378-0311.

Reaching the trailhead: From Tucson, take Interstate 10 east to Benson (Exit 302). Go south on Arizona Highway 90 for 19 miles until it intersects with Arizona Highway 82. Keep going straight on AZ 90; after an additional 8.5 miles, it turns into Buffalo Soldier Trail (Arizona 90 goes off to your left at a traffic light). Follow Buffalo Soldier Trail for 6 miles, turning right (south) onto AZ Highway 92. Go 2.8 miles and turn right onto Ramsey Canyon Road. Travel another 2.3 miles to the small parking area on your right (watch for a brown HIKER sign). *DeLorme: Arizona Atlas and Gazetteer:* Page 74 D1.

    Trailhead parking: There's a circular gravel pullout with room for three or four rigs, depending on how the passenger cars are parked. The entrance is a very tight turn for large goosenecks.

The Ride

This ride features attractive vistas of grasslands dotted with oaks, and a superb view looking across to the Mule Mountains and the Chiricahuas. In May the manzanita flowers heavily and fills the air with its aroma. If you're lucky (and quiet), you could see Coues white-tailed deer, javelina, or even a troop of coatimundi. Black bears and mountain lions have also been seen in the area.

Miles and Directions

0.0 Head west out of the parking lot.

0.6 The trail forks; take the left fork. (Soon after this point, notice the touching gravestone for someone's pet in the oak grove to your right.)

0.9 Reach a confusing-looking intersection with three possibilities. Take the middle option, and go down the hill.

1.3 At the bottom of the hill, make a hard right following the creek.

Views from the Brown Canyon Trail stretch across miles of rolling grasslands.

1.5 Go left through the gate (the sign reads PERIMETER TRAIL, BROWN/GARDEN CANYON SEGMENT), turn right onto the road, then take an immediate left. The mountains should be ahead of you and to your left.

2.9 Sign for TINKER POND.

3.2 Forest Service boundary/gate.

3.7 At a fork in the trail, go left.

3.8 Reach a sign indicating that you've been on POMONA MINE 16; go left. (If you went right, you'd come to a water trough very soon. However, there's another one in about a mile.)

4.5 The trail forks; go left.

5.0 Water trough.

5.5 Back to the three-way junction.

6.4 Arrive back at the trailhead.

Options: This entire area is riddled with four-wheel-drive roads and trails. However, *do be careful* to stay on the trails or roads while on the military post: There are large rolls of faded green razor wire and other bits of miscellaneous stray metal. If you're

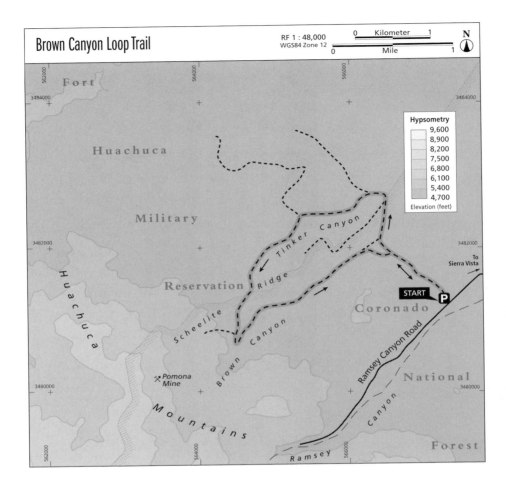

Brown Canyon Loop Trail

RF 1 : 48,000
WGS84 Zone 12

Hypsometry
9,600
8,900
8,200
7,500
6,800
6,100
5,400
4,700
Elevation (feet)

Fort

Huachuca

Military

Huachuca

Reservation Ridge

Tinker Canyon

Scheelite

Brown Canyon

Pomona Mine

Mountains

To Sierra Vista

START

Coronado

Ramsey Canyon Road

National

Ramsey Canyon

Forest

looking for strenuous climbs, after you go through the gate at 1.5 miles, take the dirt road to your left and follow the fence line toward the mountains. Another possible side trip is the old tungsten Pomona Mine, a route that provides more fine views.

35 Miller Canyon Trail

This 7.2-mile lollipop loop trail is easily accessed from Sierra Vista and features panoramic views across the valley toward the Mule Mountains to the east and beyond. The John Cooper section is narrow and frequented by mountain bikers, so this route is not recommended for novice horses.

Start: 6 miles southwest of Sierra Vista; Cochise County.
Distance: 7.2-mile loop.
Approximate riding time: 2 to 3 hours.
Total ascent: 1,150 feet.
Difficulty: Moderate.
Seasons: Best in spring and fall.
Water availability: The creek at 0.5 mile except in June.

Other trail users: Mountain bikers, hikers, and bird-watchers.
Canine compatibility: Best left at home.
Fees and permits: None needed.
Facilities: Two vault toilets.
USGS maps: Miller Peak.
Contact: USDA Forest Service, Coronado National Forest, Sierra Vista Ranger District, (520) 378-0311.

Reaching the trailhead: From Tucson, take Interstate 10 east to Benson (Exit 302). Go south on Arizona Highway 90 for 19 miles until it intersects with AZ Highway 82. Keep going straight on AZ 90; after an additional 8.5 miles, it turns into Buffalo Soldier Trail (Arizona Highway 90 goes off to the left at a traffic light). Follow Buffalo Soldier Trail for 6 miles, turning right (south) onto Arizona Highway 92. Go 6 miles and turn right onto Miller Canyon Road (Forest Road 56). Follow the road 0.8 mile through the residential area to the Forest Service boundary. The parking area and trailhead (labeled PERIMETER TRAIL PARKING) will be on your left in another 0.25 mile. *DeLorme: Arizona Atlas and Gazetteer:* Page 74 D1.
   Trailhead parking: There's a circular gravel pullout with room for six to seven rigs.

The Ride

This trail starts out across a creekbed (which often has water) before meandering through a scenic oak–juniper woodland. Beyond the Miller Canyon Trailhead, you'll take a narrow rocky singletrack that climbs along the hillside with a glorious view of Sierra Vista, the San Pedro River Valley, and the Mule Mountains.

   The people you're most likely to encounter will be out early in the morning, and they'll all be on foot and wearing binoculars. Bird-watchers from around the world flock (oops) to Miller Canyon, hoping to spot some of the 130-plus varieties of birds found in the Huachucas. The U.S. record for the largest number of hummingbird species seen in one day—fourteen—was set June 30, 2002, at Beatty's Miller Canyon Guest Ranch and Orchard, which you'll pass at 1.5 miles.

   Once you reach the John Cooper Trail, you're likely to see mountain bikers; be extra alert on weekends. Also note that summer temperatures can top 100 degrees, and in winter the upper areas of the trail can be icy.

Beautiful views—and some steep climbing—are guaranteed in the Huachuca Mountains.

Miles and Directions

0.0 From the trailhead, head south, picking up a well-used trail, crossing the creek, and picking up the trail that parallels the creek.

0.2 Turn right onto the trail that heads west and uphill.

1.0 The trail crosses the creek.

1.5 Reach a parking lot at the end of the road (near the entrance to Beatty's Miller Canyon Guest Ranch). Turn right, cross the road, and head up the trail labeled FOREST TRAIL and MILLER CANYON TRAIL (106).

1.7 Trail intersection. Go right, following a sign for CLARK SPRING TRAIL 124.

1.8 At another trail intersection, veer right onto the John Cooper Trail. You will soon have excellent views to the east.

2.9 At the end of the John Cooper Trail, go right. You're now on the Clark Spring Trail.

3.1 Fence with no gate.

3.7 The trail ends at gravel Carr Canyon Road. Turn around and retrace your steps. After about 0.25 mile on the return trip, there is a wide area on the trail with good views to the east; this is a good spot for a lunch break.

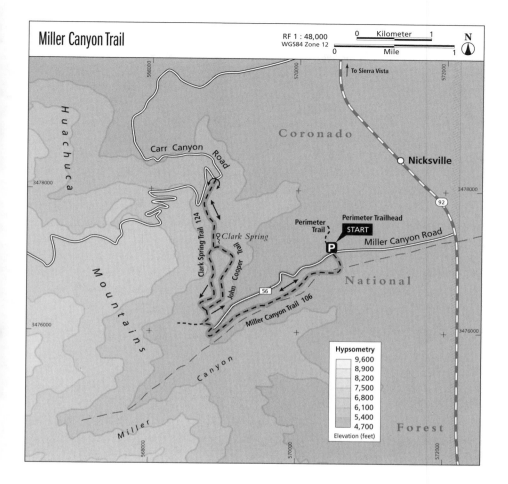

4.6 Reach the John Cooper Trail on your left. Stay straight on the Clark Spring Trail.

5.4 Reach a second intersection with the John Cooper Trail, on your left. Go straight.

5.5 At a trail intersection, go left to return to the trailhead.

5.7 The trail ends at the gravel road. Retrace your steps. From here, you can proceed down the gravel road or ride down the trail you came up. Be careful to turn left after 1.3 miles to return to the parking lot; this turn is easily missed.

7.2 Arrive back at the trailhead.

Options: This loop is short, but it's enough to give you a taste of the length and variety of trails—Hunter Canyon, Crest Trail, Carr Canyon, and more—that are available from this trailhead. Your best bet is to stop by the ranger station on AZ 92 to check on trail conditions and to pick up a Forest Service Sierra Vista Ranger District map. One possible extension for this ride is to turn left up the gravel road and continue on toward Carr Canyon Ranch (being careful of traffic on weekends).

Kofa Mountains

No, *Kofa* is not some obscure Meso-American caffeinated beverage. The name of this rugged, dramatic, and—some would say—inhospitable range comes from a famous gold mine: The branding iron used to label company property that belonged to the King of Arizona mine was KOFA.

But like mining, digging deeper reveals an even shinier gem. On the old maps this area is labeled the S.H. MOUNTAINS. According to Byrd Granger's *Arizona Place Names*, the 1860s pioneers noticed that each large peak was accompanied by a small one, just as every residence came with its smaller companion building: the outhouse. When women moved to the territory, the old-timers didn't want to offend the female sensibilities, so they began referring to these as the Short Horn Mountains, instead of the Shit House Mountains.

In 1963 the USGS officially—and humorlessly—renamed these the Kofa Mountains, thus erasing a colorful bit of historic nomenclature.

The 665,400-acre Kofa National Wildlife Refuge was established in 1939 to protect the desert bighorn sheep whose local population had dwindled to one hundred. Thanks to careful management and the artificial augmentation of some water holes, the population has now expanded to somewhere between 800 and 1,000 individuals—enough to allow some transplanting of animals around the Southwest.

As you ride, keep an eye out on the canyon walls or near potential watering places. Although rams may only drink once every two or three days and can lose up to 30 percent of their body weight without problems, ewes and lambs need to water every day. Both rams and ewes have permanent horns, but rams' horns are longer (nearly 3 feet!) and more tightly curled.

Two botanical rarities in the area include the California fan palm, which grows in Palm Canyon (you'll need to drive there, then hike in, as there's no equestrian access) and the Kofa barberry, a hollylike shrub found only in this mountain range and near Ajo.

Because it's a wilderness area, once you're off the main road, mountain bikes and ATVs are prohibited. Keep in mind some refuge regulations:

- Don't scatter manure from your camp or bury the trash; instead, take it out in large garbage bags.
- Do not remove, damage, or disturb any plant, animal, mineral, or artifacts. The exception is Crystal Hill Area, which is in the northwest corner of the wildlife area where rock collecting is permitted.
- Dispersed camping is permitted, but not within 0.25 mile of water.

- Campfires are allowed, but only with dead, down, and detached wood from areas that are not designated wilderness. (Wood is so scarce that campers are advised to bring their own from home.)

From 1860 to 1965 Arizona produced 13.3 million ounces of gold. Yuma County ranks fourth among gold-producing counties, and 237,000 ounces came from the Kofa district alone.

All that mining left its mark in the form of vertical shafts, open pits, and various tunnels that are prone to caving in or collapse. Riding close to them or attempting any kind of up-close exploration could be a fatal idea.

On another disconcerting note, the U.S. Fish and Wildlife brochure lists the following warning:

> CAUTION: Kofa NWR was included in the desert military training exercise conducted by General Patton during World War II. Unexploded ordnance may be encountered during cross-country hiking. *Do not pick up anything that appears to be military hardware.* Mark the location of the object, and report it to headquarters.

36 De La Osa Well Trail

At 18.8 miles, this out-and-back trail is long, but it's also easy, with good, sandy footing and very little climbing. Although remote, the area is an easy haul from Yuma.

Start: 50 miles northeast of Yuma; Yuma County.
Distance: 18.8 miles out and back.
Approximate riding time: 5 to 7 hours.
Total ascent: 1,300 feet.
Difficulty: Easy, but long. The footing varies from an occasionally rocky jeep road to a sandy wash.
Seasons: October through March only.

Water availability: None, except immediately after rain.
Other trail users: Unlikely.
Canine compatibility: Best left at home.
Fees and permits: None needed.
Facilities: None.
USGS maps: Livingston Hills.
Contact: U.S. Fish and Wildlife Service, Kofa National Wildlife Refuge, (928) 783-7861.

Reaching the trailhead: From U.S. Highway 95 from either Yuma or Quartzsite, between mileposts 92 and 93, take the dirt road heading east that's labeled R5W (referred to as KING ROAD on the *DeLorme Gazetteer* and as MST&T ROAD on the Kofa NWR map). Go 3.6 miles to reach the entrance of Kofa Mountain National Wildlife Refuge. Be sure to stop here to pick up a trail map. Go 4.0 miles to Junction 1—a good parking and/or camping spot. *DeLorme: Arizona Atlas and Gazetteer:* Page 54 2C.

Trailhead parking: There's a pullout camping spot large enough for several rigs.

The Ride

Unless you do a lot of trotting and cantering, this is a long day's ride. Other than being gently uphill, however, it's easy and quite lovely in its drama and desolation. From the broad alluvial valley where you parked, you'll move gradually from the creosote bush flats through several washes with palo verde, ironwood, and mesquite trees, and up into the rocky canyon habitat characterized by handsome saguaros, dramatic ocotillos, and the ever-present prickly pear and brittlebush. Keep an eye out here for bighorn sheep! As many as 161 bird species have been seen in this area at various times of year, including golden eagles, falcons, Gambel's quail, phainopeplas, cactus wrens, and Gila woodpeckers.

Bring everything you'll need for your horse and yourself: The refuge has no facilities for fuel, sanitation, towing, or drinking water. You'll also need to remove all your garbage, including horse manure.

U.S. Fish and Wildlife Service regulations stipulate that because this area is a wildlife refuge, dogs must be confined at all times, so it's best to leave your canine companion at home. (The only exception is for dogs participating in a legal hunt.)

Take note that summer temperatures can reach 120 degrees, and the canyon is narrow, so flash floods are a possibility.

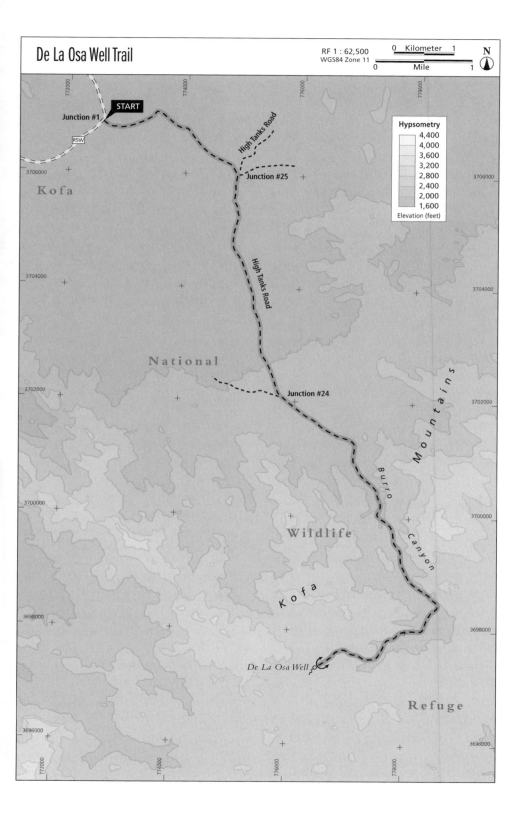

The trail to De La Osa Well meanders between dramatic rocky cliffs, home of the desert bighorn sheep.

Miles and Directions

0.0   Continue on down the dirt road (east) you're camped on. (Although most of the route you'll be on is navigable with four-wheel-drive, it is absolutely not recommended for horse trailers.)

1.8   Junction 25. Turn right (south).

4.4   Junction 24. You're now entering Burro Canyon into the interior of the Kofas in a generally southeasterly direction.

9.4   De La Osa Well. Retrace your steps.

18.8   Return to the trailhead.

Options: This area is crisscrossed by many four-wheel-drive roads and trails. You could easily spend several days camping here with hours of happy riding (just not in summer!).

37 MST&T Trail

This little 3-mile out-and-back route is just a small side trip from your camping spot along the gravel road and up to the communications tower for a superb panoramic view.

Start: 50 miles northeast of Yuma; Yuma County.
Distance: 3 miles out and back.
Approximate riding time: 1 to 2 hours, depending on how long you admire the view from the top.
Total ascent: 400 feet.
Difficulty: Easy.
Seasons: October through March only.

Water availability: None.
Other trail users: Watch for traffic on the road.
Canine compatibility: Best left at home.
Fees and permits: None needed.
Facilities: None.
USGS maps: Livingston Hills.
Contact: U.S. Fish and Wildlife Service, Kofa National Wildlife Refuge, (928) 783-7861.

Reaching the trailhead: From U.S. Highway 95 from either Yuma or Quartzsite, between mileposts 92 and 93, take the dirt road heading east that's labeled R5W (referred to as KING ROAD on the *DeLorme Gazetteer* and as MST&T ROAD on the Kofa NWR map). Go 3.6 miles to reach the entrance of Kofa Mountain National Wildlife Refuge. Be sure to stop here to pick up a trail map. Go 4.0 miles to Junction 1—a good parking and/or camping spot. *DeLorme: Arizona Atlas and Gazetteer:* Page 54 2C.

Trailhead parking: A pullout camping spot large enough for several rigs.

The Ride

This is a perfect short ride if you arrive in late afternoon and want a short jaunt before dinner, or maybe one last tiny expedition before loading up the day you leave. You'll be on the dirt road that accesses the tower, but there's very little traffic.

The view from the top is in all directions. To the north you'll be looking at the Livingston Hills and the Plumosa Mountains, while the Kofa Mountains dominate to the south and east. The Dome Rock and Chocolate Mountains are the smaller but rugged ranges to the west.

This ride is best taken during the winter, as summer temperatures can reach 120 degrees.

Bring everything you'll need for your horse and yourself. The refuge has no facilities for fuel, sanitation, towing, or drinking water. You'll also need to remove all your garbage, including horse manure.

U.S. Fish and Wildlife Service regulations stipulate that because this area is a wildlife refuge, dogs must be confined at all times, so it's best to leave your canine companion at home. (The only exception is for dogs participating in a legal hunt.)

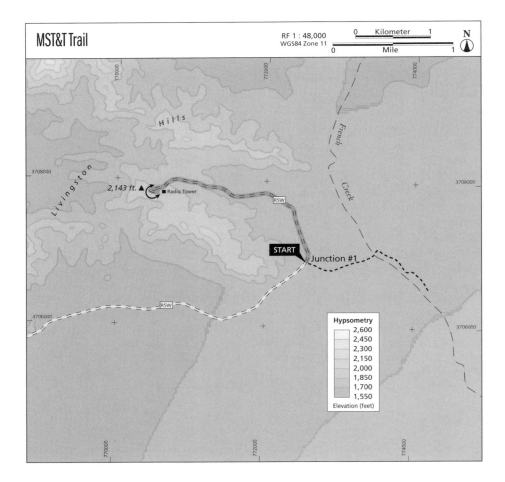

Miles and Directions

0.0 Head back to the road you drove in on, and turn right. Follow the road to the communications tower.

1.5 Admire the view, and retrace your steps.

3.0 Arrive back at the trailhead.

Las Cienegas National Conservation Area

Home of the historic Empire Ranch, this almost pristine trail riders' gem encompasses 42,000 acres of sweeping desert vistas, mountain backdrops, rolling grasslands, shady washes, and oak-and-juniper-dotted hillsides.

The original 160-acre ranch, established in the 1860s, was purchased in 1876 for $1,174 by Walter Vail, a Nova Scotian, and Herbert Hislop, an Englishman. Hislop's enthusiasm wilted two years later, but before selling his share he wrote home admiringly about the ability of Arizona's horses to do the 104-mile round trip to Tucson: "[They] only had grass to eat and one day to rest so you can judge what wiry little horses they are." At the time, a sturdy serviceable equine sold for around $40!

Vail and his other partners expanded the ranch to more than a million acres, covering much of Pima, Santa Cruz, and Cochise Counties. They later sold it to the Boice family, who in 1960 then sold it to Gulf American for commercial and residential development. That idea foundered, and Anamax Mining bought the ranch with a plan to exploit the water and mineral resources. Fortunately for all of us, that deal fell through as well. Thanks in part to a public outcry in the 1980s, the ranch is now administered by the Bureau of Land Management, and the twenty-two-room frame-and-adobe ranch house is listed on the National Register of Historic Places.

Vegetation of Las Cienegas NCA includes the best example of native sacaton grasslands in the state, luxuriant velvet ash and cottonwoods that edge the permanently flowing Cienega Creek, mesquite bosques, and, of course, the *cienegas* (marshlands) for which the area is named. It was also, until 1998, the home of the world's largest Emory oak, which blew down in a storm generated by Hurricane Lester.

Mammals of Las Cienegas include mountain lions, pronghorn antelope, both mule and Coues white-tailed deer, badgers, coatimundi, and ringtail cats. Most recently, a Mexican opossum appeared on a wildlife camera—the northernmost appearance of that species.

However, the mammals you're most likely to encounter are cattle. The Donaldson family, who have held the grazing lease since 1976, use a rest/rotation strategy to protect the land and have established twenty-eight stations around the ranch to monitor environmental impacts. They work closely with the BLM, members of the community, and a biological assessment team and have won several awards for their sensitive stewardship of this precious area.

38 North Canyon Loop

The combination of deep sand and 1,000 feet of climbing make this particular route a moderate 11.3-mile loop. In general, however, the Las Cienegas National Conservation Area (easily accessed from either Interstate 10 or Sonoita) has many miles of four-wheel-drive roads and jeep tracks, making it perfect for rookie horses and/or riders.

Start: 7 miles north of Sonoita; Pima County.
Distance: 11.3-mile loop.
Approximate riding time: 3 to 4 hours.
Total ascent: 1,000 feet.
Difficulty: Moderate; the footing is good, but young or unfit horses will notice the climb and the deep sand.
Seasons: Best in fall, winter, and spring.
Water availability: None.
Other trail users: Cattle, cowboys, ATVers, and occasional hikers.

Canine compatibility: Dogs "under control" are allowed. Bring water.
Fees and permits: Recreational pass required to access Arizona state lands.
Facilities: One rustic ramada, two vault toilets.
USGS maps: Empire Ranch, Spring Water Canyon.
Contact: Bureau of Land Management, Tucson Field Office, (520) 258-7200.

Reaching the trailhead: From Tucson, travel east on Interstate 10, and take Exit 281 to Arizona Highway 83, heading south. Go about 18 miles, and between mileposts 39 and 40 turn left (east) at the dirt road and sign for the EMPIRE CIENEGA RESOURCE AREA. Follow the road (which is also Empire Cienega 900) approximately 2.2 miles to the stop sign. Go left on Empire Cienega 901 for 1.8 miles past the corrals, and go left again onto Empire Cienega 902. You're now on the old airport strip, which is almost a mile long. Park anywhere along it. *DeLorme: Arizona Atlas and Gazetteer:* Page 73 B6.

    Trailhead parking: There's a flat unused airstrip with room for dozens of trailers. (This area is used in November and March for competitive trail and endurance events.) Arizona requires an annual recreation pass to access state land. It's easily obtained by calling (602) 542-4174.

The Ride

This loop features a variety of pleasant riding: shady mesquite bosques, sandy washes, sweeping views, and long stretches of easy footing. You'll be riding up out of Oak Tree Canyon and down into North Canyon, past the Diamond A windmill. Once the North Canyon wash reaches the road, you'll turn back toward the broad open valley of Oak Tree Canyon, picking up the trail that parallels the road and follows the telephone line.

    BLM regulations for this area stipulate that all pets should be "under control at all times." Because Las Cienegas is both a wildlife refuge and a working ranch, be sure that your dog is a good guest. You'll also need to carry dog water. (A one-

As you ride along the top side of North Canyon, you'll have a fine view of the distant Whetstone Mountains to the east.

gallon ziplock bag makes an easy-to-carry collapsible dog bowl—and in a pinch your horse can drink out of it as well.)

Since the Empire is still a working ranch, you're quite likely to see cattle or cowboys—be sure to leave gates open or closed as you find them. ATVers are common on weekends but are prohibited from using nonmotorized trails. The area is lightly used by hikers.

This scenic loop is but a tiny sample of the many miles of scenic riding in the Las Cienegas National Conservation Area. Each year the Old Pueblo Endurance Ride takes place here in early March. Even the 50- and 100-milers only see a fraction of this vast and beautiful area.

Remember that temperatures can exceed 100 degrees in summer. Also, much of the trail is open and exposed, so plan carefully around summer thunderstorms.

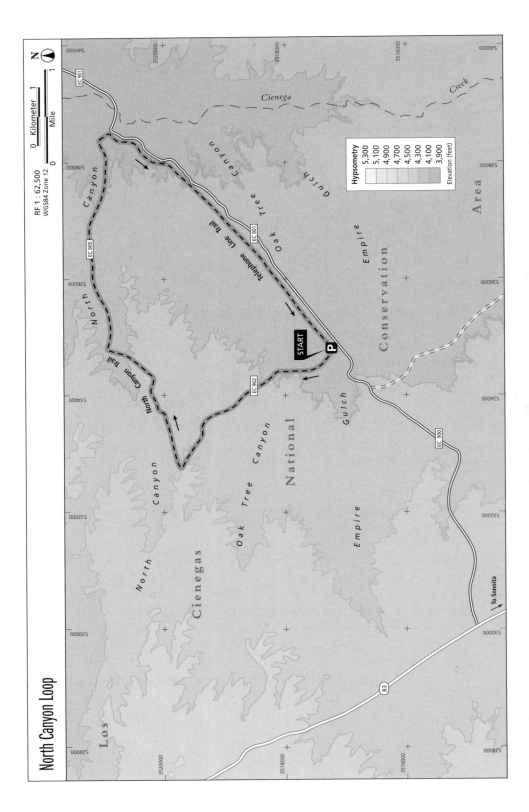

North Canyon Loop

RF 1 : 62,500
WGS84 Zone 12

N

0 Kilometer 1
0 Mile 1

Hypsometry
5,300
5,100
4,900
4,700
4,500
4,300
4,100
3,900
Elevation (feet)

Los

North Canyon

North Canyon Trail

North Canyon Trail

Cienegas

Oak Tree Canyon

Oak Tree Canyon

National

Empire

Gulch

EC 902

EC 905

EC 901

Telephone Line Trail

Cienega

Cienega Creek

Empire

Conservation

Area

EC 901

EC 900

83

To Sonoita

START

P

Miles and Directions

0.0 Take the lightly used jeep track behind the ramada that heads in a northerly direction.

0.7 Go right onto EC 902E.

2.1 Go straight onto the single track.

2.8 It looks as if the trail forks here, but the two pathways rejoin.

3.1 Go right.

4.3 Head left onto the jeep track.

5.3 Go right into the wash.

7.6 Go right up out of the wash and onto the road.

7.7 Go right onto the road.

8.6 Turn right, off the road; cross through the little wash to get on to the trail under the telephone line. (Keep an eye out; this trail is easy to miss.)

10.5 The north end of the airstrip.

11.3 Arrive back at the trailhead.

Oracle State Park

The Clovis Culture was the earliest well-established human group in North America and gets its name from the New Mexico town where a distinct type of stone projectile point was found in 1932. The Paleo-Indian culture, most likely based on nomadic hunting large game such as mammoths, flourished 10,000 years ago and spread throughout the continent, including the area we now call Oracle. Evidence also points to the Hohokam people arriving here 600 to 800 years ago to make their home in the rolling foothills of the Santa Catalina Mountains.

Kannally Wash is named for Neil Kannally, formerly from Illinois, who came to the Mountain View Hotel in Oracle in 1902 hoping for a tuberculosis cure. Apparently it worked: He recovered, then gradually convinced his siblings to join him. The family began ranching with an initial 1903 purchase of 12 head of cattle and 160 acres for $125; by 1910 the Kannally holdings had expanded to 1,100 Herefords roaming the family's 50,000 acres.

In 1929 the family built and moved into a much larger Mediterranean-style ranch house. One of their friends remembers that the shine on the slate floors came from mixing evaporated milk with the scrub water—a housekeeping technique no doubt appreciated by the family dogs.

When Neil Kannally died in 1954, the remaining cattle were sold. The last surviving member, Lucille Kannally, willed the land to the Defenders of Wildlife in 1976 along with the funds to run it for ten years. When the decade was up, DOW didn't have the money to maintain the ranch and transferred it to the State Parks Board.

The family ranch house is now the home of the park office/gift store, and well worth a visit.

39 Kannally Wash Windmill Loop

For being only a 4.9-mile loop, this route is surprisingly challenging as it takes on the foothills of the Santa Catalina Mountains. The surface is often rutted or rocky, and the climbs, totaling some 1,000 feet, are steep.

Start: Just east of Oracle; Pinal County.
Distance: 4.9-mile loop.
Approximate riding time: 2 to 3 hours.
Total ascent: Approximately 1,050 feet.
Difficulty: Moderate to slightly difficult with ruts and loose, rolling rocks.
Seasons: Best in early spring and late fall.
Water availability: Two water tanks.
Other trail users: Hikers.

Canine compatibility: Best left at home. Dogs must be leashed in the state park.
Fees and permits: Recreational pass required on Arizona state lands.
Facilities: None.
USGS maps: Campo Bonito, Mammoth.
Contact: Oracle State Park, Center for Environmental Education, (520) 896-2425.

Reaching the trailhead: From Tucson, go north on Arizona Highway 77 to Oracle Junction. Stay on AZ 77, and drive 9.2 miles to the turnoff to the Oracle business district. Turn right onto American Avenue. At 2.4 miles you'll see a sign for Oracle State Park and Mount Lemmon Road—don't take it. (That would take you to the American Flag Trailhead for the Arizona Trail.) Instead, stay on American Avenue for another 1.1 miles. The American Avenue Trailhead will be on your right. *DeLorme: Arizona Atlas and Gazetteer:* Page 67 B5.

Trailhead parking: There's a paved pull-through with room for four to six rigs. Parking at the American Avenue Trailhead is free, as of January 2006. However, that fee structure may change in the near future. No permit is needed to ride on the state park, but parts of this trail pass through state land for which Arizona requires an annual recreation pass. It's unlikely that anyone will ask to see your permit, but to be on the safe side, it's easily obtained by calling (602) 542-4174.

The Ride

Don't let the short length of this ride fool you: A young or green horse will have to concentrate for the rutted and sometimes tricky footing among loose, rolling rocks. The few areas that are flat are in a sandy wash, and for a short ride, there's a surprising amount of climbing.

The views of the Santa Catalinas from these northern foothills and of the Galiuros to the northeast are impressive—even if, for those of us who live in Tucson, having the Cats to the south instead of the north is disconcerting!

The Arizona Trail is well-traveled, particularly on weekends, and this area, although rarely crowded, is still well-used. Oracle is at 4,000 feet, and small snowdrifts on north-facing slopes in winter are not unusual, while summer temperatures can exceed 100 degrees. About half-way through the route are two water tanks fed by a windmill as well as shade and a bench.

On a hot day, this windmill and trough are a welcome sight.

Imagine riding this trail eighty years ago: no mesquite, no catclaw acacia, no cactus. The Cherry Valley Wash ran all year, and pronghorn antelope grazed alongside the cattle.

Miles and Directions

0.0   Head south out of the parking lot past the kiosk to the sign that reads POWERLINE TRAIL TO ARIZONA TRAIL. Go left (north).

0.7   You'll come to the first Arizona Trail marker: a handsome reddish 4-by-4 post with the AZT logo and a two-way arrow scratched on the north-facing surface. Go right (south) toward the wash.

0.8   Once you're in the wash, turn left (north).

0.9   Go right (east) on the four-wheel-drive road, heading up out of the wash and away from the Arizona Trail.

1.4   Go across the small wash. The pedestrian AZT goes left, but horses and bikes should go straight ahead on the power-line road.

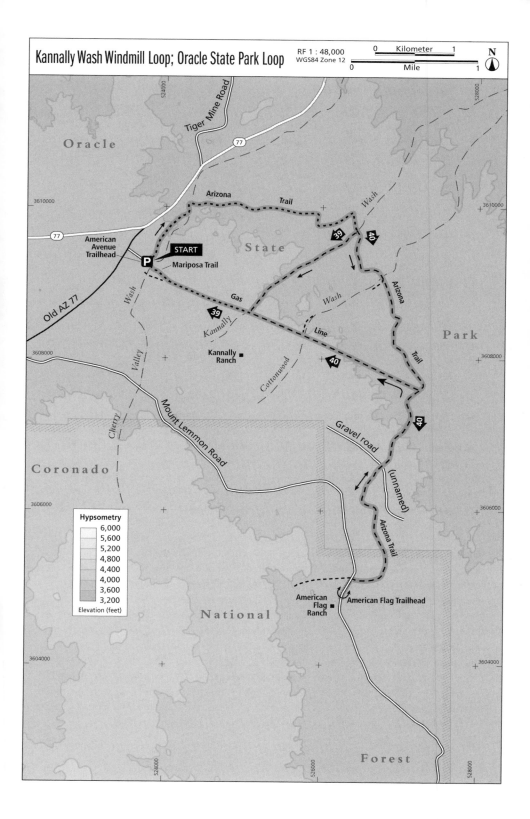

Kannally Wash Windmill Loop; Oracle State Park Loop

RF 1 : 48,000
WGS84 Zone 12

0 — Kilometer — 1
0 — Mile — 1

N

2.6 The windmill, water tanks, shade, and bench make for a great picnic spot. When you're through, turn right (south) and head down the wash (southwest). This is a lovely, shady ride among stately oaks.

3.8 Kannally Wash intersects with the Gas Line Trail. Turn right (west) for a series of hills.

4.6 Intersection of the Gas Line and Mariposa Trails. Go right (north). Even though you'll be able to see where the Gas Line Trail reaches the kiosk and parking lot, the Mariposa Trail is a more scenic way to end your ride as it winds its way down into the Cherry Valley Wash.

4.9 Arrive back at the trailhead.

Options: This trailhead is a good launching pad to hook into more miles into the Santa Catalinas.

40 Oracle State Park Loop

A 12.2-mile ride may not sound difficult, but many horses will find this lollipop loop surprisingly strenuous, thanks to the 2,100 feet of climbing with footing that some-times requires some concentration.

See map on page 163.
Start: East of Oracle; Pinal County.
Distance: 12.2-mile loop.
Approximate riding time: 4 to 5 hours.
Total ascent: 2,100 feet.
Difficulty: Moderate to difficult.
Seasons: Best in early spring and late fall.
Water availability: Two water tanks at 2.7 miles.

Other trail users: Hikers.
Canine compatibility: Best left at home. Dogs must be leashed at all times in the state park.
Fees and permits: Recreational pass required on Arizona state lands.
Facilities: None.
USGS maps: Campo Bonito, Mammoth.
Contact: Oracle State Park, Center for Environmental Education, (520) 896-2425.

Reaching the trailhead: From Tucson, go north on Arizona Highway 77 to Oracle Junction. Stay on AZ 77, and drive 9.2 miles to the turnoff to the Oracle business district. Turn right onto American Avenue. At 2.4 miles you'll see a sign for Oracle State Park and Mount Lemmon Road—don't take it. (That would take you to the American Flag Trailhead for the Arizona Trail.) Instead, stay on American Avenue for another 1.1 miles. The American Avenue Trailhead will be on your right. *DeLorme: Arizona Atlas and Gazetteer:* Page 67 B5.

Trailhead parking: There's a paved pull-through with room for four to six rigs. Parking at the American Avenue Trailhead is free, as of January 2006; however, that fee structure may change in the near future. Although no permit is needed to ride on the state park, some sections of this trail pass through state land, for which Arizona requires an annual recreation pass. It's unlikely that anyone will ask to see your permit, but to be on the safe side, it's easily obtained by calling (602) 542-4174.

Afternoon sun highlights a granite hoodoo and snow-covered Rice Mountain on the Arizona Trail near the American Flag Trailhead.

The Ride

The Arizona Trail is well traveled, particularly on weekends, and although rarely crowded, this area is still used fequently.

This trail is a strenuous workout and has lots of variety: sandy washes, rocky climbs, interesting rock formations, great views of the Galiuros and the Santa Catalinas, as well as stretches of good footing on the pipeline where you can move out.

There are two water tanks fed by a windmill as well as shade and a bench. Be sure to have horse water and a bucket waiting at your truck, however, since there's nowhere else to water your horse besides the tanks.

Oracle is at 4,000 feet, and small snowdrifts on north-facing slopes in winter are not unusual, while summer temperatures can exceed 100 degrees.

Miles and Directions

0.0 Head south out of the parking lot past the kiosk to the sign that reads POWERLINE TRAIL TO ARIZONA TRAIL. Go left (north).

0.7 You'll come to the first Arizona Trail marker: a handsome reddish 4-by4 post with the AZT logo and a two-way arrow scratched on the north-facing surface. Go right (south) toward the wash.

0.8 Once you're in the wash, turn left (north).

0.9 Go right (east) on the four-wheel-drive road, heading up out of the wash and away from the Arizona Trail.

1.4 Go across the small wash. The pedestrian AZT goes left, but horses and bikes should go straight ahead on the power-line road.

2.6 The windmill, water tanks, shade, and bench make for a great watering spot. When you're through, cross the wash and continue on the trail, heading east.

3.1 Intersection with a trail that goes to the ranch house.

3.3 Cottonwood Wash.

4.6 Intersection with a pipeline road.

4.7 Intersection with a trail to the ranch house; go straight.

5.0 Boundary of the state park, with a gate.

5.5 Cross over the gravel road; go through an equestrian-friendly green gate.

6.5 Fence with a green gate next to a pedestrian stile.

7.1 American Flag Trailhead; you and your horse have climbed 1,300 feet. This is your turn-around spot.

7.8 Fence with a green gate next to a pedestrian stile.

8.8 Cross over the gravel road; go through the equestrian-friendly green gate.

9.3 Reenter the state park through the gate.

9.7 Intersection with the Gas Line Trail. Go left onto Gas Line, instead of retracing your steps to the Kannally Wash windmill.

10.8 Cottonwood Wash and Wildlife Corridor Trail; stay on the Gas Line Trail.

11.2 Kannally Wash; stay on the Gas Line Trail.

12.0 Intersection of the Gas Line and Mariposa Trails. Go right (north). Even though you'll be able to see where the Gas Line Trail reaches the kiosk and parking lot, the Mariposa Trail is a more scenic way to end your ride as it winds its way down into the Cherry Valley Wash.

12.2 Arrive back at the trailhead.

Options: This trailhead is a good launching pad to hook into the Arizona Trail for more miles into the Santa Catalinas.

Pinaleño Mountains

The Pina-which mountains?

The Pinaleños are often called the Graham Mountains, even though only the highest peak, Mount Graham, actually bears that name. Originally called Sierra Bonita ("beautiful mountain"), it was renamed in honor of Lt. Col. James Duncan Graham, an officer with Brig. Gen. Stephen Kearney, U.S. Army Corps of Topographical Engineers.

At 10,700 feet, Mount Graham has been the site of a bitter international battle involving astronomers, environmentalists, lawyers, Apaches—and an 8-inch bushy-tailed rodent.

The peak is also called *Dzil Nchaa Si'an* by the San Carlos Apache Indians, who see the mountain as the home of their spirits *(G'han)* and a source of spiritual medicine. The Pinaleño range is the tallest and steepest of the southern "sky islands" and is the residence of Mexican spotted owls, northern goshawks, flight-less beetles, the Apache trout, and the densest concentration of black bears south of the Mogollon Rim.

At the top of the mountain is a small amount of spruce-fir habitat. Along with the Engelmann spruce and the cork bark firs comes a rare subspecies of rodent, called the Mount Graham red squirrel, thought to have been extinct but rediscovered in the 1970s.

The battle began in the 1980s when the University of Arizona wanted to clear-cut enough of the mountaintop for eighteen telescopes. Twenty years, forty lawsuits, two congressional interventions, and $120 million later, the Mount Graham International Observatory's Large Binocular Telescope received its first image in October 2005. The target was a spiral galaxy named NGC891, which is in the constellation Andromeda.

41 Shake Trail

This trail is a strenuous 10.6-mile out-and-back route with a 3,300-foot ascent of the Pinaleño Mountains. The rarely-used trail is faint in places—be sure you and your horse are ready for this one.

Start: 35 miles from Willcox; Graham County.
Distance: 10.6 miles out and back.
Approximate riding time: 5 to 6 hours.
Total ascent: 3,300 feet.
Difficulty: Difficult.
Seasons: Best in late spring, summer, and early fall.
Water availability: Water troughs at 0.6 mile and 1.3 miles.

Other trail users: Limited.
Canine compatibility: Best left at home.
Fees and permits: None needed.
Facilities: Two corrals.
USGS maps: Stockton Pass, Mt. Graham.
Contact: USDA Forest Service, Coronado National Forest, Safford Ranger District, (928) 428-4150.

Reaching the trailhead: From Willcox, travel east on Interstate 10 to the first turnoff for U.S. Highway 191 (Exit 352). New Mexicans traveling west on I-10 should take Exit 355 for the first US 191 turnoff. Take US 191 north 16 miles to Arizona Highway 266. Go left (west) 12 miles. The turnoff to the Stockton Pass Trailhead, which is unmarked, will be on your right between mileposts 115 and 116. *DeLorme: Arizona Atlas and Gazetteer:* Page 68 B3.
   Trailhead parking: There's ample pull-through parking for five or six rigs.

The Ride

The lower section of this trail is very dry, and the dead and dying junipers are a discouraging reminder of the continuing drought. The lupines in June are luxuriant, waist high, and spectacular. Views to the south look across the Sulphur Springs Valley to the Greasewood Mountains.
   Snow and ice are likely in winter, and mud in early spring.

Miles and Directions

0.0   Head northeast, across the gravel road you drove in on and along the fence line, following the sign that reads SHAKE TRAIL. You'll have to pass through a gate almost immediately.

0.6   Water trough.

1.3   Another water tank.

2.0   Reach a sign for TAP SPRING (just a few yards off the trail, but usually dry), SWIFT TRAIL (3 miles), and ALDER SPRING STOCKTON PASS (1.75 miles).

3.0   This area is much greener, with a mixture of gray and silverleaf oaks.

4.0   Pay attention to this section of the trail: In places it's indistinct and will be difficult to find when you retrace your steps coming back down. There are a few deadfalls you'll need to skirt.

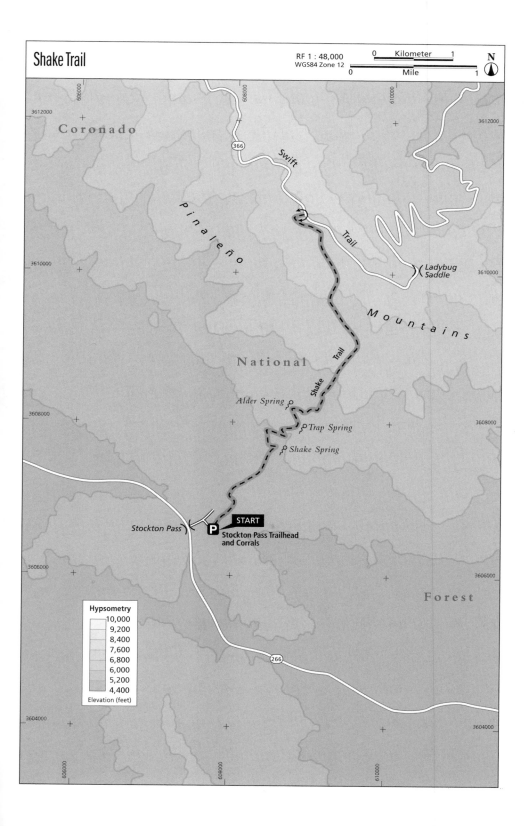

Lupines, a member of the pea family, are a June bonus on the Shake Trail. The name comes from lupus, *Latin for "wolf" because people thought the flowers devoured the soil's nutrients— after all, nothing else tends to grow near them. In actuality, the plant, being a legume, enhances the soil.*

4.5 By now you'll be among ponderosa pine, Parry's agave, and Douglas fir. In June the lupines are thick, luxuriant, and waist high.

5.1 Intersection; go straight.

5.3 The trail dead-ends at the paved Swift Trail in a paved parking lot. It's not a wonderful lunch spot, but there are a few trees where you can tie your horse to take a break.

10.6 Arrive back at the trailhead.

Options: Very few other trails take off from this one.

Rillito River Park

F ill in the blank:

The oldest known effort at settlement in the _____ Valley was that of an Arkansas pioneer who cleared a small area of bottom land just east of Fort Lowell in 1858. The entire valley was at that time unbroken forest, principally of mesquite, with a good growth of grama and other grasses between the trees. The river course was indefinite, a continuous grove of tall cottonwood, ash, willow, and walnut trees with underbrush and sacaton and galleta grass, and it was further obstructed by beaver dams.

Hard as it is to imagine beaver dams under the Dodge Road bridge, the missing word is, of course, *Rillito*. The description is from a 1910 report by hydrologist G. E. P. Smith with the title "Ground Water Supply and Irrigation in the Rillito Valley." The valley includes the drainage from the south side of the Santa Catalinas and the western slopes of the Rincons. Small wonder, then, that malaria was a considerable problem for the early residents of the Fort Lowell neighborhood.

The Rillito Creek (a somewhat redundant name, since *rillito* is "creek" in Spanish) runs from the confluence of the Tanque Verde and Pantano Washes into the Santa Cruz.

A century and a half later, what this means to a Tucson trail rider is being able to ride many miles—and right past nonhorsey establishments like Dillard's and Costco—without ever leaving the confines of the city.

42 Rillito River Park Trail

This ride is very much the urban equestrian experience since it follows the Rillito's bed either east or west, as you prefer. The route is definitely a training opportunity for your horse: You'll be riding under major thoroughfares with city buses and garbage trucks and past abandoned shopping carts, loose dogs, and the occasional homeless person's camp.

Start: Midtown Tucson; Pima County.
Distance: As long as you want to ride.
Approximate riding time: Depends on the length of the ride.
Total ascent: None.
Difficulty: Easy, although the young or unfit horses will find the deep sand discouraging. This route is also fine for barefoot horses as long as you stay down in the sandy riverbed. Recently shod horses may be tender footed on the top-side trail.
Seasons: Spring, fall, and winter (depending on rainfall).

Water availability: Trough at the trailhead. (Bring your own bucket.)
Other trail users: Everyone.
Canine compatibility: Best left at home.
Fees and permits: None.
Facilities: Hitching posts, watering trough, wash racks for horses (the water isn't always turned on), one ramada, two tables; no restrooms.
USGS maps: Tucson North.
Contact: Pima County Natural Resources, Parks and Recreation, (520) 877–6000.

Reaching the trailhead: From Interstate 10, take Exit 257 for Speedway Boulevard. Travel east (toward the University of Arizona) to Swan Road. Turn left (north), and continue through five traffic lights to just past Camp Lowell. The first opportunity to turn right will be Paseo de los Rios; a sign on the wall reads RILLITO RIVER PARK. Turn right here, and then make an immediate left. The road will dead-end at the trailhead in a few hundred yards.

When leaving, don't try to turn left with a trailer across Swan Road. Just turn right (north) onto Swan Road instead, then turn left (west) onto River Road, and take a left (south) onto any major cross street to get back to Speedway. *DeLorme: Arizona Atlas and Gazetteer:* Page 67 D4.

Trailhead parking: There's a paved parking lot with room for several trailers.

The Ride

The fun element of this ride is the contrast. You can hear the exercise drills at Tucson Racquet Club, feel the rumble of the traffic as it passes over a nearby bridge—even while you're steeped in the fragrance of a desert willow thicket. Equestrian use is also permitted above the river on the south side between Campbell and La Cholla, but be aware that you'll encounter runners, people with strollers, dog walkers, and many bicyclists. Your horse will still encounter some urban equestrian challenges in the riverbed: At the very least, he's likely to look twice at the shiny metal shopping

Rillito River Park Trail

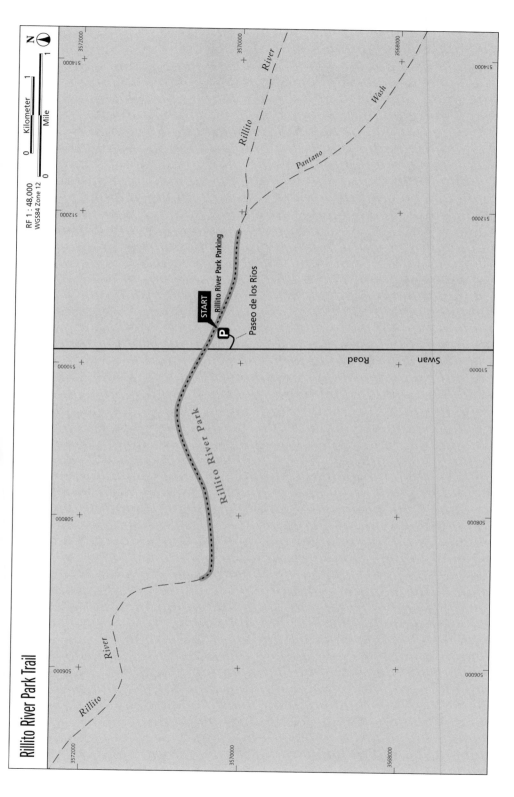

RF 1 : 48,000
WGS84 Zone 12

N

0   Kilometer   1

0   Mile   1

START

Rillito River Park Parking

Paseo de los Rios

Rillito River Park

Rillito River

Rillito River

Pantano Wash

Swan Road

carts draped with flood debris. You'll also be riding under major urban thorough-fares that carry rush-hour traffic, city buses, garbage trucks, and occasional eighteen-wheelers.

Summer temperatures are likely to be well over 100 degrees, except in very early morning. Flooding is also likely and tends to happen several times a year.

Although Tucson parks have a strictly enforced leash law (and the river park is patrolled), many people run their dogs in the riverbed. Be prepared for someone else's rowdy cur to spook and chase your horse.

(Note: The planned Brandi Fenton Memorial Park is slated for completion in late 2006. It will be located on the north side of the Rillito River between Country Club and Alvernon Way and will include a community equestrian facility, including equestrian staging area and internal equestrian trails, athletic field and soccer fields, and general park facilities, including ramadas, restrooms, and picnic areas.)

Miles and Directions

0.0   You can ride in the bed of the Rillito in either direction for as far as you like.

Rincon Mountains

S aguaro National Park is divided into east and west sections ("districts") that are 20 miles apart. The smaller, lower-elevation Tucson Mountain District lies to the west, while the Rincon Mountain District is the eastern and—at 94,000 acres—larger section. (*Rincon* means "inside corner" in Spanish, and the main ridge and Tanque Verde Ridge are at right angles to each other.) It's also taller, with a more extensive trail system that extends from desert lowlands to conifer forests at 8,500 feet. The highest elevations are accessible only on foot or horseback.

Far from empty and desolate, the lower elevations are a shining example of the lush Sonoran Desert: 2,700 different kinds of plants live here, the most majestic of which is, of course, the saguaro (pronounced *sah-WAH-row*).

Trail riding in this area is something of a scavenger hunt: The Cactus Forest is a confusing web of twenty-five-plus trails covering 40 miles, and intersections can be as frequent as 0.1 mile. You can't get very lost for very long, however, since the wall of the Rincons rises to the east, while the Santa Catalinas are always visible to the north. Signs are plentiful, although the labeling method is somewhat counterintuitive. (The trick to remember is that the largest trail name, or the title, on the sign refers to the route you'd be on if you took it, *not* the one you're already on. That nonsensical-sounding description will make much more sense once you're actually reading the signs—really.) As long as you have a map and/or directions—and you pay attention to them and where you are—you'll be fine.

As of mid-2005, both sections of the park are under management plan review, and the parking situation for equestrian use at the east end of the park may change—for better or worse.

43 Garwood/Shantz Trail

This 5.7-mile loop is both easy and scenic as it wanders among majestic saguaros with a backdrop of the Rincons and a view over the Tucson basin to the Santa Catalinas to the north.

Start: Eastern edge of Tucson; Pima County.
Distance: 5.7-mile loop.
Approximate riding time: 1 to 2 hours.
Total ascent: 456 feet.
Difficulty: Easy, with an occasional short rocky section.
Seasons: Best in winter, spring, and fall; okay as a *very* early-morning ride in summer.
Water availability: Rare, except after rain.

Other trail users: Hikers.
Canine compatibility: Dogs not permitted.
Fees and permits: None needed.
Facilities: None.
USGS maps: Tanque Verde Peak.
Contact: Saguaro National Park East, National Park Service, Rincon Mountain District Visitor Center, (520) 733-5133.

Reaching the trailhead: From Phoenix on weekends or when traffic is light, take Interstate 10 to the Speedway Boulevard exit (Exit 257) east; travel approximately 18 miles through midtown Tucson until Speedway dead-ends.

From the east, take I-10 to Houghton Road (Exit 275). Go right (north) approximately 12 miles to Speedway. Turn right (east), and go 4 miles to the trailhead.

A second equestrian trailhead is located at the eastern end of Broadway, approximately 2 miles to the south. *DeLorme: Arizona Atlas and Gazetteer:* Page 67 D5.

Trailhead parking: There's parking for twenty to forty rigs, but it's along the shoulder of Speedway Boulevard; the lot at the end of the road is reserved for passenger vehicles. On weekdays parking is plentiful and easy. On pleasant weekends, however, the area is very congested, and trailers may be parked bumper to bumper for as much as 0.5 mile from the trailhead. Drivers of large rigs may have trouble turning before the Tanque Verde Guest Ranch's private property boundary.

The Ride

Although short, this trail is a lovely early-morning or late-afternoon route that dips and twists through the Sonoran Desert at its most dramatic. Saguaros are the high point of this trail, but you also have a good chance of seeing wildlife, including deer, coyotes, javelinas, and various lizards and snakes. In a year of plentiful winter rains, the spring display of fairy dusters, brittlebush, scorpionweed, poppies, owl clover, and other wildflowers can be breathtaking.

The trails in this area are heavily used by hikers and frequently patrolled by mounted rangers and volunteers. Water is rare, except after a rain, but the creek crossings on the Garwood and Carillo Trails often run in winter and occasionally

The trails through the Cactus Forest are frequently used by equestrians. ▶

Garwood/Shantz Trail; Three Tanks/Carillo Trail

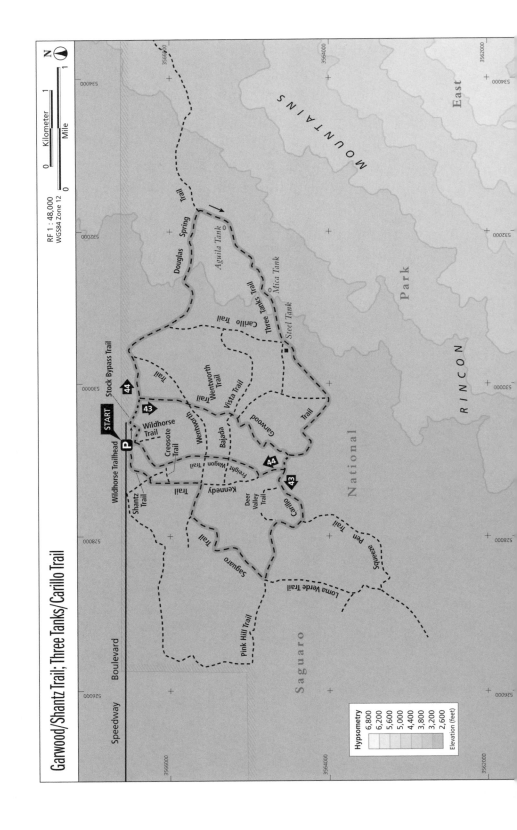

RF 1 : 48,000
WGS84 Zone 12

N

0 Kilometer 1
0 Mile 1

Speedway Boulevard

Douglas Spring Trail

Aguila Tank

Mica Tank

Three Tanks Trail

Carillo Trail

Steel Tank

Stock Bypass Trail

Wildhorse Trailhead

START

P

Wildhorse Trail

Creosote Trail

Wentworth Trail

Vista Trail

Garwood Trail

Bajada

Wentworth

Freight Wagon Trail

Shantz Trail

Kennedy Trail

Deer Valley Trail

Carillo

Saguaro Trail

Squeeze Pen Trail

Loma Verde Trail

Pink Hill Trail

Saguaro National Park

RINCON MOUNTAINS

East

Hypsometry

Elevation (feet)
6,800
6,200
5,600
5,000
4,400
3,800
3,200
2,600

have puddles at other times of year. In summer, when temperatures run 110 degrees or hotter at midday, it's best to ride this trail in the early morning.

Miles and Directions

0.0 Head south on the Wildhorse Trail. The Shantz Trail comes in immediately at your right, but you should bear left, staying on the Wildhorse Trail. (You'll be returning to this point and coming in on the Shantz Trail.)

0.1 Go left (east) onto the Stock Bypass Trail (the sign says GARWOOD 0.5 MILES).

0.6 Intersection of the Stock Bypass and Garwood Trails. Go right onto the Garwood Trail.

0.8 Intersection of the Garwood and Wentworth East Trails. Continue straight ahead.

1.0 Intersection of the Garwood and Wentworth North Trails. Continue straight ahead.

1.4 Intersection of the Garwood and Bajada Vista Trails. Go right. In less than 0.1 mile, you'll cross over the Wildhorse Trail, heading southwest and remaining on Garwood. (Ignore the fact that you can see Bajada Vista.)

1.8 As you cross the creek, look back over your shoulder at the cristate, or crested, saguaro. Scientists don't yet know why some saguaros take this abnormal fan-shaped form. This creek often has water or puddles that horses can drink from. There's a short rocky, steep area just as you get to the top of the hill.

2.1 Intersection of the Garwood and Carillo Trails. Turn right (northwest). In less than 0.1 mile, the Freight Wagon Trail comes in from your right. Ignore it, and keep going straight on Carillo.

2.3 Intersection of the Carillo and Kennedy Trails. Stay left on Carillo. **Bail-out:** If you or your horse has had enough, you can be back at the trailer in 1.3 miles by heading for home on the Kennedy Trail.

2.4 Intersection of the Deer Valley and Carillo Trails. Bear left, staying on Carillo.

2.7 Intersection of the Carillo and Squeeze Pen Trails. Bear right onto Squeeze Pen.

3.0 Intersection of the Squeeze Pen and Pink Hill Trails. Go left onto Pink Hill.

3.5 Intersection of the Pink Hill and Saguaro Trails. Go right onto Saguaro, which drops down from the top of Pink Hill.

4.4 You'll be riding along the edge of a wash that joins a larger wash (which often runs in wintertime or during the monsoon season). Keep an eye out for where the trail leaves the wash to your right.

4.5 Intersection of the Saguaro and Wentworth Trails. Go right onto Wentworth.

4.8 Intersection of the Wentworth and Kennedy Trails. Go left (north) onto Kennedy. The reason that Kennedy is so straight is that it was built in the 1960s by the county as part of a proposed housing development that (fortunately) never materialized.

5.0 Intersection of the Kennedy and Creosote Trails. Stay straight on Kennedy.

5.2 Intersection of the Kennedy and Shantz Trails. Go right, down the steps, on Shantz. This trail is named in honor of Homer Shantz, a noted botanist and former University of Arizona president who in 1933 helped convince President Herbert Hoover to set aside Saguaro National Park.

5.3 Intersection of the Shantz and Palo Verde Trails. Bear left, remaining on Shantz.

5.4 This is an unmarked intersection where the trail looks equally well traveled in either direction. Go left (north). Within less than 0.1 mile, you'll come to a second unmarked intersection. Again, go left.

5.7 Shantz comes into the Wildhorse Trail, and you'll be able to see the trailhead.

Options: When at 2.7 miles, you reach the intersection of the Carillo and Squeeze Pen Trails, you can ride an additional 5 miles by going left onto Squeeze Pen and zigzagging back to the trailhead on the Loma Verde, Mesquite, Cactus Forest, Cholla, Loma Verde, Pink Hill, Shantz, and Wentworth Trails before rejoining this route at Saguaro and Wentworth.

You can easily ride 40 miles in this area, but trail maps are strongly recommended due to the number of intersections. Maps are available at the visitor center (3693 South Old Spanish Trail, Tucson) and, occasionally, from the mounted rangers and volunteers.

44 Three Tanks/Carillo Loop Trail

Although it's only a 7.5-mile loop, this route is strenuous, narrow, rocky, and treacherous in places. You are also quite likely to encounter hikers and backpackers. Do not take an inexperienced horse or rider on this trail.

See map on page 178.
Start: Eastern edge of Tucson; Pima County.
Distance: 7.5-mile loop.
Approximate riding time: 3 to 4 hours.
Total ascent: 1,300 feet.
Difficulty: Difficult, due to the rocky and narrow trail in places, the climb, and the rutted, tricky footing around Three Tanks. Be prepared to dismount and lead if your horse is new to this kind of terrain.
Seasons: Best in winter, spring, and fall; okay

as a *very* early morning ride in summer.
Water availability: The trough at Three Tanks except during drought years.
Other trail users: Hikers and backpackers.
Canine compatibility: Dogs not permitted.
Fees and permits: None needed.
Facilities: None.
USGS maps: Tanque Verde Peak.
Contact: Saguaro National Park East, National Park Service, Rincon Mountain District Visitor Center, (520) 733–5133.

Reaching the trailhead: From Phoenix on weekends or when traffic is light, take Interstate 10 to the Speedway Boulevard exit (Exit 257) east; travel approximately 18 miles through midtown Tucson until Speedway dead-ends.

From the east, take I–10 to Houghton Road (Exit 275). Go right (north) approximately 12 miles to Speedway. Turn right (east), and go 4 miles to the trailhead.

A second equestrian trailhead is located at the eastern end of Broadway, approximately 2 miles to the south. *DeLorme: Arizona Atlas and Gazetteer:* Page 67 D5.

Most hikers are agreeable about giving way to horses on the trail. Agua Caliente Hill and the Santa Catalinas are in the background.

Trailhead parking: There's parking for twenty to thirty rigs, but it's along the shoulder of Speedway Boulevard; the lot at the end of the road is reserved for passenger vehicles. On weekdays parking is plentiful and easy. On pleasant weekends, however, the area is very congested, and trailers may be parked bumper to bumper for as much as 0.5 mile from the trailhead. Drivers of large rigs may have trouble turning before the Tanque Verde Guest Ranch's private property boundary.

The Ride

The trails in this area are heavily used by hikers and frequently patrolled by National Park Service rangers and mounted sheriff's posse volunteers. Water is generally available at the trough at Three Tanks—but not always during drought years.

The three tanks the trail is named for are Aguila Tank, Mica Tank, and Steel Tank (which is at Rock Spring, the intersection of the Carillo and Three Tanks Trails). If you have someone to hold your horse, check out the metal reservoir that feeds the drinker at Steel Tank. Sometimes you can see the goldfish introduced by cowboys to control algae before the area became a national park. (Some of the fish are *huge*.)

Seven and a half miles of trail may not sound like much, but your equine companion at least is likely to feel as if he's done some work. The best time to do this trail is at either end of the day, so that you can see the folds of the nearby hills highlighted by morning or evening light. In summer, when temperatures run 110 degrees or hotter at midday, it's best to ride this trail in the early morning.

Miles and Directions

0.0 Head south from the trailhead on the Wildhorse Trail.

0.2 Intersection of the Wildhorse and Stock Bypass Trails. Go left onto Stock Bypass.

0.7 Intersection of the Stock Bypass and Garwood Trails. Go left onto Garwood. Take an immediate right onto the Douglas Spring Trail.

1.1 Intersection of the Douglas Spring and Wentworth Trails. Stay to the left on Douglas Spring.

1.5 Intersection of the Douglas Spring and Carillo Trails. Stay on Douglas Spring (left).

2.7 Intersection of the Douglas Spring and Three Tanks Trails. Go right onto Three Tanks.

4.2 Intersection of the Three Tanks and Carillo Trails. Continue on Carillo to the south of the tank. **Bail-out:** If you take the Three Tanks Trail, you'll be back at the trailhead in 1.9 miles. However, parts of the trail are very steep and rutted.

5.1 Intersection of the Carillo and Wildhorse Trails, with a sign reading STOCK PROHIBITED to your left. Continue straight on Carillo.

5.6 You'll pass the dam that was part of a ranch established by Tucson businessman Nelson Garwood in the mid-1950s.

5.8 Intersection of the Carillo and Garwood Trails. Continue straight on Carillo.

5.9 Intersection of the Carillo and Freight Wagon Trails. Go right onto Freight Wagon.

6.4 Intersection of the Freight Wagon and Bajada Vista Trails. Continue straight on Freight Wagon.

6.5 Intersection of the Freight Wagon and Wentworth Trails. At this intersection you can see what's left of an old airstrip used by the Garwood family in the 1950s. Continue straight on Freight Wagon.

6.7 Intersection of the Freight Wagon and Wagon Spur Trails. Continue straight on Freight Wagon.

7.0 Intersection of the Freight Wagon and Creosote Trails. Continue on Freight Wagon. At the next intersection, which is confusing and unmarked, bear right.

7.2 Intersection of the Freight Wagon and Wildhorse Trails. Go left onto Wildhorse.

7.3 Intersection of the Wildhorse and Stock Bypass Trails (where you went east earlier). Stay to the left on Wildhorse.

7.5 Arrive back at the trailhead.

Options: This area is a complicated web of trails with intersections as frequent as 0.25 or 0.5 mile. (Note: Horses are not permitted on the Tanque Verde Ridge Trail, Miller Creek Trail, or Rincon Peak Trail.) Trail maps are strongly recommended and are available at the visitor center and, occasionally, from National Park Service rangers and mounted sheriff's posse volunteers you may encounter in the park.

Santa Catalina
Mountains

I t's hard to get lost in Tucson—at least in daylight.

The city is surrounded by four mountain ranges: the Santa Ritas in the distant south, the jagged Tucson Mountains to the west, the rounded lump of the Rincon Mountains to the east, and the hulking, handsome Santa Catalina Mountains to the north.

The Santa Catalina front range that provides the main backdrop for Tucson extends some 20 miles from west Tucson to Redington Pass. Mount Lemmon is the highest point in the range, rising to just over 9,100 feet. It was named in 1880 for Sara Lemmon, a botanist and the first white woman to ascend the mountain. Trail riders especially will appreciate the fact that she and her husband, also a botanist, were on horseback on their honeymoon. She was forty-five at the time.

The Cats, as they're affectionately known to locals, were also home to some Douglas firs that, according to University of Arizona tree ring scientists, started life in the 1300s. In June billowing clouds usually signal the chance of early-summer monsoons, but in 2003 they signaled a much less welcome event. The Aspen Fire burned 86,000 acres—including much of the vegetation on these 133 square miles. Just as heartbreaking was the loss of four of the five ancient Douglas firs.

Many trails, not just the northwest side of the range, are available to equestrians—more than enough for an entire book. Most of the trails on the south side are narrow, rocky, and heavily used by hikers, so they're less appropriate for horses.

45 Cañada del Oro Loop

This is a moderate 12.1-mile lollipop loop with occasional rocky sections. If the weather is cool, or if the creek is running, and your horse doesn't need the water at 6.3 miles, you could skip going to Golder Ranch corrals, making this an 8-mile loop.

Start: 6 miles south of Catalina; Pima County.
Distance: 12.1-mile reverse lollipop loop.
Approximate riding time: 3 to 5 hours.
Total ascent: 932 feet.
Difficulty: Moderate, with one steep, rocky creek crossing.
Seasons: Winter, spring, and fall are ideal; okay as a very early-morning ride in summer.
Water availability: Water tank inside the cattle pens at Golder Ranch Road.
Other trail users: Mountain bikers and hikers.

Canine compatibility: Best left at home. Dogs must be on a leash no longer than 6 feet.
Fees and permits: $6.00 day-use fee; recreational pass required on Arizona state lands.
Facilities: Three pipe corrals available on a first-come, first-served basis; there's also a vault toilet, water/hose (bring your own bucket), picnic tables, and some shade.
USGS maps: Oro Valley.
Contact: USDA Forest Service, Coronado National Forest, (520) 388-8300; Catalina State Park, (520) 628-5798.

Reaching the trailhead: From Tucson, go north on Arizona Highway 77 through Oro Valley. At the intersection of First Avenue and AZ 77, there'll be a brown recreation sign for Catalina State Park in 1 mile. Cross over the Cañada del Oro wash, and the turn for the state park will come immediately after the wash on your right.

From Phoenix, take Interstate 10 east to Tangerine Road (Exit 240). Take Tangerine Road east until it dead-ends at AZ 77. Go right (south), and the state park will be on your left in 1.2 miles. *DeLorme: Arizona Atlas and Gazetteer:* Page 67 C4.

Trailhead parking: There's ample pull-through room for ten to twelve rigs. There's a $6.00 day-use fee. It costs $45 for an annual pass, or $15 for overnight use of the corrals. Once you leave the state park at 3.7 miles, you'll be riding on state land for which Arizona requires an annual recreation pass. This is easily obtained by calling (602) 542-4174.

The Ride

A river crossing, the saguaros, the rugged Pusch Ridge, wildflowers in spring, snowy mountain backdrop in winter—this route is scenic with a variety of footing and terrain. The one thing it doesn't have in abundance is signs. In fact, except for the 50-Year Trail, this ride has no signs whatsoever. You'll need to pay attention to all the intersections and ride with either a GPS or an excellent sense of mileage.

Miles and Directions

0.0 Head out behind the vault toilet and bear right (north) toward the hill. Almost immediately you'll have to choose between going up the hill on the 50-Year Trail (the way you'll

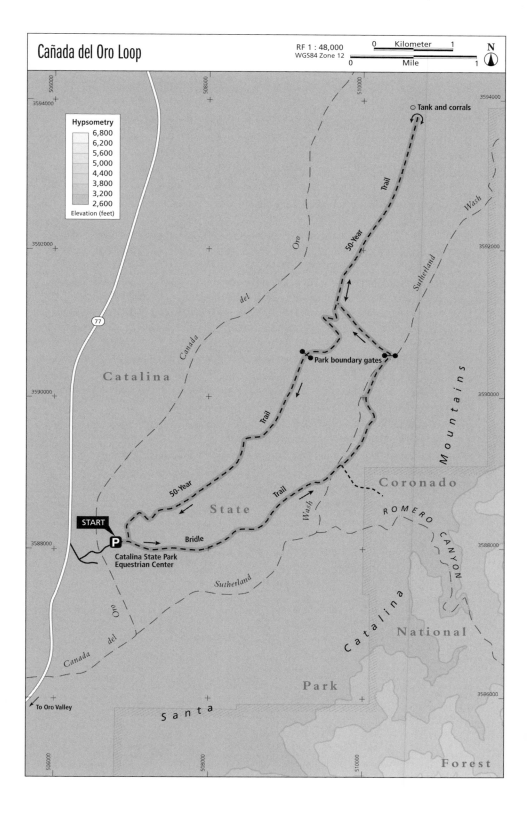

be returning) or taking a small trail with a sign that says BRIDLE TRAIL. Take the Bridle Trail (briefly).

0.3 The Bridle Trail will angle off to your right heading toward the group campground. Go left (northeast).

1.5 A rather indistinct four-way intersection. Go left (north), which is slightly uphill.

2.6 Reach a wide creek crossing that's lovely for watering horses when it's running. Cross the creek. The rock cairn that indicates the trail is a few yards upstream.

2.9 You'll be crossing back over the creek, this time in a westerly direction. This crossing is a steep, rocky descent into the creek, and your horse will need to pay attention.

3.0 Trail intersection: Go left (west). Keep heading downhill toward the wash, which you'll cross again.

3.7 Catalina State Park equestrian-friendly boundary gate. Go on through the gate (closing it behind you), and go left (southwest), following the fence line. Now that you're out of the state park, you may encounter cows.

4.3 Intersection with the 50-Year Trail, which is marked clearly with white arrows on brown posts. Go right (north). Be aware that mountain bikers use this section of the trail and are sometimes moving fast downhill. **Bail-out:** If you and/or your horse has had enough, you can turn left onto the 50-Year Trail instead of right and be back at the trailhead in 3.7 miles.

5.2 The 50-Year Trail crosses a dirt road. Keep on following the brown-and-white trail markers.

6.1 The trail crosses a jeep track. Almost immediately the trail forks, and the 50-Year Trail goes off slightly to the right. Don't take it; instead, bear left.

6.3 You'll come to the Golder Ranch corrals. The water trough inside the corrals has reliable water. When you're ready, retrace your route.

8.4 This is where you turned onto the 50-Year Trail. This time, keep going straight (south).

9.4 Catalina State Park equestrian-friendly boundary gate. Go on through the gate (closing it behind you), and keep going straight (south), following the 50-Year Trail. The trail is easy to follow but rocky in places.

12.1 Arrive back at the trailhead.

Options: The 50-Year Trail extends beyond the corrals and connects to trails that continue on up into the Santa Catalinas. In addition, this area is rich with four-wheel-drive tracks and social (unofficial) mountain bike trails that can provide many hours of happy riding.

46 Charouleau Gap Trail

This 13.2-mile out-and-back route encompasses 2,500 feet of climbing. Some sections are rocky—be sure your horse is ready for this one.

Start: 3 miles north of Catalina; Pinal County.
Distance: 13.2 miles out and back.
Approximate riding time: 4 hours.
Total ascent: 2,500 feet.
Difficulty: Difficult. The entire route is on a 4-by-4 road, much of which is rutted and rocky. Your horse will need to be in excellent shape to handle the climb, especially in hot weather.
Seasons: Best in spring and fall; okay as a very early-morning ride in summer.
Water availability: Intermittent creek.

Other trail users: Mountain bikers and four-wheelers.
Canine compatibility: Well-conditioned dogs will enjoy this trail. Bring water.
Fees and permits: Recreational pass required on Arizona state lands.
Facilities: None.
USGS maps: Oracle.
Contact: Arizona State Land Department, (602) 542-4631; USDA Forest Service, Coronado National Forest, (520) 388-8300.

Reaching the trailhead: From Tucson, take Arizona Highway 77 (Oracle Road) north. At 9.1 miles past the entrance to Catalina State Park, turn right (east) onto Golder Ranch Road; continue 1.3 miles before turning left (north) onto Lago del Oro Road at the bottom of the hill. After 3 miles, past Miraval and Sierra Tucson, you'll see a small brown sign on your right that reads CHAROULEAU GAP 4X4 ROAD #736. (If you go into the Saddlebrooke community, you've gone too far.) This is also the parking lot for horse trailers. *DeLorme: Arizona Atlas and Gazetteer:* Page 67 C4.

Trailhead parking: There's enough room for four to six smaller rigs. Turning left out of the parking area onto Lago del Oro Road is *very* tight for large gooseneck trailers. Arizona requires an annual recreation pass to access state land. This is easily obtained by calling (602) 542-4174 or going to www.land.state.az.us.

The Ride

Charouleau Gap is named for a French pioneer family that arrived in the late 1880s. The pioneer spirit apparently made it to the next generation: According to the Arizona Historical Society, on August 16, 1948, Anna Charouleau departed from Los Angeles on a 23,000-mile trip around the world. She was Tucson's first global traveler and was a passenger on what was then known as Pan American World Airways.

This trail is heavily used by equestrians, mountain bikers, and four-wheelers, particularly on weekends. In fact, it's so heavily used that you may prefer to ride it during the week. Be sure your canine friend is fit, and carry dog water. (A one-gallon ziplock bag makes a collapsible dog bowl. In a pinch your horse can drink out of it as well.)

There's enough room at the top of Charouleau Gap for several horse-and-rider teams to spread out and enjoy lunch while partaking of the great views of the Tortolita, Tucson, and Santa Rita Mountains from Samaniego Ridge. Note that the upper areas may be icy in winter.

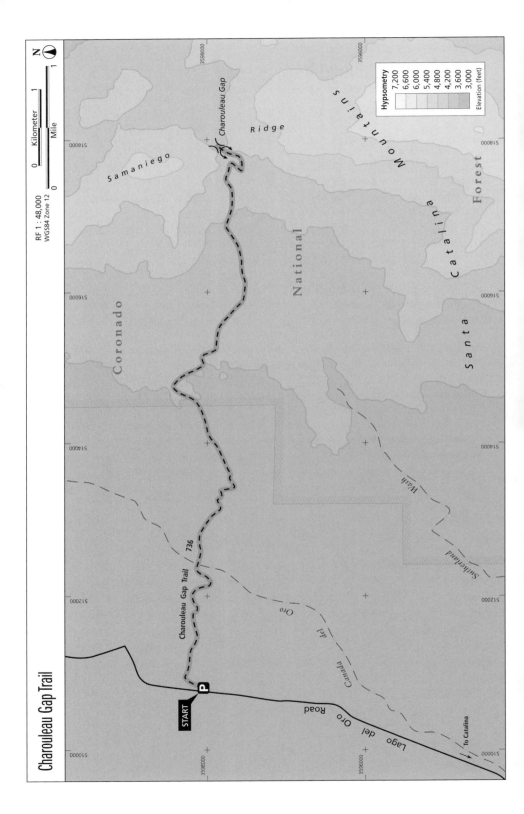

Charouleau Gap Trail

In a year when the winter rains have been plentiful, flower buds sprout in profusion from saguaro branches. Each flower opens at night—but only once. The blooms for each plant are staggered over a month's time, usually in May or June. Saguaros are usually around 75 years old when they grow arms, and some live to be as much as 200 years old.

Miles and Directions

0.0 Head northeast toward the mountains from the trailhead.

1.4 Cross the Cañada del Oro Wash.

2.4 The trail forks; take the pathway to your right, which is less rocky.

3.4 Go through the gate to the left of the cattle guard, leaving it as you found it.

4.0 Intersection with a north–south jeep track. Keep going straight ahead.

5.2 The trail starts to climb more steeply as it passes into the area burned in the 2003 Aspen Fire.

6.6 Go through the gate to the left of the cattle guard—you made it! To return, retrace your steps.

9.8 Cattle guard.

11.8 Cross the Cañada del Oro Wash.

13.2 Arrive back at the trailhead.

Options: The trail continues on toward Pig Spring and the Samaniego Ridge Trail for those with very fit horses.

Santa Rita Mountains

T he story of the Santa Ritas is all about mining, and especially all about gold.
In 1874 the richest placer deposit in southern Arizona was discovered in Greaterville. The limiting factor was not the gold but the amount of water needed to separate it from the surrounding sand and gravel. In 1902 James Stetson, the load engineer of the Santa Rita Water and Mining Company, devised a plan to channel winter runoff through 3 miles of 24-inch pipe to a reservoir of several million gallons, enough to operate the mine until the next year's rain. From then until 1906, Kentucky Camp was the headquarters for the operation, but in 1905 Stetson died in an inexplicable fall from the third-story window of the Santa Rita Hotel in Tucson. He was to have met with stockholders the next day.

By 1910 the operation was defunct, and Coronado National Forest was able to acquire the area by a land swap.

Biologically, one of the most interesting residents of the Santa Ritas is a greenish brown 4.5-inch amphibian. Once counted in the thousands, Tarahumara frogs were common in Santa Cruz County—but nowhere else in the United States. In 1983 the last one was found dead, due to a fungus or possibly particulates from a nearby copper smelter (now closed down).

Twelve years later, with the combined help of a dozen U.S. and Mexican wildlife agencies, the frogs were back. Over several years, scientists gathered egg masses where the frog populations in Sonora were still strong and raised them to tadpoles on a diet of cucumber, zucchini, boiled eggs, and baby spinach.

On June 26, 2004, the Tarahumara Frog Conservation Team backpacked 47 adults, 138 juveniles, and 229 tadpoles to several of the frogs' former locations in the Santa Ritas and released them.

Long may they live!

47 Baldy Saddle Trail

This 16.6-mile out-and-back route is a strenuous workout, with 3,800 feet of climbing and some narrow, rocky segments.

Start: North of Sonoita; Santa Cruz County.
Distance: 16.6 miles out and back.
Approximate riding time: 5 to 7 hours.
Total ascent: 3,800 feet.
Difficulty: Difficult, due to the climb and occasional narrow rocky stretches.
Seasons: Best in late spring and fall.
Water availability: At beginning and end of ride and Cave Creek.

Other trail users: Hikers.
Canine compatibility: Best left at home.
Fees and permits: None needed.
Facilities: None.
USGS maps: Mount Wrightson.
Contact: USDA Forest Service, Coronado National Forest, Nogales Ranger District, (520) 281-2296.

Reaching the trailhead: From Tucson, travel east on Interstate 10 to Arizona Highway 83 (Exit 281, to Sonoita and Patagonia). Exit right (south) onto AZ 83, and travel 21 miles to the turnoff to Gardner Canyon Road on your right, between mileposts 38 and 37. Turn right onto Gardner Canyon Road and go straight at the turnoff to Kentucky Camp; at the turnoff to Apache Springs Road 4.5 miles later, stay right on Gardner Canyon Road. Continue another 1.2 miles to the trailhead, which is on your right and well marked. *DeLorme: Arizona Atlas and Gazetteer:* Page 73 B5.
    Trailhead parking: There's ample for ten to twelve rigs, as well as some shade.

The Ride

Old Baldy is the not-very-dignified nickname for Mount Wrightson, which at 9,453 feet is the tallest peak in the Santa Ritas. Sweeping spectacular vistas of the Rincons and Santa Catalinas to the north, and past the Whetstones all the way to the Chiricahuas to the east, make this trail a winner. Snow may linger in the higher areas into May. In summer, plan your ride carefully to avoid afternoon thunderstorms.

    Most of the trail is on the north-facing slope as it climbs through a ponderosa pine forest, along with some Chihuahua pines. Once you're in the Mount Wrightness National Wilderness, you won't see mountain bikers; however, this is a popular route for hikers.

Miles and Directions

    0.0   Head west out of the parking lot on the dirt road and cross the creek, which has water most of the year.

The climb from the Gardner Canyon Trailhead to Baldy Saddle has plenty of ▶
opportunities for your horse to drink. (Mount Wrightson is in the background.)
Photo by Heidi Vanderbilt

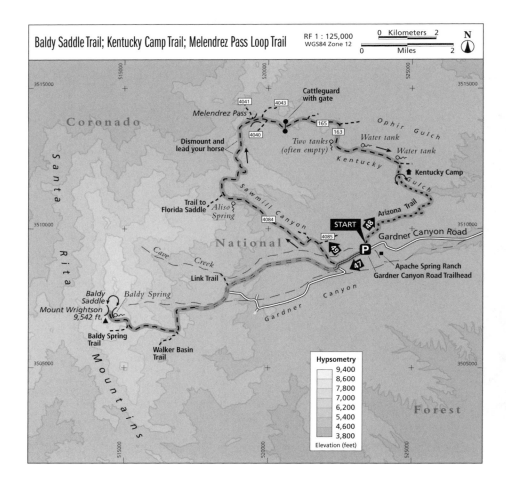

0.7 Cattle guard. Go through the gate and continue up the gravel road.

3.4 Link Trail turnoff. Take the next turn left, through the gate, and continue straight.

4.0 Intersection of Gardner Canyon and Cave Canyon Roads. Turn right, uphill, to remain on Gardner Canyon. This is also the first vista point.

4.1 The road ends and dwindles to a trail.

6.1 Intersection of Gardner Canyon Road and the Walker Basin Trail. Turn right to remain on Gardner Canyon.

7.2 Intersection of Gardner Canyon Road with the Walker and Baldy Spring Trails (Gardner becomes the Super Trail here). Turn right onto the Baldy Spring Trail. Even in late April, this section of trail can be snow covered. Be prepared to turn back.

8.3 Baldy Saddle. Retrace your steps.

16.6 Arrive back at the trailhead.

Options: The lower–elevation area of this route is crisscrossed with many four-wheel-drive roads, offering plenty of opportunities for exploration.

48 Kentucky Camp Trail

This is an easy 7.2-mile out-and-back route that's both scenic and historic.

See map on page 194.
Start: North of Sonoita; Santa Cruz County.
Distance: 7.2 miles out and back.
Approximate riding time: 4 hours.
Total ascent: 750 feet.
Difficulty: Mostly easy, with an occasional rocky stretch.
Seasons: Best in late spring and fall.
Water availability: Beginning and end of the ride.

Other trail users: Hikers, mountain bikers, and an occasional pack group with llamas.
Canine compatibility: Best left at home.
Fees and permits: None needed.
Facilities: None.
USGS maps: Sonoita, Mount Wrightson.
Contact: USDA Forest Service, Coronado National Forest, Nogales Ranger District, (520) 281-2296.

Reaching the trailhead: From Tucson, travel east on Interstate 10 to Arizona Highway 83 (Exit 281, to Sonoita and Patagonia). Exit right (south) onto AZ 83, and travel 21 miles to the turnoff to Gardner Canyon Road on your right, between mileposts 38 and 37. Turn right onto Gardner Canyon Road and go straight at the turnoff to Kentucky Camp; at the turnoff to Apache Springs Road 4.5 miles later, stay right on Gardner Canyon Road. Continue another 1.2 miles to the trailhead, which is on your right and well marked. *DeLorme: Arizona Atlas and Gazetteer:* Page 73 B5.

Trailhead parking: There's ample room for ten to twelve rigs, as well as some shade.

The Ride

This section of the Arizona Trail is well marked and winds its way through shaded mesquite woods and across an open mesa with sweeping views of the grasslands. Since you're on the Arizona Trail, you're quite likely to encounter plenty of hikers, mountain bikers, and other equestrians, and the occasional pack group with llamas. In summer, plan your ride carefully to avoid afternoon thunderstorms.

In the 1870s Kentucky Camp was a thriving, rowdy community with hundreds of miners. Now listed on the National Register of Historic Places, it's being restored with the help of the Forest Service's Passport in Time program volunteers, along with Friends of Kentucky Camp. Allow a little extra time to ride this trail so that you can enjoy the excellent interpretive signs along the way, which provide more historical detail on the water and mining system. The adobe headquarters can be rented overnight; a restroom and spigot are sometimes available to those passing through.

Miles and Directions

0.0 To water your horse before the ride, head west on the dirt road out of the parking lot to the creek, which has water most of the year. Then return to the parking lot, taking the trail that leaves from the back of the camping area: the Arizona Trail. It skirts the parking lot

Mariposa lilies are perennials that emerge in spring from bulbs after plentiful fall and winter rains. Mariposa means "butterfly" in Spanish, and with a bit of imagination the markings inside the flower could be interpreted as butterfly-like.

and heads northwest up a small ridge. This is the only serious ascent of the whole trail.

0.6 Equestrian-friendly gate. On this part of the trail, you'll be following a pipeline installed by the Santa Rita Water and Mining Company to supply water to gold-mining operations at Kentucky Camp.

0.9 The trail merges with a forest road with extensive views to the north and east of the Rincon, Dragoon, Whetstone, and Huachuca Mountains.

1.9 Turn left. The trail leaves Forest Road 410 and becomes a singletrack again; it's well marked with brown Arizona Trail carsonite markers.

2.3 The trail goes through a small canyon with oaks.

2.5 Equestrian-friendly gate.

2.8 Head straight across the gravel road.

2.9 Equestrian-friendly gate. The trail passes through a grassy valley with numerous remnants from the 1870s gold mining.

3.4 Equestrian-friendly gate.

3.6 Kentucky Camp. Retrace your path.

7.2 Arrive back at the trailhead.

Options: This area is an excellent base camp for many miles of riding.

49 Melendrez Pass Loop Trail

This route is a long, strenuous 16.2-mile loop with one short but treacherous section where leading your horse is highly recommended. The trail is ideal for endurance riders wanting a tune-up before tackling a 50-miler, but definitely not a ride for the novice horse and/or rider.

See map on page 194.
Start: North of Sonoita; Santa Cruz County.
Distance: 16.2-mile loop.
Approximate riding time: 5 to 6 hours.
Total ascent: 2,800 feet.
Difficulty: Difficult. Much of the trail is wide with good footing, but several ascents/descents are steep and narrow, and dismounting and leading your horse is recommended for one 1-mile stretch.
Seasons: Best in late spring and fall.
Water availability: Aliso Spring at 4.4 miles; stock tanks at miles 10.6, 11.4, and 12.1 might not be full.
Other trail users: Hikers, mountain bikers, and an occasional pack group with llamas.
Canine compatibility: Best left at home.
Fees and permits: None needed.
Facilities: None.
USGS maps: Mount Wrightson, Helvetia, Sonoita.
Contact: USDA Forest Service, Coronado National Forest, Nogales Ranger District, (520) 281-2296.

Reaching the trailhead: From Tucson, travel east on Interstate 10 to Arizona Highway 83 (Exit 281, to Sonoita and Patagonia). Exit right (south) onto AZ 83, and travel 21 miles to the turnoff to Gardner Canyon Road on your right, between mileposts 38 and 37. Turn right onto Gardner Canyon Road and go straight at the turnoff to Kentucky Camp; at the turnoff to Apache Springs Road 4.5 miles later, stay right on Gardner Canyon Road. Continue another 1.2 miles to the trailhead, which is on your right and well marked. *DeLorme: Arizona Atlas and Gazetteer:* Page 73 B5.
   Trailhead parking: There's ample room for ten to twelve rigs, as well as some shade.

The Ride

Although this ride has a lot of jeep roads that are open and exposed in hot weather, the views are magnificent, and there are plenty of long trotting stretches. Plan your ride carefully to avoid afternoon thunderstorms in summer. Snow may linger in the higher areas into May. You'll pass the communications towers at Melendrez Pass, home of the broadcast towers for WNEX482 and television station KWBA.

   It's unlikely you'll see other trail users until you reach Greaterville. Once you're on the Arizona Trail, you're quite likely to encounter hikers, mountain bikers, other equestrians, and the occasional pack group with llamas.

The climb to Melendrez Pass provides an excellent view of Mount Fagan with the Santa Catalina and Rincon Mountains in the distance.

Miles and Directions

0.0 Head west out of the parking lot on the dirt road and cross the creek, which has water most of the year.

0.7 Don't cross the cattle guard. Go right off Gardner Canyon Road, down the hill and across the creek, which often has water.

1.5 Intersection of Forest Roads 4084 and 4085. Stay on FR 4084.

1.7 Again, stay left on FR 4084.

2.0 Go through the gate (always leave gates open or closed, as you found them).

2.7 Go through the gate.

3.3 Creek crossing. There's good water here for much of the year.

4.4 Aliso Spring (*aliso* is "alder tree" in Spanish). Cross over the creek and head up the hill, remembering to enjoy the view of the Whetstones to your right as you ascend.

4.7 Trail junction. Go right, following a sign that says 2.5 MILES TO MELENDREZ PASS.

5.6 Caution: Reach a gate with a low overhead wire. Oddly, there's no fence, so you can just go around it.

6.0 Go through the gate. This is a great lunch spot with stately junipers, shade, and a terrific view north to the Rincons. **Bail-out:** The next section is tricky, so if you have any doubts about your mount's reliability, this is the time to backtrack. *Dismounting and leading your horse for the next mile is strongly recommended.* The view is spectacular, and most of this section is easy—except for three short sections that are narrow with slick rock and a potential drop of many hundreds of feet if your horse were to take a wrong step.

6.5 The fence line will be on your left. You've still got one tricky rock section and then a steep narrow descent on loose, gravelly sand.

6.9 The trail widens to a two-wheel-drive dirt road as you approach the TV repeater. (Don't be surprised if you see the cable guy: COX Communications sends someone up to maintain the repeater.)

7.7 Forest Road 4041 takes off to your left.

7.9 Forest Road 4043 takes off to your left.

8.1 Forest Road 4040 takes off to your right.

8.6 When you see a cattle guard, but no gate around it, you'll need to backtrack a few yards and drop off the road down into the creekbed to get to the gate.

9.2 You've now joined the Arizona Trail. It takes off to the north (your left), but you should stay on the jeep road south toward Kentucky Camp.

10.0 Again, you'll need to go down into the creekbed to get through the cattle guard gate. Immediately afterward, leave Forest Road 165 and head right onto Forest Road 163. You'll pass through the ghost town of Greaterville and remnants of old mining activity.

10.6 You'll reach two stock tanks at the top of the hill. Unfortunately, they're often empty, but you'll reach two more soon.

11.0 Cattle guard with a gate.

11.4 A welcome stock tank that usually has water.

11.8 An equestrian-friendly gate!

12.1 A stock tank that usually has water. This is also an excellent location to see yellow mariposa lilies, sometimes called desert roses, in late April if spring rains have been plentiful.

12.4 Parking lot for Kentucky Camp with an equestrian-friendly gate. A bathroom and spigot are available at the camp, and you may get the opportunity to introduce your horse to llamas. The rest of the way is on the Arizona Trail, which is well marked and winds its way back to the Gardner Canyon Trailhead through shaded mesquite woods and partly across an open mesa with sweeping views of the grasslands.

16.2 Arrive back at the trailhead.

Options: This area is laced with many old mining roads, providing opportunities for many hours of exploration.

Tubac

I n 1774 Juan Bautista de Anza was the captain of the Presidio of Tubac. At that point Tubac was still part of Sonora, a Spanish territory; it wasn't until 1848 that Tubac become part of the Arizona Territory, thanks to the Gadsden Purchase. Spain wanted an overland route from what is now Mexico to Alta California (Upper California, as opposed to Baja, or Lower, California), and Anza led a successful scouting expedition.

Two years later he enlisted 200 wannabe settlers, along with translators, cowboys, Indian guides, and 1,000 head of livestock, and they set out from Culiacan, a town in the Mexican state of Sinaloa, on their 1,200-mile journey. Five months later they arrived in what is now Monterey, and Anza wrote: "Indeed, although in my travels I saw very good sites and beautiful country, I saw none which pleased me so much as this. And I think that if it could be well settled like Europe there would not be anything more beautiful in all the world."

Before returning to Tubac four weeks later, Anza was ordered to explore the "River of Saint Francis," and he made a quick side trip to choose the site for what would become San Francisco. On March 28, 1776, he dedicated the site for the new town on what is now the south side of the Golden Gate Bridge.

This trail is a short section of the Juan Bautista de Anza National Historic Trail that commemorates the route used by the expedition. Eventually it will include another 600 miles to Culiacan, the starting point of the Anza expedition, and will be the world's first International Historic Trail.

Currently the United States has twelve National Historic Trails; this is the only one in Arizona.

50 Anza Trail

This is a wide, flat, sandy, and safe 11.6-mile out-and-back trail that meanders along the Santa Cruz between Tubac and Tumacácori, approximately 40 miles south of Tucson. Although this trail is easy, you should plan to walk most of it since it's heavily used by hikers and bird-watchers.

Start: Between Tubac and Tumacácori; Santa Cruz County.

Distance: 11.6 miles out and back.

Approximate riding time: 1.5 to 2 hours each way.

Total ascent: 220 feet.

Difficulty: Very easy. The trail is wide with good, sandy footing and is fine for barefoot horses.

Seasons: Spring, fall, and winter.

Water availability: None.

Other trail users: Hikers and bird-watchers.

Canine compatibility: Best left at home.

Fees and permits: None.

Facilities: None at the parking area, but restaurants, shops, and the historical park are within easy walking distance.

USGS maps: Tubac.

Contact: Tumacácori National Historic Park, (520) 398-2341.

Reaching the trailhead: From Tucson or Nogales, take Exit 29, Tumacácori, off Interstate 19. Go left (north) on the frontage road, following signs to Tumacácori National Historic Park, which you'll reach in about 1 mile. *DeLorme: Arizona Atlas and Gazetteer: Page 73 C4.*

Trailhead parking: There's pullout parking in a gravel lot on the right side of the road just southeast of the national park. Because of space limitations at the Tubac (north) end, parking your rig at the Tumacácori end is recommended.

The Ride

There are no fees to use this trail; however, this route is on private land and is managed by the Anza Trail Coalition of Arizona. The landowners, Baca Float Land Development Ltd. Partnership and Tumacácori Mission Land Development Ltd. Partnership, do not guarantee that the premises are safe for such use and are not liable for any injury to persons or property caused by a recreational user.

Most of this trail winds its way along the banks—and occasionally across—the Santa Cruz River in what's known as a riparian habitat. Although many people don't think of moist riverbanks as being prevalent in Arizona, these areas are vital for 85 percent of the state's wildlife. The most common trees include the tall handsome Fremont cottonwoods, as well as Goodings willows, velvet mesquite, and Mexican elders. Bird life is plentiful and, depending on the time of year, you may see or hear the gray hawk, hooded oriole, Bell's vireo, vermillion flycatcher, belted kingfisher, and green-backed heron, among many other species. Mammals include bobcats, coyotes, javelinas, and mule deer.

This trail is heavily used. Hikers and bird-watchers tend to amble on this trail, so be prepared to slow down as you approach them. Remember to bring your own

You'll ride under many tall, handsome Fremont cottonwoods (called álamos in Spanish), which are in the willow family. In springtime the female trees release millions of downy seeds that settle on the ground in snowlike drifts. Although the seeds look like cotton, John C. Frémont actually named this species for its pale color and lightweight wood.

horse and human water. (Do not drink the river water!) Temperatures reach more than 110 degrees in summer, and flooding is likely in some areas.

Do not plan on extra miles—the trail is on private property.

Miles and Directions

0.0   Head through the gate, east of the parking lot.

0.9   The trail takes a sudden and surprising U-turn.

2.0   You'll pass the remains of an old adobe building.

4.1   The trail splits. The left fork goes 0.6 mile to the Tubac Presidio. The right fork continues on a new section of the Anza Trail, which ends at the golf course (1.7 miles). Retrace your steps to the trailhead.

11.6   Arrive back at the trailhead.

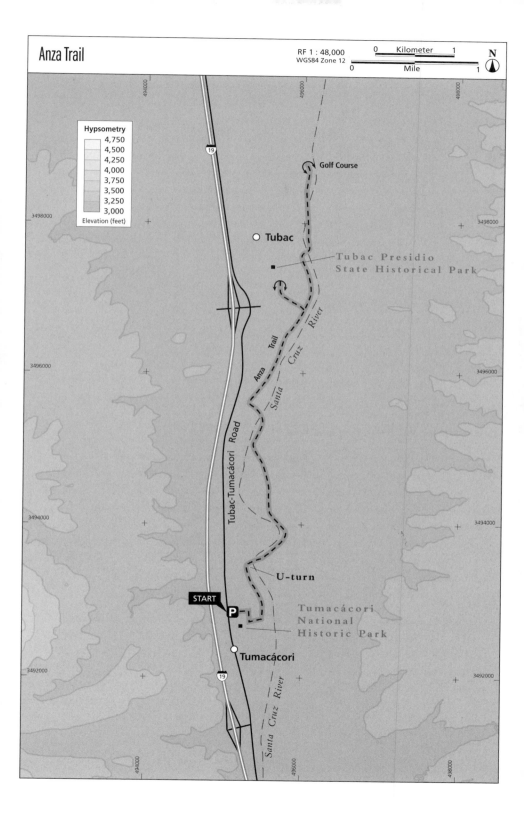

Anza Trail

RF 1 : 48,000
WGS84 Zone 12

0   Kilometer   1

0   Mile   1

N

Hypsometry

4,750
4,500
4,250
4,000
3,750
3,500
3,250
3,000

Elevation (feet)

Golf Course

○ Tubac

Tubac Presidio
State Historical Park

Anza   Trail

Santa   Cruz   River

Tubac-Tumacácori   Road

U-turn

START

P

Tumacácori
National
Historic Park

○ Tumacácori

Santa Cruz River

Historic Trails

The residents of North America have a long history of hitting the road, and evidence of their travels can be found all over the state. Some of the historic trails are thoroughly documented and maintained; others are catch–as–catch–can with only sporadic sections available to equestrians.

Below you'll find a sample. Complete descriptions of two others are found in their relevant geographic sections: The Anza Trail is in Southern Arizona, and one segment of the Moqui Stage Route is described in Northern Arizona. See this book's appendix for complete contact information for all these trails.

Beale Wagon Road Historic Trail

In the 1860s and '70s, this trail was a major thoroughfare between Fort Smith, Arkansas, and the Colorado River. Contemporary travelers can follow almost 20 miles of the Beale Trail between Flagstaff and Williams, and there are several access points to the trail. For more information and maps, contact the USDA Forest Service, Kaibab National Forest, Williams Ranger District, (928) 635–2633.

Butterfield Stage Route at Apache Pass

The Butterfield Overland Mail Company carried mail and passengers from St. Louis to San Francisco. The route initially went through Texas, southern New Mexico Territory, and southern California (including current-day Arizona), but was rerouted north after the outbreak of the Civil War. The Butterfield Stage stopped at Fort Bowie, which is now Fort Bowie National Historic Site, south of Bowie. The 3-mile loop trail from the parking lot to Fort Bowie itself, which is open to equestrians, crosses the stage route, and you can follow the mail route a short distance in either direction. For more information, contact the National Park Service, Fort Bowie National Historic Site, (520) 847–2500.

General George Crook Trail

This trail runs for 138 miles in central Arizona from Dewey, near Prescott, to near Pinedale. The trail was built under General Crook's command in 1872 to connect Fort Whipple and Fort Apache and to patrol the northern boundary of the Apache Reservation. Although much of it is either paved, unavailable, or impractical for equestrians, some sections are wonderful and still marked with the original chevrons.

For maps and more information, contact the USDA Forest Service. Try the Tonto National Forest's Payson Ranger District, (928) 474–7900; or the Prescott National Forest's Verde Ranger District, (928) 777–2200.

Mohave and Milltown Railroad Trails

These two trails follow the route of an old railroad grade for 7 miles, about 5 miles southwest of Oatman, and include separate trailheads for equestrians and off-highway vehicles. Signs at both trailheads describe the history of the railroad. For more information and maps, contact the Bureau of Land Management, Kingman Field Office, (928) 692–4400.

Moqui Stage Route

From 1892 to 1901—and for $20—you could take the Moqui stagecoach from Flagstaff to the Grandview Hotel at the Grand Canyon. The stagecoach took a whole day to make the journey and was replaced when the Grand Canyon Railroad reached Williams. Equestrians can ride the whole 70 miles or a shorter section from the Moqui Stage Station to Russell Tank and on to Grandview Lookout. (See Russell Tank/Grandview Lookout passage for a full description.) For more information, contact the USDA Forest Service, Kaibab National Forest, Tusayan Ranger District, (928) 638–2443.

Overland Road Historic Trail

The Overland Road connected Flagstaff with Prescott after gold was discovered in Prescott. Today this trail offers many glimpses into the early history of the Williams area, including the remains of early cabins, an abandoned logging camp, a Depression-era Civilian Construction Corps camp, and the Bear Springs Sheep Driveway. The Overland Road Trail covers 25 miles of easy to moderate trail with several access points. For more information and maps, contact the USDA Forest Service, Kaibab National Forest, Williams Ranger District, (928) 635–2633.

Stoneman Historic Trail

This historic trail was constructed in the 1870s under the command of Gen. George Stoneman and became a major supply road between Fort Whipple in Prescott and Fort McDowell. Equestrians can travel along 7.5 miles of the trail in McDowell Regional Mountain Park, near Phoenix. For more information, contact McDowell Mountain Regional Park, (480) 471–0173.

Appendix A: Further Reading

Beakley, Paul. *Mountain Bike America Arizona.* Guilford, Conn.: The Globe Pequot Press, 2002.

Carlson, Jack, and Elizabeth Stewart. *Hiker's Guide to the Superstition Wilderness.* Tempe, Ariz.: Clear Creek Publishing, 2002.

Chronic, Halka. *Roadside Geology of Arizona.* Missoula, Mont.: Mountain Press Publishing, 1984.

Cowgill, Pete, and Eber Glendening. *The Santa Catalina Mountains: A Guide to the Trails and Routes.* Tucson, Ariz.: Rainbow Expeditions, 1998.

DeLorme. *Arizona Atlas and Gazetteer.* Yarmouth, Maine: DeLorme, 2002.

Equine Travelers of America. *Nationwide Overnight Stabling Directory, Volume 23.* Arkansas City, Kans.: Equine Travelers of America, 2004.

Granger, Byrd H. *Arizona Place Names.* Tucson: University of Arizona Press, 1960.

Hancock, Jan. *Horse Trails in Arizona.* Phoenix, Ariz.: Golden West Publishers, 1998.

Hayes, Alden. *A Portal to Paradise.* Tucson: University of Arizona Press, 1999.

Hodge, Hiram. *Arizona as It Is; Or, The Coming Country. Compiled From Notes of Travel During the Years 1874, 1875, and 1876.* Cambridge, Mass.: The Riverside Press, 1877.

Jones, Tom Lorang. *Arizona Trail: The Official Guide.* Englewood, Colo.: Westcliffe Publishers, 2005.

Rak, Mary Kidder. *A Cowman's Wife.* 1934. Reprint with an introduction by Sandra L. Myres. Austin: Texas State Historical Association, 1993.

Ray, Cosmic. *Fat Tire Tales and Trails: Arizona Mountain Bike Trail Guide.* Flagstaff, Ariz.: Cosmic Ray, 2003.

Sheridan, Thomas E. *Arizona: A History.* Tucson: University of Arizona Press, 1995.

Smith, Ronald H. *Prescott and Central Highlands Trails.* Prescott, Ariz.: Castle Rock Publishing, 2002.

Sweeney, Edwin R., editor. *Making Peace with Cochise: The 1872 Journal of Captain Joseph Alton Sladen.* Norman: University of Oklahoma Press, 1997.

Tighe, Kelly, and Susan Moran. *On the Arizona Trail: A Guide for Hikers, Cyclists, and Equestrians.* Boulder, Colo.: Pruett Publishing, 1998.

Trimble, Marshall. *Roadside History of Arizona.* Missoula, Mont.: Mountain Press Publishing, 1986.

Appendix B: Contacts

Northern Arizona

Bill Williams Mountain
USDA Forest Service
Kaibab National Forest
Williams Ranger District
742 South Clover Road
Williams, AZ 86046
(928) 635–2633
www.fs.fed.us/r3/kai

City of Williams/Forest Service Visitor
Center
200 West Railroad Avenue
Williams, AZ 86046
(800) 863–0546

The Far North
Navajo Parks and Recreation
Department
Window Rock Office
P.O. Box 2520
Window Rock, AZ 86515
(928) 871–6647
www.navajonationparks.org

Bureau of Land Management
Arizona Strip District
345 East Riverside Drive
St. George, UT 84790
(435) 688–3200
www.blm.gov/asfo/index.htm

Grand Canyon National Park
North Rim Backcountry Information
Center
P.O. Box 129
Grand Canyon, AZ 86023
(928) 638–7875 (information only)
www.nps.gov/grca/grandcanyon/north
-rim/index.htm

USDA Forest Service
Tusayan Ranger District
P.O. Box 3088
Tusayan, AZ 86023
(928) 638–2443
www.fs.fed.us/r3/kai/

Arizona Trail Association
P.O. Box 36736
Phoenix, AZ 85067
(602) 252–4794
www.aztrail.org

San Francisco Peaks
USDA Forest Service
Coconino National Forest
Peaks Ranger District
5075 North Highway 89
Flagstaff, AZ 86004
(928) 526–0866

Coconino County Parks and
Recreation Department
HC 39, Box 3A
Flagstaff, AZ 86001
(928) 679–8000
http://co.coconino.az.us.parks/ftpark.asp

Spring Valley Cross-Country Ski Trails
USDA Forest Service
Kaibab National Forest
Williams Ranger District
742 South Clover Road
Williams, AZ 86046
(928) 635–2633
www.fs.fed.us/r3/kai/

City of Williams/Forest Service Visitor
Center
200 West Railroad Avenue
Williams, AZ 86046
(800) 863–0546

Central Arizona

Bradshaw Mountains
USDA Forest Service
Prescott National Forest
Bradshaw Ranger District
344 Cortez Street
Prescott, AZ 86303
(928) 443–8000
www.fs.fed.us/r3/prescott

Estrella Mountain Regional Park
Maricopa County Sheriff's Office
(602) 876–1011

Estrella Mountain Regional Park
14805 West Vineyard Avenue
Goodyear, AZ 85338
(623) 932–3811
www.maricopa.gov/parks/estrella

Maricopa County Parks and
Recreation Department
Headquarters Administrative Offices
411 North Central Avenue, Suite 6400
Phoenix, AZ 85004
(602) 506–2930

Granite Dells
Parks, Recreation and Library
Department
City of Prescott
125 North Arizona
Prescott, AZ 86302-2059
(928) 777–1122
www.cityofprescott.net

Lake Havasu
Bureau of Land Management
Lake Havasu Field Office
2610 Sweetwater Avenue
Lake Havasu City, AZ 86406
(928) 505–1200 or (800) 213–2582
www.blm.gov/az/lhfo/index.htm

Pinal Mountains
USDA Forest Service
Tonto National Forest
Globe Ranger District
7680 South Sixshooter Canyon Road
Globe, AZ 85501
(928) 402–6200
www.fs.fed.us/r3/tonto/home.shtml

Superstition Mountains
Arizona Public Lands Information
Center (PLIC)
222 North Central Avenue, Suite 101
Phoenix, AZ 85004
(602) 417–9300
az_plic@blm.gov

Arizona Trail Association
P.O. Box 36736
Phoenix, AZ 85067
(602) 252–4794
www.aztrail.org

USDA Forest Service
Tonto National Forest
Globe Ranger District
7680 South Sixshooter Canyon Road
Globe, AZ 85501
(928) 402–6200
www.fs.fed.us/r3/tonto/home.shtml

Timber Camp Mountain
USDA Forest Service
Tonto National Forest
Globe Ranger District
7680 South Sixshooter Canyon Road
Globe, AZ 85501
(928) 402–6200
www.fs.fed.us/r3/tonto/home.shtml

White Mountains
Hon–Dah Ski and Outdoor Sport
787 Highway 260
Pinetop–Lakeside, AZ 85935
(928) 369–7669 or (877) 226–4868
www.hon-dah.com

USDA Forest Service
Lakeside Ranger District
2022 West White Mountain Road
Lakeside, AZ 85929
(928) 369–5111
www.fs.fed.us/r3/asnf

USDA Forest Service
Springerville Ranger District
P.O. Box 760
165 South Mountain Avenue
Springerville, AZ 85938
(928) 333–4372
www.fs.fed.us/r3/asnf

Southern Arizona

Chiricahua Mountains
USDA Forest Service
Coronado National Forest
Douglas Ranger District
3081 North Leslie Canyon Road
Douglas, AZ 85607
(520) 364–3468
www.fs.fed.us/r3/coronado/index.shtml

Huachuca Mountains
USDA Forest Service
Coronado National Forest
Sierra Vista Ranger District
5990 South Highway 92
Hereford, AZ 85615
(520) 378–0311
www.fs.fed.us/r3/coronado/index.shtml

Kofa Mountains
U.S. Fish and Wildlife Service
Kofa National Wildlife Refuge
356 West First Street
Yuma, AZ 85364
(928) 783–7861
www.fws.gov/southwest/refuges
/arizona/kofa.html

**Las Cienegas National Conservation
Area**
Bureau of Land Management
Tucson Field Office
12661 East Broadway
Tucson, AZ 85748-7208
(520) 258–7200
www.blm.gov/az/tfo/index.htm

Oracle State Park
Oracle State Park
Center for Environmental Education
P.O. Box 700
3820 Wildlife Drive
Oracle, AZ 85623
(520) 896–2425
www.pr.state.az.us/Parks/parkhtml
/oracle.html

Pinaleño Mountains
USDA Forest Service
Coronado National Forest
Safford Ranger District
711 14th Avenue, Suite D
Safford, AZ 85546
(928) 428–4150
www.fs.fed.us/r3/coronado/index.shtml

Rillito River Park
Pima County Natural Resources
Parks and Recreation
3500 West River Road
Tucson, AZ 85741
(520) 877–6000
www.co.pima.az.us/pksrec/home2
/home2.html

Rincon Mountains
Saguaro National Park East
National Park Service
Rincon Mountain District Visitor Center
3693 South Old Spanish Trail
Tucson, AZ 85730
(520) 733–5133
www.nps/gov/sagu

Friends of Saguaro National Park map
www.friendsofsaguaro.org/map_cactus
foresttrails.gif

Santa Catalina Mountains
USDA Forest Service
Coronado National Forest
300 West Congress Street
Tucson, AZ 85701
(520) 388–8300
www.fs.fed.us/r3/coronado

Catalina State Park
P.O. Box 36986
Tucson, AZ 85740
(520) 628–5798
www.pr.state.az.us/parks/parkhtml
/catalina.html

Arizona State Land Department
1616 West Adams Street
Phoenix, AZ 85007
(602) 542–4631
www.land.state.az.us/index.html

Santa Rita Mountains
USDA Forest Service
Coronado National Forest
Nogales Ranger District
303 Old Tucson Road
Nogales, AZ 85621
(520) 281–2296
www.fs.fed.us/r3/coronado

Tubac
Tumacácori National Historic Park
1891 East Frontage Road
Tumacácori, AZ 85640
(520) 398–2341
www.nps.gov/tuma/index.htm

Historic Trails

Beagle Wagon Road Historic Trail
USDA Forest Service Visitor Center
Kaibab National Forest
Williams Ranger District
200 West Railroad Avenue
Williams, AZ 86046
(928) 635–1417
www.fs.fed.us/r3/kai/oldrec/trwc_beal
.html

Butterfield Stage Route at Apache Pass
National Park Service
Fort Bowie National Historic Site
3203 South Old Fort Bowie Road
Bowie, AZ 85605
(520) 847–2500
www.nps.gov/fobo/index.htm

General George Crook Trail
USDA Forest Service
Tonto National Forest
Payson Ranger District
1009 East Highway 260
Payson, AZ 85541
(928) 474–7900
www.fs.fed.us/r3/tonto/index.shtml

USDA Forest Service
Prescott National Forest
Verde Ranger District
P.O. Box 670
300 East Highway 260
Camp Verde, AZ 86322
(928) 567–4121
www.fs.fed.us/r3/prescott/index.shtml

Mohave and Milltown Railroad Trails
Bureau of Land Management
Kingman Field Office
2755 Mission Boulevard
Kingman, AZ 86401
(928) 718–3700
www.blm.gov/az/kfo/index.htm

Moqui Stage Route
USDA Forest Service
Kaibab National Forest
Tusayan Ranger District
Highway 64, Administrative Site
P.O. Box 3088
Grand Canyon, AZ 86023
(928) 638–2443
www.fs.fed.us/r3/kai/index.shtml

Overland Road Historic Trail
USDA Forest Service Visitor Center
Kaibab National Forest
Williams Ranger District
200 West Railroad Avenue
Williams, AZ 86046
(928) 635–1417
www.fs.fed.us/r3/kai/visit/oldrec/trwc
_over.html

Stoneman Historic Trail
McDowell Mountain Regional Park
16300 McDowell Mountain Park Drive
MMRP, AZ 85255
(480) 471–0173
www.maricopa.gov/parks/mcdowell

About the Author

Writer, editor, poet, illustrator, and photographer Wynne Brown has been riding horses since childhood. She has completed nearly 6,000 miles in endurance and competitive trail riding and was a member of the U.S. Southeast Team in the 1994 Race of Champions. A resident of southeastern Arizona, she holds an interdisciplinary master's degree in biology and scientific illustration from the University of Arizona as well as a master's degree in communication from the University of Tennessee. She has taught college-level journalism and has been published in numerous books and periodicals, including *Popular Science, Western Horseman, Equus,* and *Arizona Highways,* in addition to online venues such as DiscoveryHealth.com, Desert USA.com, and EnvironmentalNewsNetwork.com. The author of *More than Petticoats: Remarkable Arizona Women* by Globe Pequot Press, Brown develops multimedia science materials for grades K through 12. In her spare time she is helping her husband build a straw bale house under the supervision of their various horses, dogs, and cats.